Encyclopedia of
HOME SEWING

Marshall Cavendish London & New York

Edited by Yvonne Deutch
Designed by Linda Cole

Published by Marshall Cavendish
Books Limited
58 Old Compton Street
London W1V 5PA

Some of this material has appeared in
other Marshall Cavendish publications

This volume first published 1977

Printed in Great Britain

ISBN 0 85685 305 4

Introduction

An upstairs/downstairs, all around the house manual for today's needlewoman, *The Golden Hands Encyclopedia of Home Sewing* will appeal to everyone who wants a comfortable and beautiful home on a shoe-string budget.

Even if you have never made your own soft furnishings before, you can learn all the necessary techniques in no time, plus some useful hints on how to estimate quantities, how to cut out basic shapes, and how to sew a variety of seams. You'll be able to give your home a really personal touch—you can transform a room dramatically by introducing a new window vista or scattering a myriad coloured pile of cushions on a couch. Try a fresh-as-morning look with some crisp café curtains, or make a gorgeous patchwork quilt as a family heirloom.

Every project is clearly set out, and explained with concise instructions, helpful diagrams and attractive illustrations, so that even a beginner can achieve gorgeous results. The variety of projects is amazing too, ranging from curtains, cushions, patchwork and appliqué accessories, fashionable duvet sets, luxurious bed linen, table linen and lampshades—right through to upholstery and loose covers.

We've remembered the children too. They'll be thrilled with our brightly embroidered sheets, and will snuggle happily into a giant squashy floor cushion. *The Golden Hands Encyclopedia of Home Sewing* will be a constant source of ideas and inspiration for every home maker, as well as an unbeatable money-saver.

Contents

Basic know how

The success of any job depends upon your choice of tools. Having the right tools makes your work easier, quicker and more enjoyable.

Basic equipment

A sewing machine. There are three main types: straight stitch, swing needle (zig-zag), and swing needle automatic.

Straight stitch. This type will sew only in a straight line. It is the least expensive and is perfectly adequate for basic sewing. It is also possible to buy attachments, such as a piping foot for stitching close to a zip.

Swing needle. As well as straight stitching this machine does zig-zag stitching which is useful for neatening seams and hems, for making buttonholes for stitching stretch fabrics, and for sewing on buttons. It is also possible to do simple embroidery stitches. Swing needle machines are in the medium price bracket.

Swing needle automatic. This machine does embroidery as well as the stitches which the other two types offer. But this type of machine is the most expensive and rather a luxury unless you intend to do a good deal of decorative stitching and embroidery.

Note: Make sure that the machine you buy has a clear instruction book. It is also important, particularly with a more complex machine, to have it explained by an expert and if possible to take a few short lessons in its use. In order to get the best possible results, it is essential to get to know your machine really well.

Machine needles. Use size 70–80 (11–12) for medium fabrics, size 80–90 (12–14) for heavy cottons and blended cloth, and size 100–110 (16–18) for heavy coatings and plastic. Continental sizes are given first here followed by British sizes in brackets.

Ballpoint machine needles should be used for jersey fabrics to prevent cutting the thread and laddering.

Sewing needles. Use size 8 or 9 for most fabrics, size 6 or 7 for fabrics such as heavy linen and for stitching on buttons, and size 10 for fine work.

Pins. Use steel dressmaking pins, at least 2.5cm (1in) long. Nickel-plated pins sometimes bend during use and could damage fine cloth. Glasshead pins are very sharp but have limited use as the heads easily break.

Tape measure. Buy one with centimetre and inch markings. The fibre glass type is the best as it will not stretch. One with a metal strip attached at one end is useful, especially when taking up hems.

Thread. For man-made fibres use a synthetic thread, such as Trylko, Drima or Gutterman. Linens and cottons require either cotton or Sylko, 40 or 50. For woollen fabrics use either a silk or synthetic thread as the cloth has a certain amount of elasticity and the thread should have the same quality.

With all types of thread the higher the number given on the label, the finer the thread.

Scissors. Small shears, 18cm – 20.5cm (7-8in) long as best for cutting out most fabrics as they are heavier than scissors and glide through the cloth more easily. Larger shears are advisable when making up heavy fabrics. The handles should comfortably fit the hand (left-handed shears are available).

Small scissors are useful for clipping seams and threads.

Unpicker. This is better than scissors for cutting machine-made buttonholes, and for removing buttons and snap fasteners, as well as being useful for unpicking. Various types of unpicker are available at most haberdashers.

Iron. It is necessary to have a good medium-weight iron with thermostatic controls. If you use a steam iron you must use distilled water.

Ironing board. An essential item for pressing seams flat. It should stand firmly and have a smooth-fitting cover. A sleeve board is useful.

Pressing cloth. A piece of finely woven cotton or lawn, 61cm (2ft) square, is essential for steam pressing. Your cloth should not have holes, frayed edges or prominent grains, as these can leave an impression on the fabric being pressed. Nor should the cloth contain any dressing as this will stick to the iron and mark the fabric.

Tailor's chalk. Have two pieces for marking your fabric, white for dark fabrics and dark for light fabrics.

Tracing Wheel. Use this for marking pattern outlines onto fabric. One made from steel with sharp points is best.

Thimble. This should fit the middle finger of your sewing hand. Choose a metal one as the needle can penetrate through a plastic one while sewing.

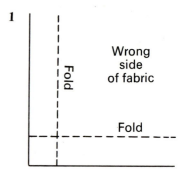

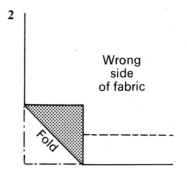

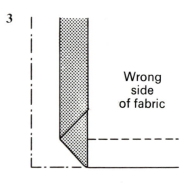

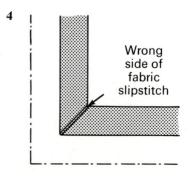

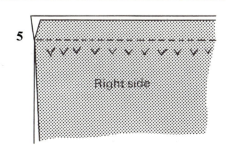

5

Right side

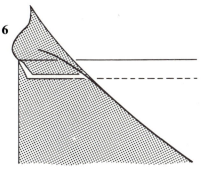

6

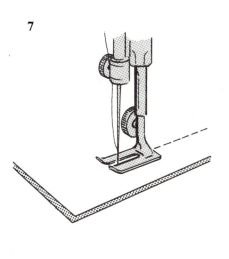

7

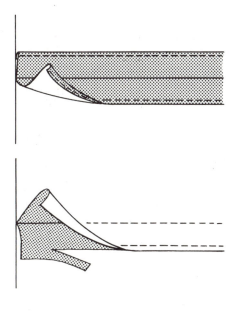

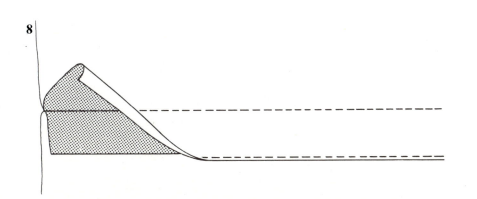

8

1. To mitre corners, first find the fold on the wrong side of the fabric

2. Still on the wrong side, fold the corner over at right angles

3. Fold over left hand edge of fabric

4. Fold over bottom edge to match up with corner angle, and stitch with very tiny slip stitches

5. To make a French seam, first stitch seam with wrong sides together, then turn inside out and stitch along the original seamline, enclosing raw edge

6. To finish seams, stitch then turn raw edge under and machine or hand stitch close to the edge

7. To make a flat fell seam, trim one edge of a plain seam, and fold over the other edge to enclose trimmed edge. Tack and machine stitch near the edge to make a neat finish. By learning how to sew these seams, you will have some useful basic skills.

Pinking shears. Not essential but useful to give a neater finish to seams, particularly when working with knitted and non-fraying fabrics.

Storing tools. As well as making sure that your tools are all in one place, it makes sense to store pins, needles and threads in small plastic boxes with lids, available in a variety of sizes.

Choosing fabrics

Always check when purchasing whether a fabric can be hand-washed or must be dry cleaned. If in doubt, wash a small test piece before making up. This is especially necessary when making an item in two different coloured fabrics or when using a loosely woven fabric which may shrink easily.

To find out whether a fabric is colour-fast wash a small square about 7.5cm (3in) square. Press while still damp onto some white fabric. The colour will run onto the white fabric if it is not colourfast.

To test for shrinkage measure a similar square of fabric, or draw around it, before washing and measure again when dry and then compare the two.

Know How
Plain seam

With right sides together, machine or back-stitch to the distance of the seam allowance from edge of fabric.

Neatening seams

Either use the zig-zag on your machine or turn under the raw edge of seam allowance and machine close to edge, or oversew closely by hand.

Flat fell seam

Join as for a plain seam and trim one side of seam allowance to within 6mm ($\frac{1}{4}$in) of stitching line. Turn over raw edge to the other side and fold over trimmed edge. Tack and machine near the edge.

French seam

With wrong sides facing, pin and stitch seam 6mm ($\frac{1}{4}$in) from seam line inside seam allowance. Trim close to stitching and lightly press stitched seam towards front. Turn article inside out. Working on wrong side, pin, tack and stitch along original seam line, encasing raw edges in seam.

Stitch library

Stitch library

The stitches shown are easily worked. Allow the threads to lie easily on the surface of the fabric. It should not be pulled out of shape by the stitch. To prevent threads from knotting: with a woollen thread stitch in the direction of the natural lie of the wool. Run a hand along the thread. In one direction the hairs lie flatter than in the other. For 6-strand floss: cut the length of thread, not more than 45.5cm (18in) for an easy needleful. Divide at the centre for the number of strands required. They will separate easily without knotting.

Stem stitch

Use for straight and curved lines. Notice the position of the thread for left-and right-hand curves. Begin on the traced line and work inward when use to fill a shape.

French knot

To make a well-shaped knot, as the needle returns into the fabric, keep the thread taut.

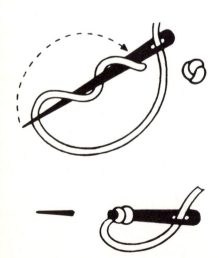

Cross-stitch

For an even appearance, work one row below another. The stitches should cross in the same direction throughout the work.

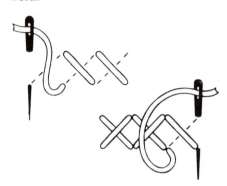

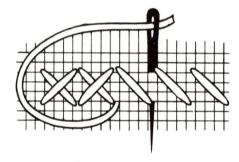

Herringbone stitch (closed)

The movements of the needle are the same as for open herringbone stitch, but the needle comes out close to the previous stitch.

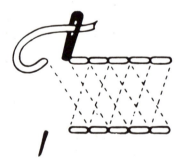

Herringbone stitch (open)

Work vertically upward, or from left to right.

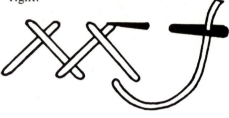

Feather stitch (half)

The needle goes in to one side of the previous stitch. The position of the needle and thread is the same as in chain stitch.

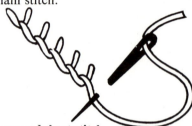

Long and short stitch

Work it as in the diagram for a broken surface. For a smooth surface, work the first row as shown. On the second row, bring the needle UP through the previous stitch. Best worked in a frame.

Rumanian stitch

Take a long stitch across the shape to be worked and tie it down with a slanting stitch.

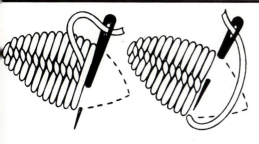

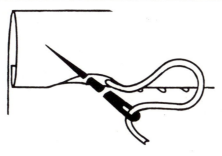

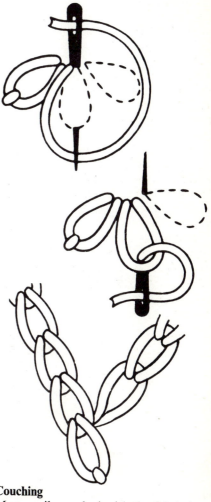

Running stitch
Use the stitch as an outline, or in rows as filling stitch.

Satin stitch
Most easily worked in a frame. The movements of the needle are simple. Hold the thread in position before inserting the needle. The stitches will lie smoothly side by side. For a raised effect, first pad with running stitches.

Blanket stitch
The thread loops underneath the needle which lies vertically in the fabric.

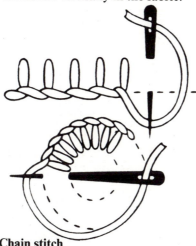

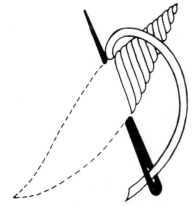

Surface satin stitch
Economical in thread. In relation to satin stitch, it has a slightly broken surface.

Chain stitch
The needle returns to the place where it came out. The thread loops under it. Chain stitch may be worked in straight or curved lines. Use it in circles or rows to fill a shape. When used as a filling, begin at the outer edge and work inward.

Couching
More easily worked with the fabric in a frame. With a large needle, take a thick thread to the back of the fabric. On the surface, tie it down with small stitches in a color-matched, thin thread. If the embroidery is to be laundered, stitch at frequent intervals to prevent the line pulling out of shape. Work it as a single line or in rows.

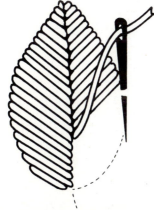

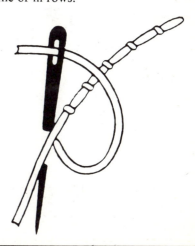

Slip stitch
Holds the hem in position with very little stitching showing on the right side.

Detached chain
Each stitch is held down separately with the working thread. Finish a row of chain stitch in this manner. The method for making a point in a line of chain stitch is also shown.

CURTAINS

Curtains are usually the most important focal point in a room, so choosing the right style and fabric can be a problem. All too often, ready-made designs are impossible to integrate with your furnishing scheme, as well as being alarmingly expensive. The answer is to make your own. There are so many gorgeous fabrics available nowadays that sewing your own curtains is a positive pleasure. You'll be inspired by the following projects – they're so easy to make, and you'll also be delighted with the range of ingenious gadgets and aids such as special tapes, hooks and tracks, all designed to give your work that extra professional touch.

Curtains have two main functions—first, to screen windows at night, giving privacy to lighted rooms and shutting out the darkness; and second, to form part of the room's decoration, by softening the hard outline of the windows during the day and by becoming an expanse of wallcovering at night when they are closed. To decide on the style of curtaining, have a good look at your windows in relation to the room and its other furnishings. Curtains can enhance or disguise the shape of windows and, if the window is out of proportion to the rest of the room, you can alter its apparent shape or size by adjusting the position of the curtain track. If daylight is restricted, the maximum amount of glass should remain uncovered when the curtains are drawn back. For this reason it is usually better to hang curtains outside reveals, but if you do have to hang them inside, take the track right around to the sides of the reveals so that no light is lost.

Sash windows

Double-hung sash windows—common in Britain in Georgian, Victorian and Edwardian houses—tend to be narrow and tall and often in rooms with high ceilings, so they look splendid with heavy, floor-length curtains. To make the windows appear wider, the curtain track should extend either side of the window so that the curtains can be pulled right back.

Casement windows

Casement windows can be of all sizes, with two, three of more sashes, but they are usually not very high, nor in high-ceilinged rooms. Full-length curtains can give them importance in a living room. Often they have to be ruled out, however, because of the siting of a radiator. Or, because many casement windows with two or three sashes are only about half the height of the walls, full-length curtains look odd when drawn back—and furniture cannot be pushed against the wall under the window, which is a snag in a small room.

Picture and pivot windows

Curtains for these should be full and heavy, so they drape well, and should have a decorative heading rather than a pelmet. Instructions for making these are given further on.

Top: A 'sham' curtain breaks up the broad window expanse.
Far left: Curtain for a French window.
Left: Where the window is small, take the curtain track around the sides.
Above: A period room with magnificent draped-swag curtain headings.

Estimating curtains

Curtain fabric (standard headings)

The width of fabric needed depends on the weight of the fabric but varies between 1½ to 2 times the track length. Lighter fabrics look better with more fullness. So, depending on fabric, measure length of curtain track and multiply by 1½ to 2 (for double fullness). To this add 5cm (2in) on each side for hems. Add a further 15cm (6in) to each curtain width if they are to overlap in the centre. Total is width of fabric needed for a pair of curtains. For windows more than 1.2m (4ft) wide, fabric must be joined for width needed for gathering.

To measure length, use steel tape or yardstick. Measure length from curtain track to either window sill or floor. Add 15cm (6in) for a double 7.5cm (3in) hem and 6.5cm (2½in) for a standard gathered heading. This measurement, multiplied by the number of widths required will give you the length of fabric needed for a pair of curtains. If you choose a pattern with a large repeat, extra will have to be allowed for matching. As a general rule you will need an extra pattern repeat for each curtain length. Check that washable fabrics are shrink-resistant, otherwise add about 2.5cm (1in) per foot of curtain length.

Estimating tie-backs

Loop the tape measure around curtain as if it were a tie back. Measurement of the loop is length of finished tie back. Straight tie backs would take about 23cm (¼yd) of curtain fabric or straight braid, 6.5cm (2½in) wide to required length, plus 2.5cm (1in) turning allowance. Also 23cm (¼yd) each of heavy buckram or pelmet buckram, interlining and lining, 4 brass curtain rings and 2 cup hooks. For shaped tie backs, draw pattern of shape required. Measure length of tie back as before, then halve this measurement. Draw pattern on brown paper folded as in diagram. Leave 7.5cm (3in) clear all around for turnings. Length and depth of opened out pattern will give amount of fabric needed for each tie back. Add same quantities of buckram, interlining and lining, rings and hooks, as for the straight tie backs.

Above: Sheer curtains are ideal for letting in the maximum light. Use them in studio and attic rooms.

Estimating cafe curtains

Decide on the finished length of the curtain. Café curtains usually cover half the window, but sometimes two curtains are used, one for the top half of the window and one for the lower half.

This type of curtain usually hangs to the sill or just below. To find the curtain width measure the track with a yardstick or steel ruler. Allow about 1½ times the length of track if a lined curtain with a scalloped heading is being used. For unlined curtains or those with more decorative headings, allow 1¼ to 2¼ times length of track. As for conventional curtains width needed depends on weight of fabric, lighter fabrics look better with more fullness.

To calculate the fabric length allow 15cm (6in) for lower hems and appropriate allowances for standard or deep heading tapes. For scalloped headings, decide on depth of scallop and add this measurement, plus 7.5cm (3in) for

Left: Full length net curtains are very graceful, and fall in gentle folds. They make a window space light and airy, where a heavier curtain would tend to look bulky. Here they are particularly suitable, since the window area is fitted with heavy shutters which open out completely. They are easy to launder.

turnings, to curtain length. Remember to allow for design repeats if using patterned fabric.

Linings

For sewn-in linings, you will need the same amount as for curtains, without allowance for pattern repeats. Lining fabrics are 1.2m (48in) wide. Check that the lining is pre-shrunk.

For detachable linings, cut linings the same size as the curtains, minus heading allowance and allowance for pattern repeats.

Heading tapes

Allow width of each curtain, plus 5cm (2in) for turnings. On lining tapes, allow 7.5cm (3in) extra. Before cutting pinch pleating tape, pleat up in arrangement you have chosen to check that finished length of tape is correct for curtain track.

Draped curtains

The side of the curtain which forms the drape will be longer than the side at edge of window. Use a piece of string and drape in a curve to estimate this length. You may find it easier to experiment with a length of calico before cutting fabric. Draped net curtains can be hung from either one curtain rod or two, overlapped fully at the top or only overlapped for two-thirds of the way across top of window. Allow for these possibilities when estimating fabric. The lower half of the curtain which is tied back can be shaped and cut at the window to your own requirements.

Side frills are often used on draped net curtains. Measure along edge where frill is to be applied, add half again to this measurement, double for a really, full frill, plus 1.5cm ($\frac{1}{2}$in) seam allowances. An effective finished width is 7cm (2$\frac{3}{4}$in). So for a double frill, cut a strip 14cm (5$\frac{1}{2}$in) wide, plus 1.5cm ($\frac{1}{2}$in) seam allowances all around.

Curtain fabric (pleated headings)

Pencil pleats need at least two-and-a-half times the width of curtain track. Allow 12.5cm (5in) for heading and 10cm (4in) for hem on each width of fabric.

Pinch pleats need 13cm (5$\frac{1}{8}$in) for heading and 10cm (4in) for hem on each width.

Most manufacturers of the particular pleating tape being used will supply a quantities chart on request to help you decide the number of widths and amount of pleating tape needed. Approximately 2 to 2$\frac{1}{2}$ times width of track.

Box pleats need three times curtain width.

Unlined curtains

Some curtains look best with light filtering through them and good fabrics for this are coarsely woven linen and other semi-sheers. It may be necessary to have a second, lightweight curtain close to the window if privacy at night is necessary. Furnishing fabrics usually measure between 1.2m and 1.3m (48 and 50in) wide, while sheers and nets come in widths from 91–304cm (36 to 120in) wide.

Cutting and seaming

Widths of fabric seamed together must have perfectly matched patterns. The design must run continuously across the window and flowers should grow upward. Remember all the windows in the room must match. Try and finish curtains with a whole pattern if possible. Place fabric on a large flat surface for cutting. Straighten one end by drawing a thread through and cutting along the line. Measure and mark with pins for first width. Fold fabric along line marked with pins and cut along fold. Match pattern if necessary, then cut off second width in same way. Continue until all widths have been cut.

If it is necessary to cut half a width, fold fabric lengthwise and cut along fold. Trim away selvedges and join width and half widths if necessary with flat fell seams. Use a loose tension and a long machine stitch for seams. A good hem is required at sides to prevent curtains from curling back. Make 1.5cm ($\frac{1}{2}$in) double hems at sides, tack and machine stitch or for a really good looking result stitch by hand. Turn up and hand stitch 2.5cm (1in) double hem at bottom. Turn top edge of curtain over for 6.5cm (2$\frac{1}{2}$in) and make a tacking line 4cm (1$\frac{1}{2}$in) down from folded edge. Cut heading tape the length required plus 5cm (2in) turning allowances. Pin and tack tape to curtain along the line of tacking. Turn ends of tape under, pulling out cord from turned in ends and tack along bottom edge of tape.

Machine stitch both edges of tape to curtain. Stitch in the same direction to prevent any drag in the stitching which would show on the finished curtains.

Secure cords at ends of tape by knotting them together or stitching firmly. Draw cords up from middle of tape and ease fabric so that it is evenly gathered and the correct width for window. Knot cords in the middle and catch them to tape with one or two small stitches to prevent knot from hanging down. Gathers are easily released by cutting these stitches and undoing the knot.

Lining fabrics

Professionally made lined and interlined curtains are expensive to buy, so it is a useful accomplishment to be able to make them at home. Making good curtains is not difficult, and with a little care really fine results can be achieved.

Choosing the fabric
Choose the best quality fabric you can afford for your curtains, bearing in mind the aspect of the room and the existing colour scheme. Next to the carpet, curtains give the largest amount of colour and texture to a room so it is essential that the right fabric is chosen. Remember when choosing the curtain material that some fabrics drape better than others. Always ask to see the fabric draped before you buy it – it can look very different lying flat on a counter. Check, too, whether the fabric is washable or needs dry-cleaning, whether it is shrink-resistant and whether it will fade if exposed to strong sunlight.

Large abstract and geometric patterns are usually too overpowering for the average living room and if a patterned fabric is used it should be of a small design and in keeping with the size of the room. More fabric will be needed if it is patterned. A large pattern repeat can be expensive too; extra material must be allowed for matching the pattern and there is often some wastage.

Make quite sure that the pattern is printed correctly on the grain of the fabric as otherwise this can present problems when making the curtains.

Linings and interlinings
Linings are used in curtains for several reasons:

a A lining helps a curtain to drape better.

b A lining protects the curtain fabric from sun and light, and also from dust and dirt which damage the curtain fabric and make it wear out more quickly.

c A lining can act as an insulator if a metal insulated lining called Milium is used. Milium will also make a curtain draught-proof and is therefore particularly useful when used to curtain a door. Cotton sateen is normally used for lining curtains. This fabric is usually 122cm (48in) wide and the colours most often used are fawn and white. Although cotton sateen does come in various colours, it is desirable to line all the curtains in the house with the same colour, if possible, to give a uniform effect from the outside of the house. An exception must be made for curtains with a white background where a matching white lining is more suitable.

Interlinings
Bump and dommette are the usual fabrics used for interlining curtains although a flannelette sheet would be quite suitable. Bump is rather like a very thick flannelette sheet and is fawn or white in colour and fluffy. Domette is similar to bump but not quite so fluffy. Both materials are good insulators.

Detachable linings
It is now possible to make curtains with detachable linings if a Rufflette curtain lining tape is used. This makes it possible to wash or dry-clean the linings separately, which is quite useful as they often seem to need cleaning before the curtains do.

When a detachable lining is used the curtains and linings are very useful in some rooms although they do not have quite the professional finish of hand made lined curtains. These have the linings stitched to the curtain around the two sides and bottom. An attached lining prevents dirt and dust from getting in between the curtain and lining fabric, giving more protection to the fabric and making it last longer.

Left: Match up your curtain fabric with other soft furnishings.

Pelmets and valances

A valance is just like a very short curtain and is hung from a pelmet rail with curtain hooks. Valances can either be gathered or pleated as with curtain headings, so although you measure the pelmet rail in the same way as for pelmets, the measurements will be for the final gathered length. Decide on the depth you want the valance to be then calculate the amount of fabric necessary as for unlined curtains, or for pleated headings. For a uniform look match the valance to the curtains in both fabric and style and use the same type of curtain heading tape for both the curtains and the valance. The diagrams here will give you ideas for styles. Make the valance as you would an unlined curtain, or if you wish to line the valance use the technique for lining pelmets.

A pelmet is a length of stiffened fabric which is hung above the curtains to conceal the curtain track and help balance the proportions of the window. It can be simply or elaborately shaped and is attached to a pelmet board, to a valance shelf or rail. A pelmet board should be 10–15cm (4–6in) deep and extend at least 5cm (2in) beyond each end of curtain track. Pelmets are usually tacked to pelmet boards but can also be attached with Velcro fastening. Pelmets are attached to pelmet rails with curtain hooks.

Most fabrics, unless very lightly or loosely woven, can be used for pelmets. But if curtains are very light a valance made in the same fabric, would be more suitable.

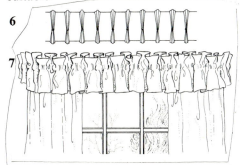

1. Plain and simple pelmet
2. Pelmet with squared ends
3. Gently curved pelmet
4. Pelmet with fringe trimming
5. Scalloped edge on pelmet
6. Pencil pleated valance
7. Simple gathered valance
Left: Gingham curtains and valance.

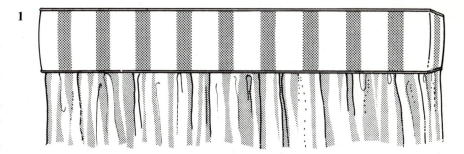

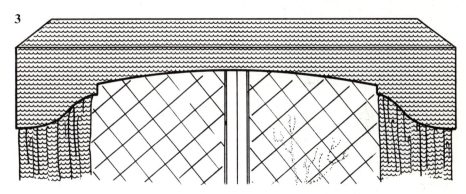

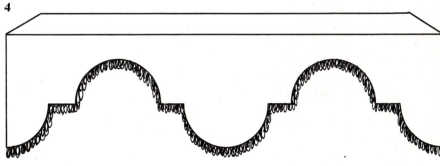

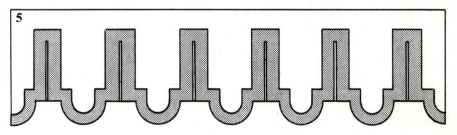

Making pattern for a pelmet

Use a sheet of brown paper sufficiently large for full length and depth of finished pelmet. Measure off length for pelmet on the paper, draw in the shape you have planned to depth required (use large plate, lid or compass to help draw any curves). Fold pattern in half to check symmetry and cut out.

Making pelmet

Pin pattern to fabric, leaving 4cm (1½in) turning allowance. Check that any de-

Below: A traditional bedroom has a pelmet covered with same fabric as curtains and bedspread.

sign is evenly placed before cutting out. Cut out lining with 1.5cm (½in) turning allowance. Cut out interlining with 1.5cm (½in) turning allowance and pelmet buckram without turning allowances. Lay interlining onto wrong side of fabric and lay buckram on interlining. Turn edges of interlining fabric over buckram, snipping into curves where necessary. The fabric should be pressed onto the pelmet buckram using a damp cloth and a hot iron.

Sew on any decorative braid or trimming before lining.

Turn under edges of lining for 2cm (¾in) and press.

Arrange in place.

If you are attaching pelmet to pelmet board, cut length of Velcro as long as finished pelmet. Stitch one half along top edge of turned-in lining on the right side. Lay lining on pelmet, wrong sides facing, and hem in place around edges. Stick other half of Velcro along pelmet board, flush with top edge, using very strong adhesive. When dry, pelmet is simply pressed in place.

The pelmet should be fixed to the board by using a strong tape sewn to the back of the pelmet and pockets should be made so that drawing pins can be used. For a pelmet rail insert the hooks into the heading tape and hang the pelmet as if it were an ungathered curtain.

Curtain headings

There are several types of attractive headings which can be made to give curtains an elegant finish, without using pelmets. The simplest to make is a standard gathered heading, which takes the least amount of fabric and is suitable for all weights of material.

Pencil pleated headings take rather more fabric and are particularly suitable for heavier fabrics which need to fall in generous but well regulated folds. For a really elegant heading, pinch pleats display satins, velvets and large prints to their fullest advantage.

Measuring for curtains
Measure the length of the curtain rail, or the combined length of both rails where two overlap. More often than not this will be wider than the window itself. Measure the overall curtain length from the height of the heading required, adding an extra 20.5cm (8in) for hems and headings.

Patterned curtains will need extra fabric so that the pattern runs on the same level on all curtains and an allowance for shrinkage should be made when buying all curtain and lining fabrics. Check with the retailer for details.

Full length curtains should finish 2.5cm (1in) above the floor to allow them to hang properly and to protect the fabric from wear. Similarly, shorter curtains should either fall just above the window sill, or just below it.

Stitching the tape
If the curtain rail is fixed to the wall, with plenty of space above it, stitch the tape with the hook pockets at the bottom. Where the curtains are suspended below the rail, such as on a decorative pole or from a rail fixed to the ceiling, stitch the tape with the hook pockets at the top.

Standard gathered headings
The fabric required to make the curtains must be at least $1\frac{1}{2}$ times the width of the curtain rail, including any overlap, plus an allowance of 7.5cm (3in) for the side hems and 3.5cm ($1\frac{1}{4}$in) for each seam. Using Standard Rufflette tape, 2.5cm (1in) wide, you will need the same amount of tape as the curtain fabric width.

Join the curtain widths where necessary taking a 1.6cm ($\frac{5}{8}$in) seam allowance.

Make side hems on the curtains taking an allowance of 4cm (1½in) each.
Pin and tack a 4cm (1½in) turning along the top edge of the curtains.

Preparing the tape
Pull out approximately 4cm (1½in) of each cord at one end of the tape, and knot them together.
Trim off the surplus tape.
Turn this prepared end under so that the knotted ends are enclosed (fig. 1).
At the other end of the tape, pull out the same amount of cord and leave the ends free for pleating.
Turn under the end of the tape to make a neat finish. The knotted end of the tape should always be stitched to the edge of the curtain which is at the centre of the rail, the loose cords can be suspended from the outside edge.
Making sure that the hook pockets are facing outwards, pin and tack the tape in position on the curtain so that it covers the raw edge of the turning, and is 2.5cm (1in) in from the top edge (fig. 2).
Stitch all around the outer edge of the tape keeping the stitching line outside the cords and as close as possible to the edge of the tape. It is advisable to machine stitch in the same direction along the top and bottom of the tape to avoid causing any drag in the stitching.

Pleating the curtains
Holding one end of the tape firmly, pull the fabric along the cords until all the fabric is packed to one end of the tape. Gently pull the fabric out again to the required width and knot the cords tightly to hold the heading in place. Insert curtain hooks at each end of the tape, and at 7.5cm (3in) intervals along

the length of the curtains.
Do not cut off the surplus cord as this allows the curtains to be pulled flat fos washing and ironing.
When the curtains have been pleated, wind the surplus cord around the fingers into a neat coil.
Secure with thread and suspend neatly out of sight at the outer edges of the curtains. Having tried the curtains for length, tack and stitch a temporary hem, which may need altering after cleaning or washing.

Pencil pleated headings
The amount of fabric required for pencil pleating must be 2½ times the width of the curtain rail, plus any overlap.
Make up the curtains as for a standard gathered heading, but make a 1.6cm (⅝in) turning along the top edge.
Prepare the tape in the same way as before, using tape especially for this.
Making sure the hook pockets are facing outward and the knotted end of the tape is to the centre of the curtain, tack the tape to the centre of the curtain, so that the edges meet along the top.
Stitch all around the edge of the tape, keeping the stitching outside the cords and as close to the edge as possible.

Pinch pleated headings
There are two versions of this type of tape, for curtains which conceal the rail and for curtains which are suspended below it. There is also a version for smaller windows and lightweight fabrics. So buy the appropriate type of tape required.
The fabric needed for pinch pleating must be at least twice the width of the curtain rail, plus the usual allowances.

You will need the same length of tape as the width of fabric required.
Make up the curtains in the usual way, and pin and tack a 1.6cm (⅝in) turning along the top edge of the curtain.
Making sure the tape is the right way up, make a cut in the centre of the first group of pleats (fig. 3).
Pull out the ends of the cord and knot them together. Trim off the surplus tape 1.5cm (½in) from the cord (fig. 4).
Turn under 2.5cm (1in) at the end of the tape, including the knotted ends of the cord (fig. 5). Lay the tape over the top of the curtain with the folded end level with the centre edge of the curtain and the top edge close to the top of the curtain.
Stitch across the folded edge and along the top edge of the tape.
If the tape ends at a space at the side of the curtain, use the point of a pair of scissors to pick out the cords, and trim the tape to within 1.5cm (½in) of the cord. Making sure that the ends of the cord are left free, turn under the raw edge of the tape and stitch along this edge, but not over the cords. Stitch along the bottom edge of the tape a little way in.

To pleat the curtains
Hold the free ends of the cord firmly, and push the first set of pleats into position along the cords. The spaces between the pleats must be kept flat and unpuckered. Push the second set of pleats into position and then push the first set into position again.
Proceed in this way until all the pleats are in position along the heading. Try the curtain on the rail and adjust the pleats if necessary so that they fit exactly.

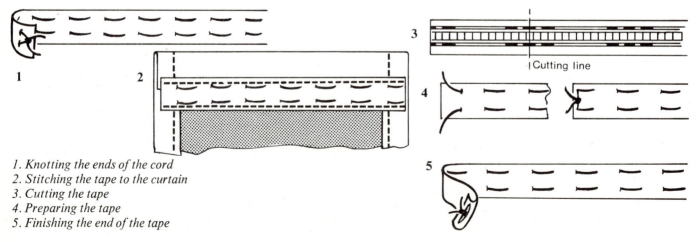

1. Knotting the ends of the cord
2. Stitching the tape to the curtain
3. Cutting the tape
4. Preparing the tape
5. Finishing the end of the tape

Curtain tracks and fittings

Detachable linings can be made if desired and attached to the curtains by the same hooks which suspend the curtain from the rail.

You will need 1½ to twice the width of the curtain rail in lining fabric, plus the usual allowances.

Make up as for the curtains, using lining tape, and pleat to match the curtain width.

Tapes and hooks

Here are some of the most widely used heading tapes:

Standard heading tape: this is a 2.5cm (1in) wide tape for even gathering on all types of fabrics where a simple gathered heading is required. The tape comes in a variety of colours and has two cords for drawing up the fullness.

Kirsch Easypleat, and similar deep pleating tapes are ideal for making pinch pleats easily. No cord is used for drawing up the tapes, but special deep pleat hooks are required and the pleated effect is achieved by inserting the prongs of the hooks in the pockets on the tape. Single, double or triple pleats can be made. When using the tapes it is necessary to work out carefully the quantity of fabric required and the number of sets of pleats in each curtain. Some companies produce a tape and fabric calculator for this purpose.

Rufflette Regis is a special tape for making pencil pleats. No special hook is required for this tape; the standard plastic hook is used. The tape is made of nylon and is hard wearing and strong, standing up well to washing and dry-cleaning. Two cords are used to draw up the tape and so form the pleats. There are other ways of making pencil pleats and special hooks are used. Various detailed leaflets are available on these and other heading styles and can be obtained from soft furnishing counters.

Curtain tracks

There are so many different types of curtain track and heading tape available that it is advisable to give your curtain headings some thought and to decide on the effect required. Decorative curtain poles are very much in fashion again and can look most attractive used with pleated or deeply gathered heading tapes. Many different effects can be achieved by using the new tracks and headings and it is advisable to find a soft furnishing or hardware store which displays some of them.

If a lined or interlined curtain is being used, make sure when choosing a track that it is strong enough to take the weight. Curtain tracks these days are made for use with or without pelmets and with conventional or deep headings. Some tracks can be bent to fit around curves; some are made in plastic or nylon, others are made from metal or wood. Some have a perfectly plain 'front', others have a decorative finish.

When you choose a track you should first consider the type in relation to the shape of the window, then to the room, its other furnishings and the style and weight of the curtains. It is always worth actually selecting the track in a store which has a large number of different types displayed so you can compare them and examine the fittings (you can always buy it locally, if that is more convenient). Many stores also show tracks complete with curtains so you can judge them for smooth running and noise.

Choosing for a window

If you windows are straight, with small spaces of wall above, almost all types of track are suitable. You simply have to decide on the best style. With bay and some dormer windows, however, the choice is more limited.

Where the bay is either square or angled, it may be possible to fit a separate track to each section. This means that on the most common style of bay, which is made up of three sections, you would need a minimum of four curtains – a pair for the centre section and one for each side. This works quite well, although it can be a little inconvenient and also reduces the amount of daylight allowed into the room when the curtains are open.

The alternative – and the only style possible on a circular bay – is to use a track which can be bent to the right shape. There are some tracks which you buy in a straight piece and bend yourself, that your local dealer can suggest. Or for heavy curtains you can have the track custom-made.

On some dormer windows, if you fit a straight track, the curtains may block out too much light when they are open.

Here it may be a good idea, if the walls at each side of the window are deep enough, to buy a track 15cm (6in) longer than the width of the window and bend it 7.5cm (3in) at each end around into the room. Then the curtains can be pulled right around to hang against the wall at each side.

It is usually best to hang curtains outside a window reveal, but often this is not practical – in a bathroom or kitchen, for example. So that the curtains do not have to rub against the window (which they might with a track fixed to the wall above it), it may be better to use an unobtrusive track, which can be fixed to the ceiling of the reveal.

Choosing for the room

In choosing the style of curtains, one of the main decisions is whether or not to have a pelmet. If you have decided against one, you are then plunged into the next decision: the style of curtain track.

The standard type of metal track which was the only sort available for many years, is considered by many people to be too ugly for use without a pelmet. The 'works' of the runners are visible from the front, and on most windows two sections of track are needed so that the curtains can overlap in the middle when they are drawn. Other disadvantages are that it collects dust and is noisy in use, although application of a little silicone wax helps this.

The nylon equivalent of this type is much quieter and easier to clean, and is often used for curtains with a plain heading where there is no pelmet. Its other advantages are that it is cheap and is easily bent to fit bays.

For a more streamlined effect, a plain strip, where the mechanics of the runner are hidden behind, is very popular. There are several different makes, all very similar. Some versions, however, look best with curtains which have deep headings, because plain headings tend to drop or fall back.

With this type of track, only one length is needed on straight runs because there is a special fitting which can be used on one of the curtains so that it will overlap the other when closed.

The overlap fitting is about 5–7.5cm (2–3in) long and slots on the track in the same way as the runners. It normally

has two or three holes into which the hooks at the end of the curtain can be fitted, and it moves along the track with the curtain. Because the arm is curved to come out about 1.5cm ($\frac{1}{2}$in) from the track, the edge of the other curtain can fit in behind it when the curtains are closed. When the curtains are open, the arm is not noticeable at all, but the curtain to which it is attached does not pull back quite as far as the other one.

Another point about this fitting, which might be a drawback in some cases, is that the curtain it is attached to has to be about 10cm (4in) wider than the other one after the gathers are pulled up. If possible, you should allow for this in the initial cutting out of the curtains. Where doing this would upset the balance of the fabric's pattern, it might be better to make both curtains the same size before gathering, and to settle for the overlapping ones being slightly less tightly pleated.

If you want the effect of the plain band, but also want to fit it around a bay, an aluminium track, may be a better choice. This track can be bent to a curve (not a sharp angle) with a 13cm (5in) radius without affecting its performance or breaking. It has a combined glide hook which is clipped onto the track from the front. The prong of the hook can be inserted into the pockets of the gathering tape, thus holding a plain heading upright. For a deep heading, separate hooks can be used and hung from the ring at the base of the glide.

Most plain tracks are designed so that they are concealed by the curtains when closed, but if you have one of the decorative types you can sew on deep heading tape so that the pockets come at the top in order to reveal the track when the curtains are closed.

Decorative poles

At the opposite end of the scale for straight runs, there are the decorative curtain poles. Curtain poles were the original way of hanging curtains with rings which were attached to the curtain and slid along the pole. They did not run very smoothly or quietly, and because the rings were sewn to the curtains these had to be removed each time the curtains were cleaned.

Nowadays this method has been modified to give the same effect, but the

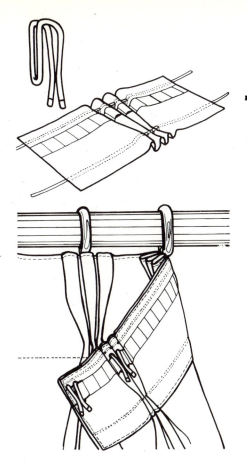

Above: Making pleats with hooks

curtains run more smoothly because the rings, which encircle the pole, have much smaller rings at their base into which the curtain hooks can be slotted. In other versions no large rings are used, but small ones glide along a groove at the base of the pole. With most poles it is possible to fit an overlap arm and a cording set.

The poles are made in different finishes – brass, aluminium or wood painted in different colours – so you can choose the best one for your room. They also have a variety of end pieces which can be screwed into place.

All these poles look best with curtains with a deep heading – pinch pleats especially – and they also need a fairly 'grand' setting. They are more expensive than most other kinds of curtain track, but some have the advantage of being expandable so if you move you can normally adjust the pole to fit another window.

Choosing for the curtains

If you are having a pelmet or valance, the best sort of track to use is the standard metal kind, or its slightly less strong nylon equivalent. It is the least expensive type of track to buy, it is easy to fit, can be bent easily, and all the mechanics are hidden by the pelmet.

If you are having a gathered valance, you can combine it with a valance rail. The curtain track is fixed in the usual way and the valance rail is clipped onto it by a nylon bracket so that it stands away from the track to allow easy movement in closing the curtains.

If you also want net curtains with this type of track, it is possible to use a bracket which holds both tracks about 2.5–5cm (1–2in) apart. Alternatively, for straight runs, you can buy a special top fixed combined track which has two channels.

If you are not using a pelmet but have curtains with a plain gathered heading, the best sort of track to use is one with a combination glide hook (see above), because this prevents the heading from falling back, and when the curtains are closed the track is completely covered.

Most kinds of track can be used with a deep heading, providing there is enough clearance above the track – a minimum of 6mm ($\frac{1}{4}$in) – to allow the curtain to move freely along. With decorative poles, however, this is not a problem because they are designed to allow the pole to be visible when the curtains are closed.

Whichever sort of track is used, it is essential to check that it will be strong enough for the weight of the curtains. With most fabrics there is no need to worry, as long as the track has been fixed securely. But on full length, lined and interlined velvet curtains, for example, a lightweight plastic or aluminium track is not strong enough and you should use a heavy-duty metal track.

Measuring for the track

In order to allow as much light as possible to come into the room when the curtains are open, it is usually better to hang curtains outside a window reveal, rather than immediately next to the window. Unless you want to use the curtains to camouflage the shape of the window, the track should be long enough to extend about 15cm (6in) on each side of the reveal so that the curtains can be pulled right back. On extra wide windows, or when the curtains are very bulky, you may want to make the track even longer.

If you are limited in space, and are using a decorative pole, remember that the end pieces may add about 5–7.5cm (2–3in) on each end but without actually increasing the length of the usable track. With some other tracks, adding a cording set may make a difference to the length of track you buy, because the fittings can add some extra width at each side.

Most tracks are sold in set lengths, increasing at 15cm (6in) or 30.5cm (1ft) intervals. You simply buy the length nearest your own, and cut it to the right size if necessary. Some other types are expandable and simply need adjusting to size.

Before you buy the track, decide on whether you are going to fix it to the ceiling or the wall above the window. Fixing it to the wall is more satisfactory in most cases, but where there is no room above the window or where the curtains are to come within a reveal, it may be preferable to fix it to the ceiling. Some tracks are supplied with brackets which can be used either way, but with others you may have to buy a special bracket.

Fitting a cording set may seem like an extravagance, but in fact they are well worth the money. Most tracks work better with one, and there is less strain put on them. They also save the edges of the curtains from soiling and wearing out through constant handling.

Some more expensive tracks are supplied already fitted with a cording set. With others you buy a kit, complete with cord, pulleys and weights, and fit it to the track yourself.

Fixing the track

Most tracks are supplied with instructions and all the necessary brackets and screws for fixing it into position. If you are securing the track to a wall, it is essential that the holes for the screws are correctly and adequately plugged and for heavy curtains it is more than likely that the screws supplied by the manufacturer will not be long enough.

One of the simplest methods of fixing the brackets for a straight run is to screw them to a wooden batten 5cm x 2.5cm (2in x 1in), which can then be screwed to the wall. In this way, you can ensure that all the brackets are level, which is never easy if you are drilling several holes into the wall, and you can use the edge of the batten to mark the fixing line.

Sheer curtains

Sheer curtains add charm and can also make a screen in a dining alcove.

The fabric

Sheer curtain fabrics fall into two categories: fine nets and semi-sheers.

Fine nets are the traditional type, hung against the window to give privacy to a room which can be seen into. The fabric used to be cotton, but these days it is more often a man-made fibre such as Terylene which is strong and resistant to the sun. Fine net curtains are normally white and are combined with heavier main curtains which give complete screening at night.

Semi-sheers, such as those shown in the photograph, are heavier than fine nets and have a more open weave. They look particularly attractive with large modern windows where they diffuse the light rather than obscure it. They can also make attractive room dividers.

Semi-sheers are made in a variety of colours, weaves and textures, mostly from acrylic fibres which give a warm feel. The curtains are decorative and heavy enough to be hung outside the window recess, and main curtains are not often necessary. For complete screening at night, however, you could make a detachable lining to hang from the same track as the sheers so that the lining is pulled across at the same time. If you wish, they can be removed in summer. Or, if you like to leave the curtains drawn across the window during the day, the lining could be made to hang from a separate track next to the window and be drawn at night.

The amount of fabric

Both types of sheer curtains are measured and made up in a similar way to unlined curtains. The main difference is that they should be much fuller – up to three times the width of the area they are to cover.

To save joining several lengths together, which can look ugly as the seams show through to the right side, it is normally better to make several curtains, each of a fabric width, instead of the traditional pair. When these are hung, the edges are hidden by the folds and the effect is one of a complete curtain.

Fortunately semi-sheer curtain fabrics are often made in extra wide widths – sometimes twice the normal 122cm (48in). With fine nets you can often buy the fabric in a set length nearest to the one you require, and the width required is measured off the roll in the same way as the length is measured off for regular fabrics. The hem and heading are already made and you simply have to finish the side hems.

Sewing sheer curtains

Sheer fabrics are not difficult to sew provided you use a fine sharp needle and set your machine with a loose tension to prevent puckering. It is always advisable to tack all folds, hems and seams as the fabric tends to slip while it is being machine stitched. You should also use synthetic thread and gathering tape as this will behave in the same way as the fabric.

If you have difficulty in feeding the fabric through the machine or if it still slips in spite of being tacked, it may help to put strips of tissue paper under the fabric as it is being fed into the machine This can be torn away afterwards.

Another important point in making sheer curtains of both types is that all the hems – side, bottom and top – must be made double with equal first and second turnings, so you will not get an ugly raw edge showing through to the right side of the curtain. With semi-sheers, you should also plan the width of the hems and turnings so that the spaces in the weave of the fabric fall on top of each other and the stitching can be worked on a solid section of the weave. In many cases you may not have to make side hems as the selvedges make perfectly good edges.

Deep headings

Because of their additional fullness, both types of sheer curtains can be made with a deep heading tape giving either pencil or pinch pleats.

These are available in a man-made fibre and are stitched on in a similar way to the narrower standard tape. The essential difference is that the top edge of the curtain should be turned over for the exact depth of the tape and the top edge of the tape should be placed just below the fold.

Right: Sheer curtains are ideal for the modern home. They are easy to launder, and let in the maximum amount of light.

See-through curtains

In a fine cotton lawn with a broderie frill these enchanting curtains are a cool cover-up for any room in the house. And they are easy enough for beginners.

The curtains

They are made from white lawn and have a gathered broderie anglaise frill along the hem and front edge, with another frill below the casing at the top. The curtains are hung on expanding wire which hooks onto the window frame, and are tied back during the day with frilled bands.

How much fabric to buy

1 First measure for the width of the fabric needed in each of the two curtains, simply by measuring the width of the window. By allowing this full width in each curtain, which covers half the width of window, you will have a pleasing double fullness.

It is normally simplest to work in full or half widths of fabric and the width of the curtains can be adjusted to suit this if necessary, but there should never be less than a fullness-and-a-half.

2 Next, measure for the length, from the top of the window to the window sill. From this, subtract the depth of the frill and multiply the final amount by the number of widths required for both curtains. Allow 1.37m (1½yd) extra for the turnings and tie backs.

3 The gathered frills are made from broderie anglaise trimming 15cm (6in) or 20.5cm (8in) wide, of the type sold by the metre. Alternatively you could use broderie anglaise fabric and trim off the required depth for the edging.

In either case for the trimming, you will need to buy an amount equal to: 6 times the width of the curtains plus 3 times the length plus about 2.30m (2½yd) for the two tie backs.

Making the curtains

1 Cut out two pieces of lawn to the measurements calculated above, but 2cm (¾in) shorter (because the casing is added separately).

2 To make the left-hand curtain of the pair, start by stitching a 2.5cm (1in) hem along the left-hand edge. To do this, turn under 6mm (¼in) onto the wrong side and press down. Turn the edge over for another 2.5cm (1in), tack and machine stitch. Press again.

3 Turn up a 6mm (¼in) fold onto the right side along the bottom and right-hand edge. Press and tack.

4 Cut off a length of trimming equal to 1½ times the combined width and length of the curtain, plus 4cm (1½in) for turnings.

5 To prepare the trimming make a small hem along the bottom edge if you are using broderie anglaise fabric. On all trimmings, turn under 1.5cm (½in) onto the wrong side along the left-hand short edge. Turn over 2.5cm (1in) more, tack and machine stitch. Leave the right-hand short edge raw.

Turn 9mm (⅜in) onto the wrong side along the top edge, tack and press.

6 Make two rows of gathering stitches (like running stitch if you are doing it by hand, or with a long machine stitch), one 6mm (¼in) below this.

7 Draw up the gathering threads so that the frill fits the bottom and right-hand side of the curtain. Lay out the curtain with the right side facing up and the bottom edge toward you. Place on the trimming, with the wrong side facing down with its top edge 1.5cm (½in) above the bottom edge of the curtain. Distribute the gathers evenly, allowing more at the corner so that the frill will hang well. The raw edge of the frill should be level with the raw edge at the top of the curtain. Pin and tack in position.

8 Stitch with two lines of machine stitches just above the gathering lines.

9 Measure the width of the curtain, including the frill, and cut a 10cm (4in) wide strip of lawn to this length, plus 2.5cm (1in) for the casing.

Fold under each short end of the strip for 6mm (¼in) on the wrong side and press. Fold over another 6mm (¼in) and tack and machine stitch. Fold the strip in half lengthwise with the wrong side inside, and work a line of machining 20.5cm (8in) from the folded edge.

10 Place the strip on the wrong side at the top of the curtain with the raw edges level, and machine stitch through the three thicknesses, 6mm (¼in) from the edge. Press the turnings onto the curtain with a moderate iron.

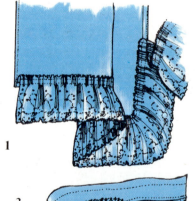

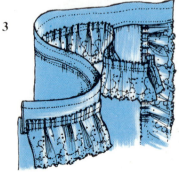

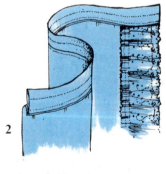

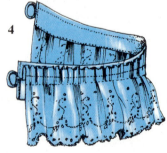

1. Place the trimming along the edge of the curtain, allowing more gathers at the corner so frill will hang well.
2. Attaching the casing to the top
3. Attaching frill to the casing
4. Tie backs with loops attached

Right: These crisp white curtains convey a delightful country cottage atmosphere. They are made in cotton lawn, and have a gathered broderie anglaise frill and tie backs.

11 Cut a length of trimming equal to 1½ times the total width of the curtain, plus 7.5cm (3in) and prepare it as before but making hems along both short edges.

12 Place it on the right side of the curtain so that its top edge is 6mm (¼in) above the seam line of the casing. Machine stitch along this line and 6mm (¼in) below, so that the raw edges of the seam are enclosed.

13 Make the right-hand curtain in a similar way, but reverse the instructions so that the frill is attached along the left-hand edge and bottom.

Tie backs

1 Cut two strips of lawn, 45.5cm x 7.5cm (18in x 3in). Make hems along the short edges as before, then make one along one of the long edges. Turn up a 6mm (¼in) fold onto the right side along the remaining edge.

2 Cut a 91cm (36in) length of trimming, make hems at each end and gather the top edge as before. Place it over the raw edge of the strip and stitch in position.

3 Sew on 6mm (¼in) diameter curtain rings at both ends of the strip, so that the tie backs can be hooked onto small

hooks screwed into the wall at the side of the curtains. These should be placed about ⅔ up the side of the wall.

Hanging the curtains

Place the curtains so that the frilled sides are in the middle. Slot the expanding wire through the casing formed between the machine stitched line and the top of the frill of both curtains. Try the curtains in position against the window and screw the side hooks to the window frame at the correct height. Arrange the gathers evenly on the wire and add the tie backs.

Unlined curtains

Unlined curtains are simple and quick to make and are ideal in a room like the lounge where they may need frequent washing. Make them in a gaily patterned cotton, or lightweight man-made fibre. Patterned curtains will need extra fabric.

The amount of fabric
This is calculated by measuring the width and height of the window area. If the curtains hang outside the window recess, take the measurements from the track from which they will hang as this probably extends some way on each side of the recess and is fixed a little above it.

Measuring the width
Ideally each curtain should be cut double the width of the area it is to cover so that when it is gathered it will have a pleasing fullness. Usually, however, it is simpler to base the width on full and half widths of fabric so there is no wastage. The small difference this makes can be adjusted in the gathering.
1 Measure the length of the curtain track with a wood or steel rule. Add 10cm (4in) and divide the width of the fabric into the total rounding it off up or down to the nearest half width.
2 This gives the number of widths required in each curtain, so double it to give the number of widths for a pair of curtains.

Measuring the length
Curtains hung inside the window recess should finish at the sill, or if they are hung outside the recess, 7.5cm–10cm (3–4in) below the sill.
1 Measure from the top of the track to the required length and add 15cm (6in) for a double hem at the foot and 4cm (1½in) for the heading.
2 Multiply this figure by the total number of widths to give the minimum amount of fabric required for the curtains.
3 If the fabric is patterned you will have to buy extra so that it can be matched on all the widths. Check on the size of the pattern repeat and as a guide allow one extra on each width. For example, if each curtain is made from two widths, you should allow four extra pattern repeats for a pair of curtains.
4 If the fabric is not guaranteed non-shrink, allow an extra 2.5cm per sq 91cm

(1in per square yard), and wash the fabric before cutting out.

Gathering tape
The easiest way of gathering the curtains is to stitch on tape which has cords along each edge which can be drawn up, and pockets for the curtain hooks to be inserted.
For unlined curtains, use tape which is 2.5cm (1in) wide. This is available in a variety of colours, in cotton for natural fibres and nylon for man-made fibres. Buy a piece equal to the width of each curtain, plus 5cm (2in) for turnings.

Cutting out
1 Iron the fabric to remove all the creases and lay it out, right side up, on a large flat surface. You must be able to see a complete curtain length at once, so use the floor if you do not have a table large enough.
2 Make the top edge square with the selvedges by pulling out a thread across the width. Cut along this line. Measure the total length of the curtain from this point, withdraw another thread and cut along it.
3 Place the top edge of the cut length alongside the next length so you can see how the pattern matches, adjust it if necessary and trim off any wastage from the top edge. Cut the next length in the same way. For a half width, fold the length in half and cut down the fold.

Joining the widths
1 For plain fabrics, pin the pieces together with right sides facing and selvedges matching. Place half widths on the outside edge of each curtain.
2 Tack and machine stitch, taking 1.5cm (½in) turnings. Trim one side of the turnings to 6mm (¼in) and press both turnings to one side so that the untrimmed one is on top. Fold under the edge of this one 6mm (¼in) and slip-stitch to complete a fell seam.
3 To join patterned fabrics, press the turnings under for 1.5cm (½in), or the width of the selvedge if this is more, on one of the pieces. Place the fold over the edge of the other piece so that the pattern matches.

Left: Unlined curtains give a light, airy atmosphere to a room, and are very convenient for easy laundering.

Above: Use unlined curtains for small windows as well as larger expanses. Co-ordinate fabric and wallpaper.

4 Pin the pieces together from the front and slip tack in place. To do this, insert the needle into the fold on the first width and withdraw it 6mm ($\frac{1}{4}$in) further on. Take it directly across to the second width and insert it. Pass it under the fabric and withdraw 6mm ($\frac{1}{4}$in) further on. Continue like this for the length of the curtains. You will then find you can stitch the pieces together on the wrong side in the normal way. Complete the join with a fell seam as for plain fabrics.

The side hems

1 Make 2.5cm (1in) double hems along the sides of the curtain as these are heavier than normal hems and prevent the sides from curling back. To make the hems, fold over the edges for 2.5cm (1in) on the wrong side of the fabric. Press.

2 Fold over the edges for a further 2.5cm (1in), tack and slip stitch or machine stitch in position. Press.

Attaching the tape

1 Fold over the raw edge at the top of each curtain for 3.8cm (1$\frac{1}{2}$in) on the wrong side and press down.

2 Cut a length of tape the width of the curtain, plus 5cm (2in). Pull out about 2.5cm (1in) of the tape. Knot the cords

together at one end but leave their other ends free for gathering.

3 Place the tape on the wrong side of the curtain so that it covers the raw edge of the turning centrally, and the top edge of the tape is 2.5cm (1in) from the top of the curtain.

4 Turn under the short ends of the tape, enclosing the knotted cords at one end but leaving them free at the other end. Tack it to the curtain all around the edge.

5 Machine stitch outside the cords on each side, stitching in the same direction on the top and bottom to prevent dragging.

Gathering the curtains

1 Pull the curtain along the cords until it is gathered tightly at the knotted end. Pull out to the correct width, distributing the gathers evenly.

2 Knot the cords to secure the width but do not cut off the surplus ends.

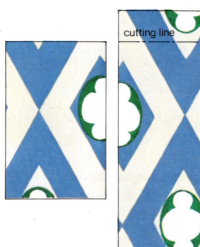

Matching the pattern widths

Slip-stitching the fell seam

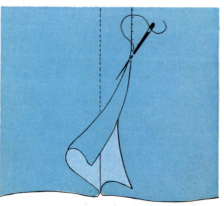

These can be wound up and caught to the tape with a few stitches and can be unpicked to release the cords when you wash the curtains.

3 Insert curtain hooks at ends of each curtain and at 7.5cm (3in) intervals between. Hang the curtains for a few days before taking up the bottom hems.

Making the hems

1 Mark the required length of the curtain with pins across the width while they are still hanging. Take them down, check that the line is level and that the sides are the same length and correct if necessary.

2 Turn up the hem along the marked line and tack loosely along it. Turn under the raw edge for half the total depth of the hem allowance and tack. Slip stitch along this fold and down the sides of the hems.

3 Press the hem, remove all tacking and re-hang the finished curtains.

Joining patterned fabrics

Stitching the sides of the hem

Lined curtains

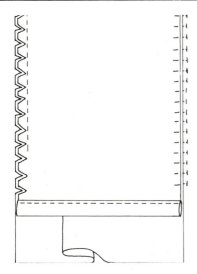

Making a tuck in curtain fabric
Making an equal border on both sides

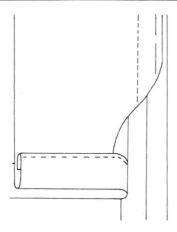

Folding in lining down seam line

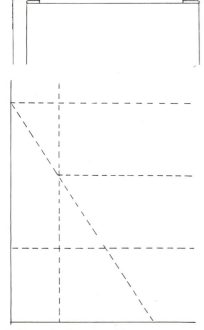

Fold marks for mitred hem
Detail of stitching on mitred hem

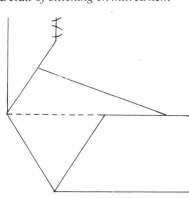

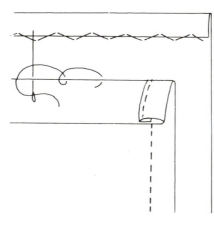

Stitching fold of lining to curtain

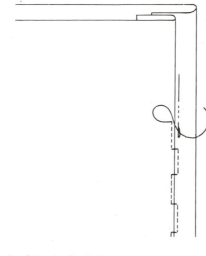

Locking in the lining

Lining improves the appearance of all curtains, making them seem fuller and better draped. For curtains hung at windows it also protects them from fading and soiling on the window side, and it intensifies their colour against daylight, makes them more opaque and helps keep out draughts.

The lining fabric
For curtains to be hung at windows, use a conventional lining fabric, such as sateen. This is sold in white, beige and a few colours in the normal furnishing width of 122cm (48in). Buy the same amount of lining as curtain fabric and wash it before cutting out to allow for shrinkage.

When the curtains are to be used as room dividers, they should be made with equally attractive fabric on each side. This can be the same fabric; in which case you should buy double the amount; or contrasting fabrics of similar weight and type, in which case you should buy the same amount of each fabric. You should also buy double the amount of gathering tape and hooks.

Machine method
1 Cut out the curtain fabric to the right size. Work a line of tacking down the centre of each length.
2 Cut out the lining fabric, making it 5cm (2in) shorter and 7.5cm (3in) narrower for each curtain. Work a line of tacking down the centre of each length.
3 Make a double hem of 7.5cm (3in) along the bottom of the lining and machine stitch.
4 Lay out the curtain fabric right side up and make a tuck of 7.5cm (3in) down the middle to make it the same width as the lining.
5 Place the lining on the curtain with right sides together so that the top and sides are level. Pin the sides together taking turnings slightly larger than the selvedges on the curtain fabric.
6 Machine stitch to within 5cm (2in) of the foot of the lining.
7 Turn the curtain right side out and match the centre point to the centre of the lining. Lay the curtain out flat with the lining side up and centre the lining on the curtain so there is an equal border of curtain showing along both sides. Press with a moderate iron.

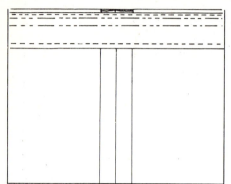
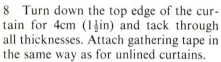
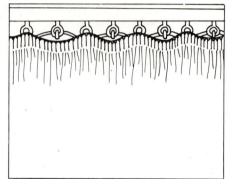

8   Turn down the top edge of the curtain for 4cm (1½in) and tack through all thicknesses. Attach gathering tape in the same way as for unlined curtains.
9   Hang the curtains for a few days to allow for the fabric dropping, then mark the hemline.

Making a mitred hem
1   Turn up the lower edge of the curtain along the marked hemline. Press lightly.
2   Measure the depth of the hem and turn under half the turning to make a double hem. Press lightly. Mark the position of the second fold on the edge of the curtain (i.e. the stitching line).
3   Unfold the hem completely and fold over the corners diagonally in a line which passes from the stitching line at the side of the curtain, through the junction of the side fold line and the second fold line of the hem, to the edge of the hem. Press.
4   Fold down the side turning of the curtain and catch in position. Turn up the hem along the same folds and pin in position. Tack and slip stitch. Catch the remaining lining in position. Press the finished hem and re-hang the curtain.

Hand-stitched method
1   Cut out the curtain fabric and join the widths if necessary. Cut out the lining, making it 5cm (2in) shorter than the curtain fabric. Mark the centre point of the top edges if the curtains are a single width. Join the widths, adjusting the turnings to match those on the curtain fabric, and press the curtains open.
2   Make 5cm (2in) single turnings on the wrong side along each side edge of the curtains and slip stitch loosely.
3   Make a double hem of 7.5cm (3in) along the bottom of lining and stitch.
4   Lay out the curtain, wrong side up,

completely flat on a large smooth surface (the floor is ideal if you haven't a table large enough). Lay the lining, wrong side down, on top of the curtain, matching the centre points of the turnings and so that the top edges are level.
5   If the curtains have more than one fabric width, fold the lining back onto itself down a seam line. Tack the turning on one side of the seam to the corresponding turning on the curtain to within 30.5cm (12in) of the bottom. Then lock in the lining as for a single width curtain.
6   If the curtains are made from a single fabric width, fold the lining back down the centre so that the side edges are level. Keeping the lining completely flat, lock it to the curtain (this process prevents the lining from billowing away from the curtain, thus helping it drape and also preventing the lining from dropping).

Locking in the lining
1   Using thread to match the curtain fabric, start 30.5cm (12in) from the bottom of the curtain and work upward. Secure the thread to the fold of the lining and pick up two threads of the curtain fabric. Work along the fold in a blanket stitch, placing the stitches about 5cm (2in) apart and keeping the loops loose to avoid puckering. Pick up no more than two threads of curtain fabric so that the stitches will not show on the right side.
2   When the first line of locking is complete, fold the lining down again and smooth it flat. Then fold it back on itself 45.5cm (18in) away from the first fold and repeat the process. Work across the width of the curtain in this way, locking the lining to the curtain fabric along the seam lines and about three times to each fabric width.
3   When all the locking is complete,

keep the lining and curtain flat and turn the side edges of the lining under to come 4cm (1½in) from the edge of the curtain (this measurement can be adjusted if necessary so that the lining completely covers the selvedge of the curtain fabric).
4   Pin in place, placing the pins at right-angles to the edge of the curtains.
5   Slip stitch the fold of the lining loosely to the turning of the curtain by inserting the needle into the fold of the lining and withdrawing it 1.5cm (½in) further on and inserting it immediately into the turning of the curtain and making a stitch on the inside of about 1.5cm (½in). Finish the stitching about 7.5cm (3in) above the hem of the lining.
6   Turn up the hem of the curtain, mitering the corners as for the machine method. Slip stitch the remaining part of the lining in position and hang the finished curtains.

Reversible method
The curtains for room dividers are really made like very wide unlined curtains which are then folded in half and joined down the side.
1   Cut and join the fabric for the curtains and the lining, making them the same length.
2   With right sides together, join the lining to the curtain down one of the side edges, taking turnings 1.5cm (½in) wide or the width of the selvedges if this is more.
3   Turn over the top edge of the curtain and lining and attach curtain tape along the entire width (including the lining).
4   Pull up the tape to make the curtain and lining double the required width, plus 2.5cm (1in). The seam joining the lining should be exactly in the centre.
5   With the right side inside, join the lining to the curtain down the remaining side edge. Turn right side out and position the seams exactly at the edges.
6   Insert the curtain hooks along the entire width of the curtain and lining and place them into the hooks of the track alternately from the lining and then the curtain and then the lining and so on. Allow to hang for a couple of days. Turn up the hem.

Right: Full length curtains look quite magnificent on poles, which come in a wide variety of styles and materials.

Tie backs

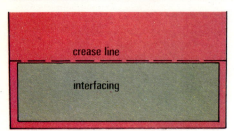

Iron-on interfacing

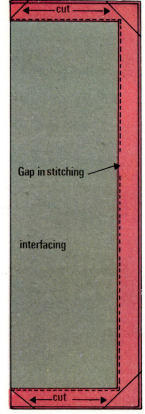

Small opening in stitching

Sew curtain rings on tie backs

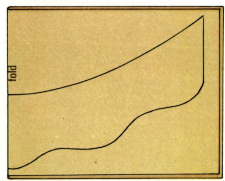

Pattern for shaped tie back

Simple tie backs can be made from straight strips, cut from the same fabric as the curtains. As a variation, if the curtains are of a patterned fabric, the tie backs can be in a plain fabric which matches one of the colours. Or, if the curtains are in a plain fabric, the tie backs can be made of a patterned fabric to match something else in the room. Straight tie backs can also be made from furnishing braid which is simpler still, as they do not need to be lined or interfaced. For a more draped effect, the tie backs can be cut in a similar way to a curved waist band so that they 'sit' well around the curtain, or they can be made with bound, scalloped or shaped edges for a more decorative finish.

The tie backs are hung with curtain rings of 1.5cm ($\frac{1}{2}$in) diameter, which are sewn to the centre of the short ends of the strips. The rings are placed onto small hooks screwed into the window frame at the required height.

Measuring the tie backs
The most attractive width is between 5cm–7.5cm (2in–3in), although you can make them up to 2.5cm (1in) wider if you prefer. To calculate the length, loop a tape measure around the curtains and adjust the length until you have the best effect. This will also give the best position for the tie backs.

Making straight tie backs
1   Cut out two pieces of fabric twice the width of the tie backs plus 2.5cm (1in) for turnings, by the length of the tie backs plus 2.5cm (1in).
2   Cut out two pieces of iron-on interfacing to the exact size of the tie backs.
3   Fold the fabric for the tie backs in half lengthwise with the right side out and press firmly along the fold. Open out the pieces and place on the interfacing strips so that one long edge lies along the crease line of the fabric and there is 1.5cm ($\frac{1}{2}$in) margin on the remaining three sides. Pin in position and iron so that the interfacing adheres to the fabric.
4   Fold the tie backs in half lengthwise again, but this time have the right side inside. Tack and machine stitch around the three raw edges, taking 1.5cm ($\frac{1}{2}$in) turnings and leaving a small opening in the stitching on the long side.
5   Trim the turnings diagonally across

the corners and turn the tie backs right side out.
6   Fold under the turnings of the opening, pin and slip stitch the folds together. Tack around the edges carefully so that the seam is exactly on the edge. Press.
7   Mark the centre of the short edges of the tie backs and sew on the curtain rings with several loose stitches.
8   Screw the hooks into position at the sides of the window and hang tie backs in place.

Braid tie backs
1   Cut the braid to the required length of the tie backs, plus 2.5cm (1in) for turnings.
2   Fold under the turnings at each end and make narrow hems. Slip-stitch.
3   Sew the curtain rings to the centre of the short ends with several loose stitches.

Shaped tie backs
1   Start by making a paper pattern of the shape you require. The simplest way of doing this is to cut a piece of paper about 7.5cm (3in) wider than the required width and about 2.5cm (1in) longer. To make sure the shape is symmetrical, fold the paper in half widthwise to make the strip half the length of the tie back.
2   Draw on the shape for half the tie back from the fold of the paper. Cut around the shape, open it out and try the pattern in position. Adjust the shape if necessary.
3   Cut out four pieces from the paper pattern, allowing 1.5cm ($\frac{1}{2}$in) all around for turnings. (If you are short of fabric, two pieces may be cut from lining fabric). Cut out two pieces of iron-on interfacing to the exact size of the pattern.
4   Place the interfacing on the wrong side of two of the tie back pieces (or the linings) so there is exactly 1.5cm ($\frac{1}{2}$in) margin all around. Iron firmly so that the interfacing adheres to the fabric.
5   Pin the interfaced pieces to the unstiffened pieces so that the right sides are facing. Tack and machine stitch taking 1.5cm ($\frac{1}{2}$in) turnings and leaving an opening in the stitching along one edge.
6   Trim the turnings diagonally across the corners and turn the tie backs right side out.
7   Finish off as for straight tie backs.

Café curtains

Café curtains are short curtains, hung from a rod which is placed halfway down the window. They are often kept closed in order to give privacy or to hide an unattractive view. They are sometimes used with other curtains made from the same fabric which are hung from the normal place above the window, and are long enough to overlap the lower tier.

The lower tier can be made in two separate curtains or for a small window, less than 91cm (36in) wide, as a single curtain. The upper tier is usually best made in two parts so that they will look balanced when drawn back. In order to let the maximum amount of light filter through, café curtains are best made in cotton or a semi-sheer synthetic fabric and left unlined.

Positioning the curtains

Although the lower tier should normally hang halfway down the window, if there is a glazing bar in a different position, the lower tier could be placed level with the bar. The curtains should be made long enough to finish at or just below the window sill. The upper tier can hang immediately above the window or, if they are to hang outside the window reveal, about 5cm (2in) above it. They should be long enough to overlap the lower tier by at least 5cm (2in).

The amount of fabric

Café curtains can be made less full than other curtains because of the scalloped heading which does not need gathering. Divide the width of the window by two and allow $1\frac{1}{4}$–$1\frac{1}{2}$ times this measurement

for the width of each curtain. Add 30.5cm (12in) to the length of each curtain for the headings and hems.

If you are using a patterned fabric which should be matched on each curtain, check the size of the design repeat, divide this into the required length of each curtain and round up the amount required to an exact multiple of the repeat measurement. For example, if you are using fabric with a repeat of 41cm (16in) and your required length is 102cm (40in), you should allow 122cm (48in) for each length. The small extra amount can be trimmed off or included in the hem.

Hanging the curtains

The most attractive method of hanging the curtains is from a rod, made from brass or wood, of about 2.5cm (1in) diameter. You can buy brass rods which can be adjusted to the exact width required, complete with fittings which screw into the window frame or into the wall on the side of the reveal. For

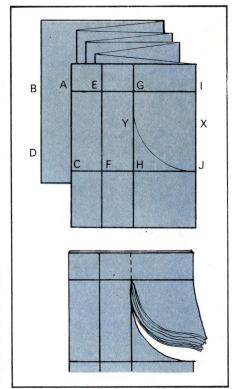

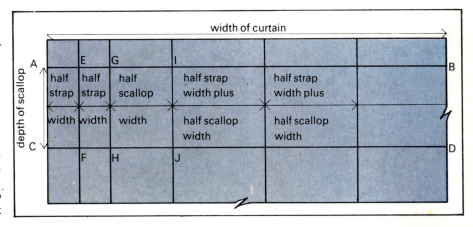

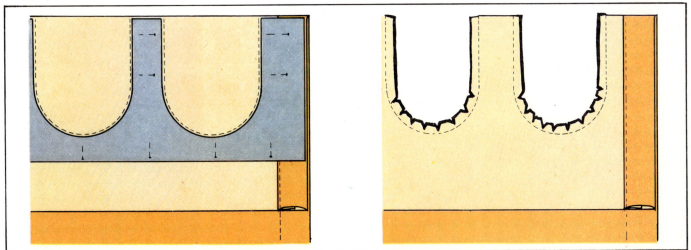

wooden rods, you can buy dowel in the required diameter and cut it to length.

The headings

The traditional heading for café curtains is scallops. The scallops can be made long enough to form loops which slip onto the rod or you can sew on hooks which slide onto the rod. Between 10cm–15cm (4in–6in) is a suitable depth for scallops without loops and 7.5cm–10cm (3in–4in) makes a good width, with 2.5cm–4cm (1in–1½in) for the straps between the scallops. Add 5cm (2in) to the depth of the straps if they are to be made into loops.

Making a pattern

The safest way of ensuring that all the scallops and straps (the pieces between the scallops) are the same width and a good shape is to make a paper pattern. Use a piece of paper the exact width of each curtain, excluding 10cm (4in) for turnings, and about 15cm (6in) deeper than the depth of the scallops.

1 Draw a line (A–B) across the width of the paper about 5cm (2in) from the top edge. Draw another line (C–D) the depth of the scallops below this.

2 Decide on the width of the scallops and the straps and add them together. Divide this measurement into the width of the paper. Use any remaining figure to make another strap so that there is a strap at both sides of each curtain. You may have to adjust the measurements slightly in order to achieve this.

3 Starting at the left-hand edge of the paper, draw a vertical line (E–F) half the width of the strap. Draw another line (G–H) the same distance away from this and then a third line (I–J) half the width of the scallop from G–H).

4 Add together half the width of a scallop and half a strap and continue marking lines equal to this measurement across the paper. At the right-hand edge this should leave an amount equal to half a scallop and a whole strap.

5 Mark a point (X) on the line I–J half the width of a scallop from the line C–D. Mark a similar point (Y) on the line G–H. Then using X as the centre, and the distance between X–Y as the radius, draw an arc to join Y–J. This gives the curve for the scallop.

6 Keeping all the marked lines uppermost, fold the paper along the line I–J,

then continue folding concertina-wise along the remaining marked lines. A section, equal in width to half the strap, will extend beyond the folds at each end.

7 Cut through all the folds along the top line A–B, then cut out the scallop along G–Y–J. When the paper is opened out, the pattern for the complete scallop edge will be formed.

Making up the curtains

1 Turn over 2.5cm (1in) onto the wrong side on each side of each curtain and press down. Turn over the same amount again and make a double hem. Stitch by hand or by machine. Press.

2 Turn over the amount allowed for the scallops plus 5cm (2in) at the top of each curtain onto the right side and press. This forms the facing.

3 If the fabric is flimsy, cut a piece of iron-on stiffening to fit the width of each curtain and slightly deeper than the scallops. Iron it onto the wrong side of the facing allowance so that its edge is level with the fold.

4 Pin on the paper pattern so that the top edge of the straps are level with the fold of the fabric. Tack around the edge of the pattern, excluding the fold, through all thicknesses, keeping your stitches small and as close to the edge of the pattern as possible. Unpin the pattern and machine stitch.

5 Cut out the scallops to within 6mm (¼in) of the stitching. Do not cut along the fold. Clip the turnings around the curves of the scallops and at the top corners of the straps. Turn the facing onto the wrong side and push out the corners of the straps carefully. Tack along the seam line so that none of the facings show on the right side. Press.

6 Turn under the raw edges at the bottom of the facing for 1.5cm (½in) and slip stitch lightly to the wrong side of each curtain.

7 If you are forming the straps into loops, turn the top edge of the straps onto the back of each curtain for 5cm (2in) and stitch down.

8 If you are hanging the curtains by brass rings, stitch these loosely in place by hand at the centre of each strap.

9 Hang the curtains in position and turn up the hems to the required length.

Right: Nothing looks quite as fresh as café curtains in crisp cotton.

Shower curtains

In most department stores you can find a large selection of shower curtains. However, you may not find the colour, style, or price you had in mind. And if you want to have matching window and shower curtains then the choice is more restricted. Fortunately, it's easy to make your own shower curtain. You don't need to make pleats (although you can if you want to); all you need to do is hem a flat piece of plastic or fabric on all four edges and make holes in the top for rings.

The fabric

If you want a plastic shower curtain you can buy plastic by the metre (or yard) in a variety of widths, colours, and designs. You may find this in the bath accessories department, rather than in furnishing fabrics.

To give yourself more scope you might prefer to buy a plain plastic curtain to use as a liner and make an outer curtain out of fabric. You can choose virtually any kind of washable material, for it will be protected from water by the liner curtain. For a glamorous look use lace or a semi-sheer drapery fabric, perhaps in white over a coloured plastic liner. For a more tailored look choose a linen-weave fabric, and for a gay, informal effect a brightly printed cotton.

To calculate how much fabric to buy, measure the width of the area to be covered by the curtain and compare it with the width of the fabric you have chosen. Include 5cm (2in) for side hems, if desired, and 2.5cm (1in) for each seam if you need to join two or more widths. To estimate the length you need, measure from the rod to approximately 5cm (2in) above the floor, if you are making an outer curtain, or the same distance above the bottom of the bathtub if you are making a plastic curtain that will hang inside the tub while in use. Add 5cm (2in) for the top hem. If you are making a plastic curtain, it is not essential to hem the sides and lower edge because the plastic will not fray, although single 2.5cm (1in) hems do make the edges firmer. If you are making a fabric curtain, you should hem all the edges. For the lower hem 5cm (2in) is sufficient. Buy enough rings to place one at each side of the curtain and at approximately 7.5cm (3in) intervals in between. If you are making an outer curtain, the placement of holes will be determined by the placement of holes in the purchased liner curtain.

You will also need an equal number of eyelet rings, called grommets, which you can find in a department store

Making a plastic curtain

1 Check that the top and bottom of the fabric is square with the sides and trim even if necessary.
2 If you are joining widths, apply adhesive in a band 1.5cm (½in) wide down the edge on the right side of one piece, and place the other, wrong side down over it. Press firmly.
3 If you are making hems at the sides and bottom, fold them over for 2.5cm (1in) and stick down with adhesive. Alternatively, sew by machine using a long stitch. It's a good idea to test the stitch first on a scrap of the plastic.
4 Fold 5cm (2in) to the wrong side at the top of the curtain and hold in place temporarily with masking tape.
5 Mark the positions for the holes with a marking pen at the correct intervals, 2.5cm (1in) from the top. Insert the grommets as directed on the package.

Making a fabric curtain

1 Trim the fabric if necessary so that the edges are on the straight of grain. To do this, pull a thread and trim along the line where it has been pulled. If the corners are not right-angles, pull the fabric on the bias until they are square.
2 If you need to join widths of fabric, make a flat felled seam. First join the two pieces with wrong sides together, so that the raw edges are on the right side. Press the seam open. Then press both seam allowances to one side, with the upper stitching thread, not the bobbin thread, upward. Trim the lower seam allowance close to the stitching. Turn under the edge of the upper seam allowance and stitch it in place, covering the other raw edge.
3 Turn under 6mm (¼in) at the top and baste or finger-press. Turn under another 4.5cm (1¾in) and machine stitch close to the folded or tacked edge.
4 In the same way, fold under and stitch the side hems, taking a total of 2.5cm (1in) hem allowance.
5 Turn up the lower edge and hem in the same way. Note: if you prefer you can, of course, hem all four edges by hand. This is recommended if you are using a fabric in a plain colour.
6 Mark and punch holes and insert grommets as directed.

A gathered curtain

If you want a shower curtain that falls in pretty folds even when it's pulled across the tub or shower stall, you can easily achieve this effect by gathering the fabric. Buy enough to cover the distance 1½ to 2 times. Hem and seam in the same way as for a plain fabric curtain, but make the top hem the same depth as the sides. Machine stitch a double gathering thread far enough down from the top hemmed edge so that the heading will cover the shower rod. Draw up the gathers to fit the distance to be covered and fasten the ends securely. Shorten the machine stitch and stitch between the two lines of gathering. You may want to add some narrow braid to cover the stitching line. Pull out the gathering threads. Buy small plastic curtain rings and sew them to the underside of the curtain at the gathered line, spacing the rings to match the spacing on the liner curtain. To hang the curtain, slip the small rings onto the larger rings on the rod.

A pleated curtain

If you prefer pleats to gathers, you can make a pleated shower curtain in much the same way as you would make pleated curtains. The top hem should have a piece of stiffening, such as petersham, inserted before stitching it in place. Figure the depth of the top hem as for the gathered curtain. The curtain should be 1½ to 2 times the width of the area to be covered. Make pleats as directed on pp. 19–20.

The essence of successful decorating is in the blending of colours and textures. And what simpler decorating device could you employ to point this up than new shower curtains to transform a rather bland bathroom. Overnight, with a bright new colour, a different fabric or material, a startling print or pattern, you can create a whole new atmosphere. A vinyl curtain in a bright colour or a designer print will give an ultra-modern look, while a formal flower print fabric can impart a traditional and luxurious feeling.

Roller blinds

Roller blinds are one of the easiest ways to give a new look to your home. Make your own and you can match them to any room. Roller blinds can easily be made to fit almost any window, using your own fabric and a roller available in kit form.

Measuring for blinds

A roller blind can be hung either inside or outside the window recess, depending on the shape of the window and the frame. If it is to hang inside the recess, check that the window fittings do not protrude far enough to touch the fabric. If the recess is shallow, or the window narrow, hang the blind outside the recess.

Measure the size of the area to be covered by the blind with a wooden yard stick or steel rule, rather than a fabric tape measure, so that the measurements are absolutely accurate.

Measuring inside the recess

1 First measure the width of the recess. The roller should be cut 2.5cm (1in) smaller than this, to allow for the pins and brackets to be fitted at either end.

The width of the fabric should be the same as the roller before the pins are attached, plus 5cm (2in) for side hems if necessary. Alternatively, the sides can be bound with bias binding, in which case the fabric is cut to the size of the roller.

2 For the length of the blind, measure the height of the recess from the top to the window sill and add 30.5cm (12in) to allow for the fabric to be attached to the roller at the top and for the lath casing at the bottom. This amount ensures that, when the blind is down, there will still be some fabric covering the roller.

Measuring outside the recess

1 Measure the width of the recess and add 15cm (6in) to this so that the roller covers the recess well by 7.5cm (3in) on each side. Cut the roller to this length. The width of the fabric should be the same as the roller, plus 5cm (2in) for the side hems. No hem allowance is necessary if sides are bound with bias binding.

2 For the length of the blind, measure the height of the blind and add 45.5cm (18in). This allows for the fabric being attached to the roller at the top, for the

casing at the bottom, and for the finished blind to be hung about 7.5cm (3in) above the reveal and come down the same amount below it.

Cutting the fabric

1 It is essential that the fabric is cut accurately on the grain, so that the blind hangs and rolls up smoothly without puckering. The safest way of doing this is to tear the fabric to the required size. Alternatively, withdraw a thread at the right point and then cut along this line.

2 If you have to join more than one width of fabric to get the right size, cut two widths of the same length and then cut one of these in half lengthwise.

If the pattern continues into the selvedge, join each half length along the selvedges to the sides of the main piece by over-lapping the edges for 1.5cm ($\frac{1}{2}$in), and machine stitching twice, one down each edge. If the selvedges do not match the fabric trim them off and then join the pieces with machine fell seams.

The fabric

Fabric for roller blinds should be firm and closely woven. Holland (a stiff linen) is widely used and it is available in a variety of widths and colours. Its advantage is that it can be trimmed to the right width and it does not fray, so you do not have to make side hems.

Closely woven cotton, hessian and canvas can also be used, although you will need to make side hems, and PVC fabrics in strong, bright colours and patterns are ideal for kitchens and bathrooms.

Making the blind

1 Finish the side edges with bias binding or make hems.

To make the side hems, fold over 2.5cm (1in) onto the wrong side along both edges and press and tack down unless the fabric is PVC coated. For PVC, crease the fold by hand, and hold in place with adhesive tape rather than using pins.

2 Machine stitch, using a large zig-zag stitch, and positioning the raw edge in the centre of the zig-zag.

3 To make the lath casing along the bottom edge, turn under 1.5cm ($\frac{1}{2}$in) on the wrong side. Turn under another 3.8cm (1$\frac{1}{2}$in) and machine stitch.

4 Cut the lath to 1.5cm ($\frac{1}{2}$in) less than

the fabric width and insert it into the hem. Stitch up the openings at each side.

5 Thread the cord through the knot holder, and screw this into the centre of the lath on the back of the blind so that the cord hangs down.

Finishing the blind

1 Before you attach the fabric to the roller, it can be sprayed with spray starch to give extra body. Iron flat.

2 Assemble the roller and pins, and screw the brackets in place, following the manufacturer's instructions. If the blind is being attached inside the recess, allow enough room above the brackets to give clearance for the fabric when it is rolled up.

3 The fabric should be attached to the roller so that it hangs next to the window, with the roll towards the room.

Place the prepared fabric right side up on the floor. Lay the roller across the top with the spring mechanism on the left.

4 Attach the fabric to the roller, using a staple gun or row of small tacks, working from the centre toward the edges.

5 Roll up the blind by hand and place it in the brackets. Pull it down and make sure it hangs properly.

6 If it does not roll up smoothly, tension the spring by taking down the blind and re-rolling by hand. Take care not to over-tension it, however, because if it snaps up too quickly, the mechanism may be damaged.

7 Thread the loose end of the cord into the acorn, and the blind is complete.

Decorating blinds

The instructions given here will enable you to make a very basic roller blind. Nowadays, most people decorate their blinds, using a wide variety of methods to do so. In the following pages we show some ideas that you may like to try. For example, the nursery blind with its attractive moon and stars motif can either be appliquéd onto the blind, or even applied with a special fabric paint. You can also use fabric paint to draw on animals, groups of any kind of flowers you please – in fact whatever you can draw. Another bright idea is to trim the blind with a fabric to match your curtains, or else you can make a decorative hem. The method is shown on page 45.

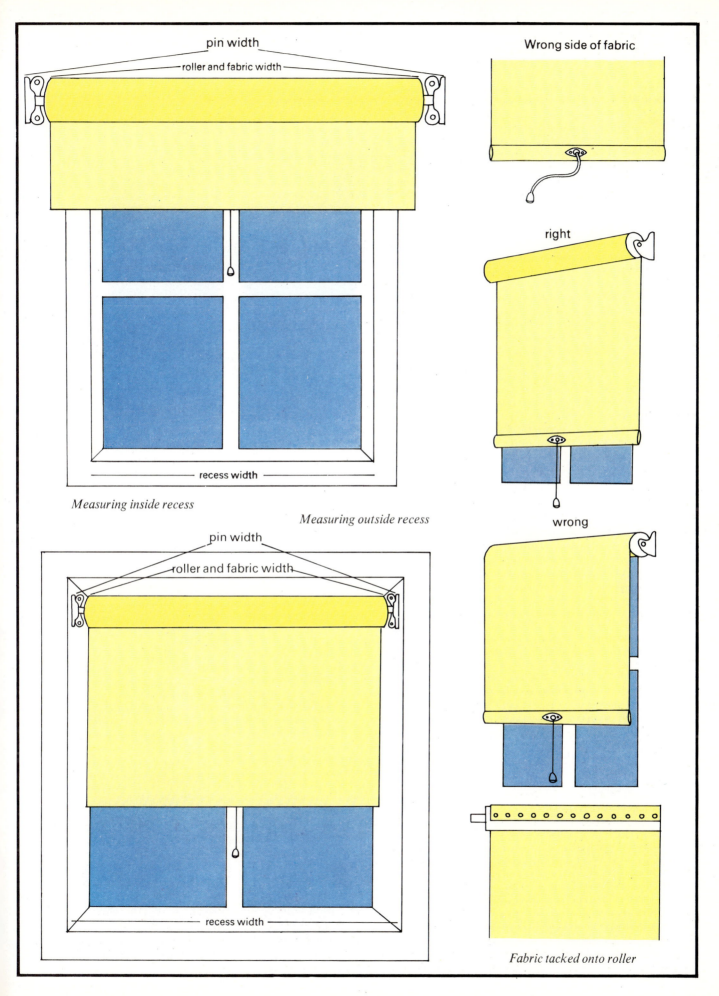

pin width

roller and fabric width

recess width

Measuring inside recess

Measuring outside recess

pin width

roller and fabric width

recess width

Wrong side of fabric

right

wrong

Fabric tacked onto roller

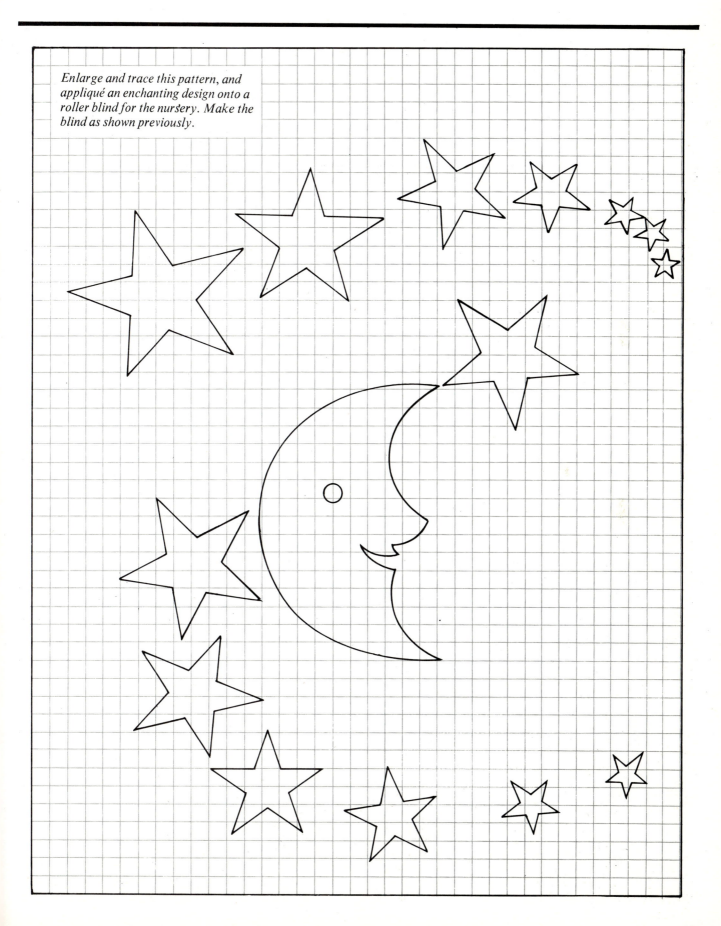

Enlarge and trace this pattern, and appliqué an enchanting design onto a roller blind for the nursery. Make the blind as shown previously.

Shaped hems for blinds

A shaped hem adds a professional and distinctive finish to a home-made roller blind and it is fairly simple to make.

The hem can look attractive on either a plain or patterned blind. The styles can be made using regular fabric which is stiffened when the blind is complete or from special blind fabric which is sold pre-stiffened and can be cut without turnings because it does not fray.

Shaped hems can either be made to come below the casing of the wooden stretcher batten or to incorporate pockets to hold a decorative pole which takes the place of the stretcher. The pole can be of the type made for café curtains, either wood or brass, about 2.5cm (1in) in diameter and available with a variety of decorative finials (end pieces).

For both styles, except where the pockets for the pole are simple strips (see below), you will need to make a paper pattern of the required shape.

For details about making basic roller blinds, see preceding pages. Add 15cm (6in) to the length of fabric required.

Making a pattern
1   Cut a strip of paper 15cm (6in) deep x the width of the blind. Fold it in half so that the shape of each side will be symmetrical.
2   Draw the shape you want onto the paper using a ruler and compasses (or a saucer) as a guide to straight lines and smooth curves. Do not make the curves deeper than about 10cm (4in). The diagrams below give some ideas for shapes.
3   For hems which incorporate straps to hang the pole, make the downwards sections about 5cm (2in) longer than the length of the blind so that the excess can be turned up.

Hems with wooden battens
1   For blinds made in unstiffened fabrics with a shaped hem below the casing for a regular wooden stretcher batten, cut a piece of fabric to match the blind, making it the same width as the blind plus 2.5cm (1in) for turnings x 15cm (6in) deep. Iron on a piece of stiffening to give the hem extra body.
2   With right sides together, place this stiffened facing onto the bottom of the blind so that the lower edges are level and 1.5cm ($\frac{1}{2}$in) of the facing extends at each side. If you are using patterned fabric check that the pattern is running

the correct way up on the facing.
3   Pin the paper pattern onto the fabric with the shaped edge 6mm ($\frac{1}{4}$in) from the bottom. Cut around, leaving a margin of 6mm ($\frac{1}{4}$in) for turnings.
4   Remove the pattern and tack and machine stitch along the shaped edge. Clip into the turnings and press the facing onto the wrong side of the blind.
5   Turn under 6mm ($\frac{1}{4}$in) along the top edge of the facing and press. Turn under the side edges of the facing and slip stitch, leaving an opening on one side until the stretcher batten has been in-

Above: A scalloped hem looks really crisp and fresh on roller blinds.

Opposite: Match up hem with curtains

serted. Tack and machine stitch along the top fold of the facing and stitch another line 2.5cm (1in) below this to form the casing for the stretcher.
6   For blinds made from stiffened fabrics, cut a strip 5cm (2in) wide from the bottom edge of the blind and reserve it for the casing.
7   Cut the shaped hem using the pattern

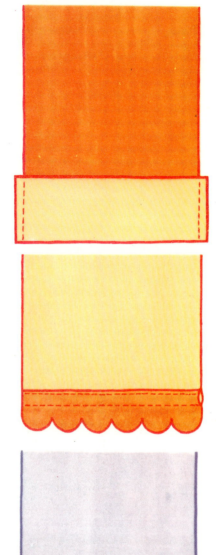

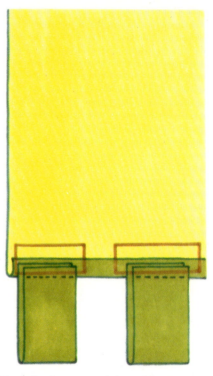

Far left: A variety of shaped hems, some with wooden battens inserted into casing above the hem, and others with poles through the pockets.

Centre: Stages in making the casing, then attaching hem or pockets.

Above: To attach the pockets to the blind, first attach them on the wrong side of the blind with adhesive tape, then stitch on the right side.

along the bottom of the blind but do not add any allowance for turnings. Place the strip for the casing into position on the wrong side of the blind and machine stitch along each edge.

Hems with decorative battens
1 For unstiffened fabrics cut and attach the facing in a similar way as for a regular casing. Turn it onto the wrong side, fold under the top edge for 6mm (¼in) and slip hem into position.
2 Turn up the bottom edges of the downward pieces for 5cm (2in) and pin in position. Try the batten in place to check for size and adjust if necessary. Machine stitch the straps in place.
3 For blinds made from stiffened fabrics, cut the hem with the sections for the straps from the paper pattern, turn them up for 5cm (2in) and machine.

Simple pockets
This method is particularly suitable for blinds made with stiffened fabric.
1 Decide on the positions for the pockets, making them 5cm (2in) wide and placing one at each side of the blind and then at equal intervals of approximately 7.5cm (3in) in between. Mark the positions lightly in pencil along the bottom edge of the blind fabric.
2 Turn up a single 2.5cm (1in) hem

along the bottom of the blind and secure temporarily with adhesive tape placed in between the positions for the pockets. (Do not use pins as these leave holes.)
3 Cut strips of matching fabric 10cm (4in) long x 5cm (2in) wide. Fold the strips in half widthways and place the doubled edges onto the wrong side of the blind, level with the raw edge of the hem. Secure temporarily with adhesive tape.
4 Machine stitch along the hem through all thicknesses from the right side to ensure a really straight line. Use a fairly long stitch and push the fabric through the foot slowly. If the machine sticks, place tissue paper over the stitching line and work through this. Pull the paper away after stitching.
5 Insert the stretcher pole into the pockets and hang the blind in position.

TABLE LINEN

Tablecloths and napkins no longer create the laundering problems our grandmothers had. With the lovely range of easy care fabrics now available, you can make non-iron and drip-dry table linen in colours to match your china, to set off a table centre-piece, or even to match wall-paper, curtains and soft furnishings. Keep hand-embroidered cloths for special occasions – you'll find that the table settings featured in the following projects are ideal for every day use, while at the same time they are beautifully designed. Use the Provençal set for an informal lunch on a sunny day, and protect your table surface with the practical pocket-style table mats.

Circular table cloth

Ready-made tablecloths can be expensive and are usually available in only a few standard sizes. By making your own tablecloth you can choose the colour and fabric to suit your room.

Fabrics

Any washable dress or furnishing fabrics, such as cottons, linen and manmade fibre mixtures are suitable. Dress fabrics are usually sold in 91cm, 115cm, and 137cm (36in, 45in and 54in) widths and furnishing fabrics in widths of 122cm-132cm (48in-52in).

Patterned or coloured sheeting, in widths of 126cm-174cm (70in-108in), is extremely practical because of its extra width.

Use leftover fabric to make matching napkins.

Circular cloths

For a small occasional table the cloth often looks best if it just clears the floor.

For a dining table a drop of 23cm-30.5cm (9in-12in) is more practical when people are seated at the table. If you want to make a floor length cloth for the dining table it is a good idea to make a smaller, matching cloth with an overhang of about 13cm (5in), with a plastic undercloth to protect the larger cloth from spills and stains (fig.1). It is much easier to wash and iron a small cloth.

Alternatively, if you're lucky enough to find a fabric with a matching, plasticized version, cover the top of the table cloth with a neat circle of the plasticized material.

Measuring is easy. First the diameter of the tabletop (the width across the centre). Then decide on the depth of overhang, measuring from the table-top downwards.

To find the overall diameter of cloth required, add 1.5cm (½in) hem allowance to the depth of overhang, then

Right: Circular tablecloth matches valance and soft furnishings.

1. *Make a small cloth to cover top*
2. *Measure for circular tablecloth*
3. *Cutting plan for cloth*
4. *Assembling the fabric for cloth*
5. *Cloth with braid trimming*
6. *Notched and tacked hem*
7. *Attaching bias binding*

Calculating side panels
Diameter (width) of tabletop=105cm (41in). 2 × overhang of 30cm (12in) plus 1.5cm (½in) hem allowance= 63cm (25in).
Diameter (width) of unfinished cloth =168cm (66in).
Finished width of centre panel= 122cm (48in) minus 3cm (1in) for joining seams=119cm (47in).
Therefore, combined width of panels needed=168cm (66in) minus 119cm (47in)=49cm (19in) plus 3cm (1in) for seams.
Cut width of each panel=24.5cm (9½in)+1.5cm (½in)=26cm (10in).

diameter of cloth=
diameter of table top +
2 x (overhang +1.5cm (½in) hem allowance)

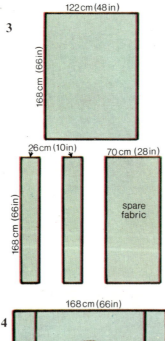

122cm (48in)

168cm (66in)

26cm (10in)   70cm (28in)

168cm (66in)

spare fabric

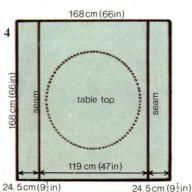

168cm (66in)

168cm (66in)   seam   table top   seam

119cm (47in)

24.5cm (9½in)   24.5cm (9½in)

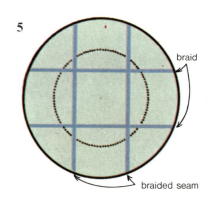

braid

braided seam

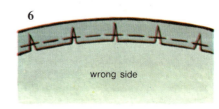

wrong side

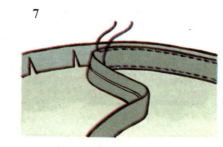

double this total and add it to the diameter of the table (fig.2).

The quickest way of joining fabric to make a circular tablecloth is to cut it from a square of fabric with each side equal to the diameter of the unfinished cloth. This avoids the necessity of seaming ànd of pattern matching. It is also the most economical method as you only need one length of fabric equal to the unfinished diameter.

If your chosen fabric is not wide enough to do this, join equal widths of fabric to each side of the main section, to make a square of fabric with sides equal to the diameter of the unfinished cloth (figs.3 and 4).

The main section of fabric should be wide enough to cover the tabletop (fig.4). You will need to buy a length of fabric twice the diameter of the unfinished cloth (allow extra for matching a pattern).

Figs. 3 and 4 show how to cut and assemble fabric to make a cloth with a diameter of 165.5cm (66in) from 122cm (48in) wide fabric. For a cloth of another size make your own calculation by using the formula given in fig.4.

When the cloth is on the table the seams will fall in an uneven arc on the overhang. These will be unobtrusive on a patterned fabric.

With a plain fabric a feature can be made of the seams by covering them with braid or ribbon and thèn stitching corresponding lines of braid to the cloth to cross the seams at right angles (fig.5). This looks attractive only if the centre panel is narrower than the table.

Make a paper pattern. A pattern ensures an accurate shape when cutting out a circular tablecloth. You need an exact square of paper with each side a little longer than the radius (half the diameter) of the unfinished cloth.

Draw a quarter-circle on the paper with a radius of the finished cloth, plus 1.5cm (½in) hem allowance. Cut along the pencilled line. This gives the pattern for one quarter of the unfinished cloth.

It is essential in making up to make sure that, when cutting out and tacking, you match the pattern of the fabric.

Cut out the side panels and tack them to the main section of fabric 1.5cm (½in) from the edge, with right sides together (figs.3 and 4).

Machine stitch the seams using a plain seam or, if the cloth is to be washed regularly, using a flat fell seam to enclose the edges.

If the seams are to be covered with braid or ribbon sew plain seams, with wrong sides together, trim seam allowances to 6mm (¼in) and press them open. Cover raw edges with the trimming.

The resulting square should have sides equal to the diameter of the unfinished tablecloth.

Fold the square of fabric into quarters to make a square with sides equal to the radius of the cloth. Pin paper pattern on to the fabric so that its square corner is in the corner of the fabric where the folds meet. Cut through the fabric along the curved edge of the pattern. Do not cut along folds. Unpin pattern and unfold fabric.

To make the hem, snip little 'V' shaped notches into the edge at 2.5cm (1in) intervals, 9mm (⅜in) deep. Turn in 1.5cm (½in) all around, pin and tack. The notches will close up allowing the hem to lie flat (fig.6).

Neaten the hem with bias binding. Measure around the hem to determine the amount of bias binding needed, adding on an extra 5cm (2in) for overlapping the binding.

Pin and tack bias binding over the turned hem to cover the raw edge, then machine stitch the binding into place (fig.7), neatening the ends by turning in 6mm (¼in) and overlapping. Press the cloth.

To trim around the edge of the cloth choose a braid or fringe with enough 'give' to enable you to ease it smoothly around the curve (bias binding will not be needed).

Snip small 'V' notches, 9mm (⅜in) deep, into the edge of the cloth at 2.5cm (1in) intervals. Turn up a 1.5cm (½in) hem onto the right side of the cloth and attach the braid over the raw edge in the same way as you would attach the bias binding for an untrimmed hem. Press the finished cloth.

Drape cloth over the table, making sure folds are hanging evenly.

Breakfast table set

This bright and attractive matching tablecloth and napkin set makes the perfect setting for a cheerful breakfast table. The combination of cotton gingham and polka dot fabrics creates an interesting border design, and the mix and match napkins complete the picture.

Polka dot border

Cut two lengths of polka dot fabric each 137cm (54in) long. Cut these in half lengthways to give four lengths each measuring 137cm (54in) by 45.5cm (18in).

With wrong sides together, fold each strip in half lengthways and press.

Pin and tack a 1.5cm (½in) turning along the long edges of the strips and press (fig.1). This tacking is left in position until the tablecloth is completed. Following the steps illustrated in fig.2a-d, make a paper template.

Open out one of the polka dot strips and place it wrong side up on a flat surface. Pin the template in position, with point A 2.5cm (1in) in from one short edge of the fabric strip (fig.3). Check that the edges of the template and the edges of the fabric match up exactly.

Using a ruler and a soft pencil, lightly mark in the diagonal edges of the template on the fabric.

Remove the template, and repeat the pencil markings on the other end of the strip as shown here (fig.4).

To make up the border

With right sides together, pin and tack two of the strips together and machine stitch along the pencil guide lines (fig.5). Trim the seam allowance to 1.5cm (½in). Turn to the right side and press, to form

Below: The newest idea in table linen is to combine contrasting prints in matching colourways. Here a set of tablecloth and napkins has been made up in polka-dot and gingham patterns.

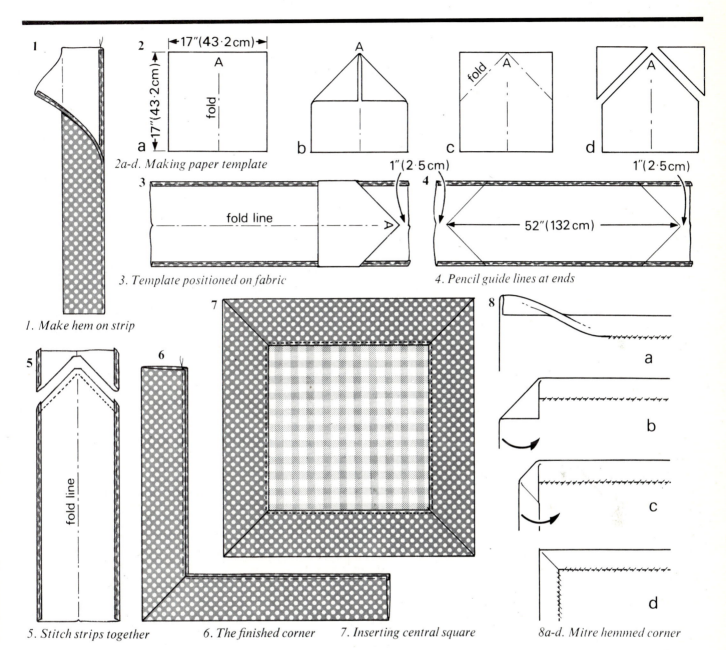

1. Make hem on strip

2a-d. Making paper template

a ←17"(43·2cm)→

A

fold

17"(43·2cm)

b A

c fold A

d A

3 fold line 1"(2·5cm) A

3. Template positioned on fabric

4 1"(2·5cm) 52"(132cm) 1"(2·5cm)

4. Pencil guide lines at ends

5 fold line

5. Stitch strips together

6

6. The finished corner

7

7. Inserting central square

8 a

b

c

d

8a-d. Mitre hemmed corner

the first corner (fig.6).
Tie the loose ends of the machine stitched thread together, and sew them by hand into the line of stitching, to neaten.
Open out the unstitched end of one of the strips and with right sides together pin and tack to a third strip, taking 1.5cm (½in) seam allowance. Stitch along the guide lines as before to form the second corner.
The third and fourth corners are both formed in the same way.
Press the finished border carefully.

To make up the centre
Cut a piece of gingham fabric to measure exactly 91cm (36in) square.
Place the polka dot border on a flat surface and lay the gingham square in the centre. Sandwich the edges of the gingham between the two layers of the border, so that the gingham is overlapped by 1.5cm (½in) all around.
Use the lines on the check fabric to make sure that the gingham square is exactly centred.
Tack the gingham in position and machine stitch approximately 6mm (¼in) in from the inner edge of the polka dot border (fig.7).
Tie the ends of the thread together neatly and remove all the tacking, including the original tacking along the turned edges

of the border. Press the cloth.

Napkins
From the remaining fabric pieces cut two 38cm (15in) squares of gingham fabric and two 38cm (15in) squares of polka dot fabric.
Fold over 6mm (¼in) along one side of the napkins and then fold over a further 6mm (¼in) and hem stitch neatly in place (fig.8a). Make a 1.5cm (½in) fold at the corner (fig.8b) and then fold the second side over 6mm (¼in) (fig.8c). Fold over a further 6mm (¼in) and hem stitch neatly in place (fig.8d).
Repeat for all sides of the napkins and press carefully.

Scalloped table cloth

All measurements must be absolutely accurate, so check everything twice. Trim along one edge of each piece of fabric by pulling a thread and cutting along this line. Take all subsequent measurements from this straight edge.

To make the tablecloth
Working on the patterned fabric, draw a thread to get a straight edge and cut off exactly 180.5cm (71in) of fabric. Measure off a second 180.5cm (71in) piece and trim the edge straight by drawing another thread. If the fabric is patterned and needs to be matched, do this before cutting the second piece.
Working on the plain fabric, measure off and cut another two 180.5cm (71in) lengths in the same way. Cut the remaining plain fabric into four 39.5cm (15½in) squares, for the napkins.

Below: Detail of scalloped edge

Place the patterned fabric pieces right sides together and stitch, taking a 1.5cm (½in) seam allowance. The joined piece should measure exactly 180.5cm (71in) square. Press the seam open. Join the patterned fabric in exactly the same way. Place the patterned fabric right side up on a large flat surface, with the seam running horizontally. Place the plain fabric on top, right side down, with the seam running vertically. Match the edges exactly. Pin and tack the two layers together, running lines of tacking stitches from A to B, A to C, A to D, A to E, A to F, A to G, A to H, and A to I (fig.1). Remove the pins. Working on the plain side, measure 2.5cm (1in) in from the edge EC and draw a line, using a pencil and the yard rule, parallel to and 2.5cm (1in) from the edge. Repeat with the other three sides. Measure 7.5cm (3in) in from the edge EC and draw a line, using a pencil and the yard rule, parallel to and 7.5cm (3in) from the edge. Repeat with the other three sides (fig.2).

The scalloped edging
The scallops each measure 10cm (4in) across and 5cm (2in) in depth. They are set apart with 14 scallops on each side of the cloth. Set the compasses so that the lead point is exactly 5cm (2in) from the metal point. The scallops are drawn from the inner line with their lowest point touching the outer line. Working on the plain side, mark a point on the inner line 6.5cm (2½in) from the central seam. Place the compass point on the

mark and draw a semi-circle to form the first scallop. The edge of this scallop falls 1.5cm (½in) from the central seam. From the right-hand edge of the first scallop measure a point 7.5cm (3in) further along the inner line. Mark this point and draw the next scallop from this (fig.3). Continue drawing scallops in this way until the corner is reached. The final scallop on each side curves right around the corner (fig.4). Continue until scallops are drawn right around the cloth. Tack all around the scalloped lines. Using a short machine stitch around all the scallops on the pencilled line. Remove tacking, trim and clip (fig.5).
Press back the seams along three scallops on one side and unpick the stitching on these scallops. Turn the cloth right side out, then retack and hem the opening. Press the tablecloth carefully. It is important to do this unpicking and re-sewing to keep the shape even.
If desired, two rows of top-stitching can be worked around the scallops 6mm (¼in) and 1.5cm (½in) in from the edge. This helps to keep the scallops in position, and makes pressing easier.

The napkins
To make the napkins, tack two 39.5cm (15½in) squares right sides together as shown in fig.1. The scallops are 2.5cm (1in) deep and 5cm (2in) across, and are set 1.5cm (½in) apart. Draw a line parallel to each edge and 1.5cm (½in) in from the edge. Draw a second line parallel to each edge and 4cm (1½in) in from the edge. Fold the napkin exactly in half, and mark the centre line, Measure 3.5cm (1¼in) from the centre line along the inner line and mark this point. Set the compasses so that the lead point is exactly 2.5cm (1in) from the metal point. Place the metal point of the compasses at the marked point and draw a scallop. From the right-hand edge of the first scallop mark a point 4cm (1½in) along the inner line and draw the second scallop from this. Continue drawing scallops in this way right around the square. Tack and stitch the scallops exactly as described for the tablecloth. Turn the napkin to the right side and hem the opening. If desired, a double row of top-stitching, in a toning or contrasting colour, can be worked around the scallops 6mm (¼in) and 1.5cm (½in) from the edge of the napkin.

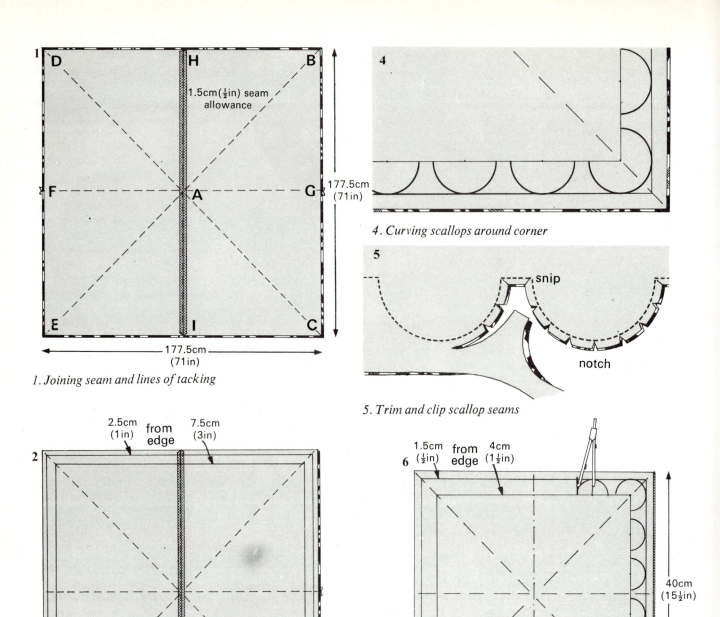

1. *Joining seam and lines of tacking*

D · · · · · · H · · · · · · B
1.5cm(½in) seam allowance

F · · · · · · A · · · · · · G
177.5cm (71in)

E · · · · · · I · · · · · · C
177.5cm (71in)

4. *Curving scallops around corner*

snip

notch

5. *Trim and clip scallop seams*

2.5cm (1in) from edge 7.5cm (3in)

2. *Drawing parallel lines along edges*

1.5cm (½in) from edge 4cm (1½in)

40cm (15½in)

1.5cm
3.1cm(½in) 5cm
(1¼in) (2in)

40cm (15½in)

6. *Marking scallops on napkin*

3. *Marking the scallops*

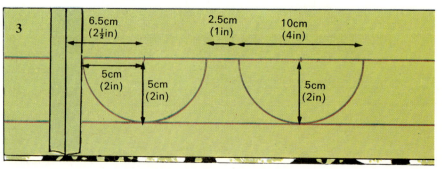

6.5cm (2½in) 2.5cm (1in) 10cm (4in)

5cm (2in) 5cm (2in) 5cm (2in)

Liberty print table set

This delicate tablecloth and napkin set is made up from two different Liberty prints and incorporates three colourways. The subtly matching fabrics complement each other and create an attractive, traditional setting.

You will need
To make a tablecloth 132cm (52in) square and four napkins each 30.5cm (12in) square
2.8m (3yd) 91cm (36in) wide small flower print fabric
0.4m (⅜yd) 91cm (36in) wide fabric in two different colourways
matching thread
tape measure, ruler, soft pencil

To make the cloth

Cut the fabric for the cloth in half lengthways and trim each half to exactly 134.5cm (53in).

Trim 23.5cm (9¼in) off one side of each piece to give two lengths of fabric each 134.5cm (53in) by 66.5cm (26¾in).

With right sides together, join the two halves of the cloth along the selvedge, taking a 6mm (¼in) seam allowance. Press the seam open.

Turn under 6mm (¼in) along one side of the cloth and then fold over a further 6mm (¼in). Hem stitch neatly in place, or alternatively machine stitch in position.

Make a fold 1.5cm (½in) from the corner, turning the corner over diagonally.

Fold over and stitch the second side in the same way as the first, thus forming a neat mitred corner.

Repeat for all sides of the cloth and press carefully.

To make the napkins

Take the two pieces of fabric, each in a different colourway, and cut 25.5cm (10in) off one short side of each.

Trim one long side of each piece by approximately 1.5cm (½in) to give two rectangles of 33cm (13in) by 66cm (26in). Cut each piece of fabric in half widthways to give four equal squares.

Finish off each napkin in the same way as the cloth, taking a total of 1.5cm (½in) seam allowance on each side.

Left: Combine subtly toning floral prints in this delightful traditional table setting in feminine mood.

Place mats and accessories

To make the roll holder

Mark and cut out three circles in the plain brown fabric 27.5cm (11in) in diameter, using a large plate as a guide. If a sewing machine is not available, tack and hem each circle with a 6mm ($\frac{1}{4}$in) turning.

Pin the broderie anglaise edging to each circle and stitch on by hand.

Alternatively, if a sewing machine with zig-zag stitch is available, tack the broderie anglaise to the raw edge of the circles and machine on with a narrow zig-zag stitch (fig. 1).

Place two circles of fabric with right sides together. Divide them into six equal sections by folding first in half and then into three. Mark the sections very lightly with tailor's chalk. Machine stitch the two circles together along these sections, being careful not to stitch over the edging (fig.2).

Place the third circle, right side up, under the other two circles. Pin and tack between the sections of the top two circles. Machine stitch the bottom and middle circles together 6.5cm (2$\frac{1}{2}$in) in from the outside (fig.3).

Turn over the circles and sew the press studs in place (fig.4).

Press flat.

To make the place mats

Mark and cut out four circles in the brown fabric 28cm (11in) in diameter. Cut 5cm (2in) wide bias strips from the gingham fabric, joining them together to make four strips each long enough to go around the mats (approximately 0.9m (1yd) for each mat). With right sides together and having raw edges level, carefully pin and tack the strips to the circles 1.5cm ($\frac{1}{2}$in) in from the edge (fig.5). Turn under 1.5cm ($\frac{1}{2}$in) on the raw edge of the bias strip and hem to line of stitching (fig.6).

Press the mats flat.

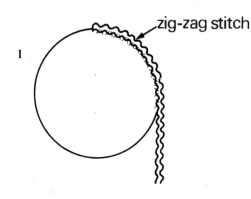

1. Machine-stitch broderie anglaise using a narrow zig-zag stitch

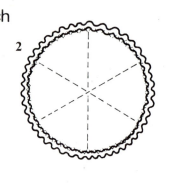

2. Place circles together and divide them into six equal sections

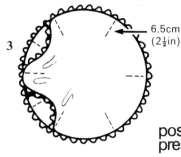

3. Place third circle under the other two, and stitch bottom and middle

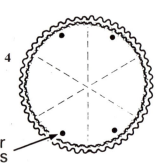

4. Turn over the circles and then sew press studs into place

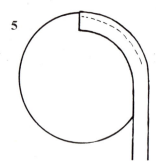

5. Tack bias strips onto the outer hem of the table mat

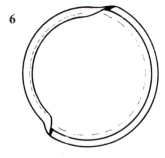

6. Turn under raw edge of bias strip and hem to line of stitching

To make the napkins

Cut four squares of gingham fabric 45.5cm × 45.5cm (18in × 18in). Turn under a 6mm ($\frac{1}{4}$in) double hem all the way around. Tack and machine the hem using a small stitch.

Press the napkins flat.

Right: This charming table setting is ideal for the breakfast table. This design is made up in gingham, but any washable cotton would be suitable. The roll holder can also be used to hold fresh fruit, or fragrant, warmed croissants.

Pocket table mats

Cutting out the mats

1 From the patterned fabric cut four pieces 107cm (42in) wide by 4.5cm (or 13½in) deep. The shorter sides should be cut parallel with the selvedges.

2 From the remaining patterned fabric cut four pieces 15cm (6in) wide × 20cm (8in) deep for the napkin pockets. The longer sides of the pockets should be cut parallel with the selvedge.

3 From the plain fabric cut four pieces 45.5cm (18in) square for the napkins. The simplest way of doing this is to withdraw threads at the required places and cut along their lines.

Making up the mats

The mats are made like large pockets in to which firm tablemats can be inserted for extra protection against heat. Onto one side of these large pockets smaller pockets are sewn to hold the napkins.

1 Fold over the bottom and side edges for 1.5cm (½in) onto the wrong side of each of the napkin pockets. Tack to hold in place.

2 Fold over the top edge of each pocket for 2.5cm (1in) and make a hem 2cm (¾in) deep. Machine stitch in place.

3 Place the pieces for the mats with the right sides facing up and with the longer sides at the top and bottom. Place the napkin pockets, wrong side down, onto the pieces for the mats so the pockets are 5cm (2in) from the left hand edge and 3.5cm (1⅜in) from the bottom edge. Tack and machine stitch the pockets to the mats along the side and bottom edges.

4 Fold the mats in half, with right sides together and with the shorter sides meeting. Tack and machine stitch along the top and bottom edges, taking 1.5cm (½in) turnings.

5 Trim off the excess fabric at the corners

and turn the mats right side out. Tack along the seam line so that it lies exactly along the edge of the mat. Press.

6 Fold under 2.5cm (1in) onto the wrong side all along the open side of the mat and make a hem 2cm (¾in) deep. Tack and machine stitch in place. Press.

The napkins

These are made with mitred corners for a really neat finish.

1 Fold over each side of the napkins on to the wrong side for 6mm (¼in) and press. Make another fold 1.5cm (½in) from the first fold and press again.

2 Open out the second folds and turn in the corners on a diagonal line going through the point where the fold lines meet and at an equal distance from the corners on the adjoining sides.

3 Leaving the first folds turned in, trim off the corner 6mm (¼in) outside the diagonal line, cutting firmly through the folded edges.

4 Find the centre of the diagonal line and fold the corner, with right sides together, at this point so that the adjoining sides of the napkin are together. Stitch along the diagonal line and then turn it right side out, easing out the point carefully with a knitting needle.

5 Re-fold the hems along the original creases and machine stitch or hem by hand.

Finishing off

Fold the napkins into four and then fold in half again. Insert it neatly into the pocket of the place mat.

1. Turn in the corners on a diagonal line going through the point where the fold lines meet
2. Trim off the corner outside the diagonal line, cutting firmly through the folded edges.
3. Fold the corner with right sides together so that the adjoining sides match up. Stitch along diagonal

Left: A really snazzy geometric pattern is used for this thoroughly modern table setting. The mats are made like pockets, so that you can slip in firm mats for extra protection against heat. Each mat has a convenient pocket sewn on the side to hold individual napkins. Make these in a toning solid colour.

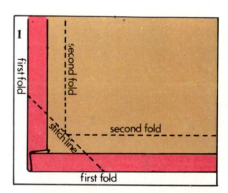

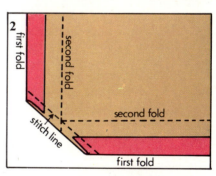

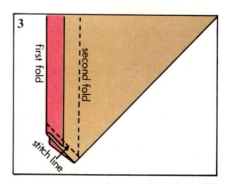

Provençal luncheon set

This charming luncheon set can be made with any washable printed cotton fabric. The one we use here is in a typical Provençal design, in brightly contrasting blue and red. Use with boldly patterned pottery for a gay and inviting luncheon table. The mats are open along one side to allow you to slip a hard mat inside for insulation if you wish.

You will need
4 mats, 4 napkins with rings and breadholder
1.15m (1¼yd) main blue cotton fabric 91cm (36in) wide
0.90m (1yd) contrasting blue fabric 137cm (54in) wide
2.8m (3yd) plain red cotton fabric 91cm (36in) wide
1.40m (1½yd) 2oz Terylene wadding matching sewing cotton
0.50m (½yd) Permastiff
1.8m (2yd) piping cord No. 1
Note: 1.5cm (½in) *seams are allowed on all pieces.*

To make the napkins
Cut out four pieces from the contrasting blue fabric 38cm (15in) square. Cut out 32 equal strips from the red fabric 43in × 5cm (17in × 2in). Turn down the corners of each strip and trim along the fold (fig.1). With right sides facing, stitch the four strips together to form a square (fig.2). With right sides together, stitch the square of fabric into the red square and press the turnings outwards. With right sides and raw edges together tack and stitch another red square to the napkin. Trim the turnings, clip corners and turn the facing to the wrong side. Turn in the raw edge and slip stitch to the stitching. Make three more napkins in the same way.

The napkin rings
Cut out four strips from the contrasting blue fabric 20.5cm × 7.5cm (8in × 3in) and four strips from the red fabric 20.5cm × 9cm (8in × 3½in). Cut four strips of wadding 20.5cm × 7.5cm (8in × 3in). Tack the wadding to the wrong side of the blue fabric and work diagonal lines of quilting through both layers, keeping lines parallel and equidistant (fig.3). With raw edges and right sides together, tack and stitch the red fabric to

the quilting on both long edges. Trim away the excess wadding and turnings and turn the strip through. Press the strip so that the red binding is the same width on both sides. Turn in the seam allowance on the short ends and top-stitch along the seam line on both long edges (fig.4). Ladder stitch the short edges together on the right side and slip stitch the seam on the inside of the ring (fig.5). Make three more rings in the same way.

The place mats
Cut out four rectangles from the main blue fabric 43cm × 30.5cm (17in × 12in) and four identical rectangles from the red fabric. Cut out four more rectangles 44.5cm × 30.5cm (17½in × 12in) from the red fabric. Cut out four rectangles from the wadding the same size as the blue fabric and tack them to the wrong side of the blue fabric. Work quilting on the mats as for the napkin rings following the diagram shown for the mats. Lay one longer rectangle of red fabric over the quilting, matching one short edge. Stitch along the short edge only, taking 1.5cm (½in) turnings. Trim away the wadding and excess turnings and press the red fabric to the wrong side leaving 6mm (¼in) showing on the right side (fig.6).
Cut out two strips of red fabric 45.5cm

1. Trim along the fold of the strip
2. Stitch strips to form a square
3. Diagonal lines of quilting
4. Top stitch along seam line
5. Ladder stitch short edges
6. Press red fabric to the wrong side
7. Tack binding to blue fabric
8. Cut wadding to fit base
9. Tack piping to the fabric
10. Stitch cords to the corners

×4cm (18in×1½in) and one strip of red fabric 33cm×4cm (13in×1½in) to bind the three edges of the mat. Tack the binding to the blue fabric with raw edges together and mitring the corners (fig.7). With wrong sides together and matching edges, tack and stitch the lining to the place mat through all thicknesses. Trim turnings and clip corners. Turn the binding to the wrong side, turn in the raw edge and slip stitch to the stitching. Make three more mats in the same way.

The bread holder

Cut out two rectangles from the main blue fabric 51cm×38cm (20in×15in). In the centre of the rectangles on the wrong side mark rectangles 38cm×25cm (15in×10in) with tailor's chalk and extend the lines to the raw edges. Cut pieces of wadding to fit the base rectangle on one piece of fabric and the four side rectangles on both pieces of fabric (fig.8). Tack these to the wrong side of the fabric and work the quilting as for the napkin rings. Cut pieces of Permastiff to fit the side rectangles and the base from double fabric.

Cut a length of piping cord to fit around the seam line of the rectangle and cover it with a bias strip of red fabric 4cm (1½in) wide. Tack the piping to the piece of fabric with a quilted base on the seam line, matching the raw edges (fig.9). With right sides together tack and stitch the two rectangles together leaving a 15cm (6in) opening in one side to turn through. Insert the Permastiff into the sides and base and top-stitch around the pieces. Slip stitch the opening.

Cut out eight lengths of red fabric 10cm×4cm (4in×1½in). Fold each strip in half with right sides together and stitch the long edge and one short end. Trim the turnings and turn through. Turn in the raw edge and stitch the cords to the top corners of the quilted rectangles (fig.10). Tie the cords together.

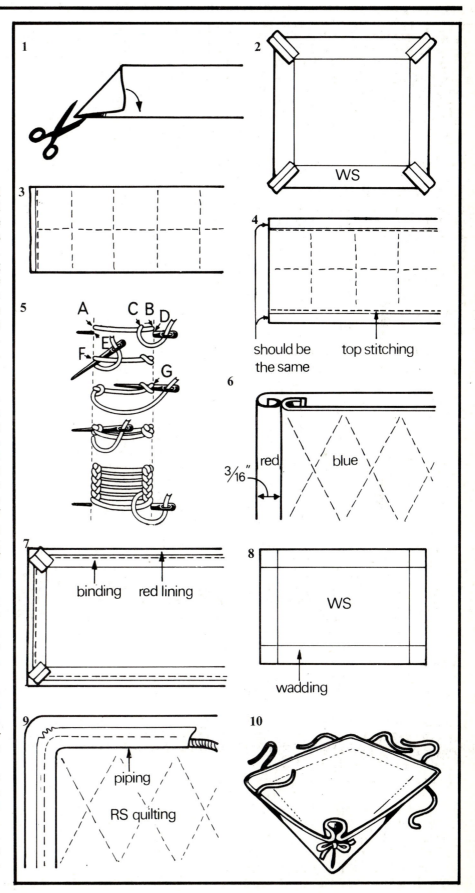

Embroidered table cloth

Size
The embroidery is designed for
a cloth of 180cm (72in) diameter, but
can be adapted for cloths of 152cm–
228cm (60–90in) diameter.

You will need
For a cloth with 183cm (72in)
diameter:

1.9m (2yd) white medium-weight
embroidery linen, 183cm (72in)
wide.
For different sized cloths:
buy a length equal to the required
diameter of either 183cm (72in) or
229cm (90in) wide linen and trim the
width to equal the length.
Clark's Anchor Stranded cotton, 24

skeins Cobalt blue 0134 (used with
three strands throughout)
5.95m (6½yd) white cotton fringing,
5cm (2in) wide
1 crewel needle No.7
Paper for making pattern, 91cm ×
183cm (36in × 72in)
Pencil, length of string and a drawing
pin, tracing paper and transfer pencil

Making the pattern

1 Lay out the paper flat on a surface into which you can stick a drawing pin, and find the centre point on one long edge of it.

2 Tie one end of the string around the pencil and measure 91cm (36in) – or half the required diameter – back along the string. Secure the string at this point to the centre point of the paper with the drawing pin.

3 Holding the pencil upright with the string taut, draw a semi-circle on the paper. Shorten the length of the string to 45.5cm (18in) – or half the radius – and move the drawing pin to the point on one side of the semi-circle where the pencil line intersects the edge of the paper (point A).

4 Keeping the string taut and the pencil upright, draw an arc through the semi-circle (point B). Move the string to point B, keeping it the same length, and draw another arc through the semi-cricle. Repeat this until you reach the opposite side of the semi-circle, thus dividing it into six equal sections.

5 Using a long ruler, draw a straight line from the point where each arc intersects the semi-circle to the centre point of the straight edge of the semi-circle (radii).

6 Cut around the semi-circle.

Cutting out the fabric

1 Press the fabric to remove any creases, lay it out flat and fold it in half. Place on the semi-circle pattern so that its straight edge lies along the fold of the fabric. Pin pattern in position and cut around. Do not cut along the fold.

2 Mark the centre point of the straight edge on the fabric with a tailor's tack and make a few more tailor's tacks along the centre fold and the radii out to the edge of the fabric.

3 Remove the paper pattern, cut through the tailor's tacks and open out the fabric. Mark the centre line and the radii right across the fabric with lines of tacking, It is also wise to overcast the raw edge of the circle to prevent the fabric from fraying while your work the embroidery.

Tracing the design

1 Using the transfer pencil, trace the design within section 1 onto tracing paper. Trace on the parts indicated with dotted lines in ordinary pencil as these are for guidance only and should not be transferred onto the fabric.

2 On a second sheet of paper, trace the design within section 2. Trace on the areas in dotted lines in ordinary pencil.

3 Lay out the fabric on your ironing board with the centre point on the ironing surface. Place on the design from section 1 and position it so that the dotted lines of the radii correspond with those on the fabric. Iron off, using a hot temperature.

4 Go over the design with transfer pencil and place it onto the fabric again so that the dotted lines showing the position of the previous motif correspond with the previous transfer. Iron off. Repeat this until the circle is complete.

5 Place on the design for section 2 so that there is a space of 49cm (19¼in) between the small buds in section 1 and 2. Iron off. Repeat this until you have traced the motif between the radii all around the cloth. The dotted lines on the tracing should correspond with that area of the previous motif.

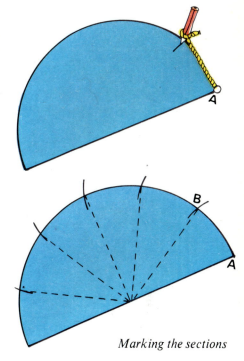

Marking the sections

Key to Diagram
1 Satin Stitch
2 Back Stitch
3 Buttonhole Stitch
4 French Knots
5 Double Knot Stitch
6 Chain Stitch
7 Stem Stitch

Double knot stitch

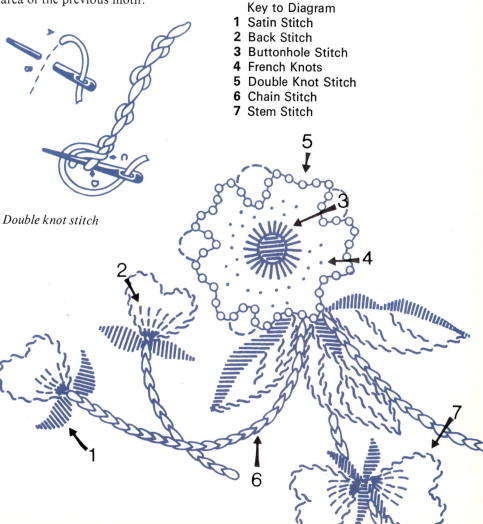

For a different size cloth

If you are making a cloth of a different size, you may wish to alter the position of the outer ring of embroidery so that it is shown to best advantage on your table.

1 Trace the two main motifs in section 2 of the embroidery onto separate sheets of paper.

2 Place the cloth onto your table so there is an equal overhang all around. Place on the flower tracings arranging them between two radii of the cloth. They will probably look most attractive on the edge of the table so adjust the spacing between them to fit, overlapping the small flowers if necessary.

3 When you have decided on the best position, iron off the transfers and repeat until the circle is complete.

Below: Trace off this attractive floral design and transfer onto a crisp tablecloth. None of the stitches used is difficult, and the results are well worthwhile.

Key to Diagrams

Diagram **A**
Diagram **B**

Working the embroidery

Work the embroidery, following the diagram and numbered key as a guide to the stitches. Work each similar part in the same stitches.

Double knot stitch

1 Bring the thread through at point A. Take a small stitch across the line at point B. Pass the needle downwards under the surface stitch just made without piercing the fabric, as at point C.

2 With the thread under the needle, pass the needle again under the first stitch as at point D. Pull the thread to form a knot. The knots should be spaced evenly and closely to obtain a beaded effect.

Finishing off

1 Press the embroidery on the wrong side.

2 Turn up the raw edge around the circumference of the cloth for 6mm ($\frac{1}{4}$in) onto the right side.

3 Place on the fringing so that the top edge covers the raw edge of the fabric. Tack the machine stitch along both sides of the braided section of the fringe.

A

Embroidered napkins

Six bright little birds, each perched on a blossoming branch, decorate an unusual and stylish set of table napkins. Their plumage is realistically shaded with long and short stitch, while satin stitch is used for claws and legs.

You will need
1.15m (1¼yd) fine ecru linen or cotton, 91cm (36in) wide, or six fine linen napkins approximately 35.5cm (14in) square
Milward 'Gold Seal' crewel needle No. 7
Anchor Stranded cotton in the following colours and quantities for each bird:

Chaffinch 1 skein each 048 rose pink, 0160 and 0164 kingfisher, 0168 peacock blue, 0244 grass green, 0255 parrot green, 0301 gorse yellow, 0336 terra cotta, 0355 oak brown, 0360 peat brown, 0378 and 0379 beige, 0382 coffee, 0402 white, 0403 black

Nuthatch 1 skein each 048 rose pink, 0128 and 0130 cobalt blue, 0142 electric blue, 0164 kingfisher, 0255 parrot green, 0323 orange, 0339 terra cotta. 0355 oak brown, 0366 cinnamon, 0379 beige, 0382 coffee, 0401 grey, 0403 black

Blue Tit 1 skein each 0140 electric blue, 0158, 0160 and 0164 kingfisher, 0278, 0279, 0280, 0281 muscat green, 0267 moss green, 0300 gorse yellow, 0355 oak brown, 0368 cinnamon, 0402 white. 0403 black

Gold Crest 1 skein each 0212 laurel green, 0268 moss green, 0278, 0280 and 0281 muscat green, 0300 gorse yellow, 0332 flame, 0355 oak brown, 0368 and 0371 cinnamon, 0402 white, 0403 black

Wren 1 skein each 048 and 052 rose pink, 0213 forest green, 0244 grass green, 0266 moss green, 0293 buttercup, 0306, 0307, 0308 and 0309 amber gold, 0371 cinnamon, 0402 white, 0403 black

Robin 1 skein each 048 and 052 rose pink, 0244 grass green, 0266 moss green, 0326 orange, 0332 flame, 0371 cinnamon, 0372 and 0375 snuff brown, 0378 beige, 0380 coffee, 0391 0398 grey, 0402 white, 0403 black

To make the napkins
Cut six pieces 37cm (14½in) square from the fabric. Using dressmaker's carbon

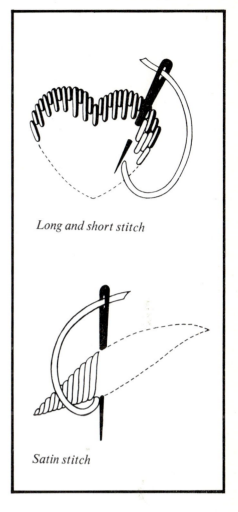

Long and short stitch

Satin stitch

paper or an embroidery transfer pencil, transfer each design onto the lower left hand corner of a napkin 6.5cm (2½in) from the edges.
Use three strands of thread throughout. Each bird is worked in long and short stitch with satin stitch worked for the claws and legs. Follow the coloured drawings for the placing of the colours. To make up, turn back 6mm (¼in) hems, mitre the corners and slip stitch.

Left: A project which will appeal to the dedicated embroiderer, the gorgeous table napkins would make a wonderful wedding gift for a new bride. They'll become heirloom items, brought out with the best silver for special occasions. Each napkin is decorated with a different bird – a chaffinch, nuthatch, blue-tit, goldcrest, wren and a jolly robin. The birds are perched on blossoming branches, looking just as bright and alive as if they were in your own garden.

Chaffinch

Nuthatch

Blue tit

Goldcrest

Wren

Robin

68

BED LINEN

And so to bed. . . . where you can luxuriate in some of the stunning bed linens featured in the following projects. The bed itself is a central focus in the room, and the rest of the decor should harmonize in colour and mood. Easy care quilt covers and matching sheets and pillowcases have revolutionized bed-making – and by making your own you are able to choose the most up-to-date fabrics and designs. The nursery is as much fun to furnish as your own bedroom, and there are some delightful embroidered sheets to brighten a child's dreams. There are also some easy-to-make bedspreads, one in frothy lace, which will appeal to everyone.

Soldier sheets

Use 178cm (70in) wide fabric for child's bed. Subtract width of mattress from fabric width. Add difference to length of mattress for each sheet.

1 Cut the fabric to the length calculated above. Halve the difference between the width of the mattress and fabric, subtract 1.5cm ($\frac{1}{2}$in) and measure this amount from the corners in both directions on each side of the fabric. Mark.

2 Make a dart at each corner by folding the adjacent edges together diagonally so that the marks match and the right side of the fabric is inside. Pin the dart from the marks to the fold on the straight grain of the fabric.

3 Machine stitch the dart, curving the stitching out slightly towards the corners in the middle of the dart. This gives extra ease when the sheet is put onto the bed.

4 Trim the excess fabric to within 6mm ($\frac{1}{4}$in) of the stitching, press the turnings to one side and overcast them together.

5 Fold under 2.5cm (1in) onto the wrong side all around the edge of the sheet. Turn under the raw edge for 6mm ($\frac{1}{4}$in) to make the hem 2cm ($\frac{3}{4}$in) wide. Machine stitch, leaving an opening in the stitching about 2.5cm (1in) long on both long sides of the sheet, 23cm (9in) from the darts at each end.

6 Cut a piece of elastic to fit the short ends of the sheet between the darts. Insert it into the hem through the opening at one end. Secure one end of the elastic there, thread the remaining length through the hem along the short

end of the sheet to the opening on the opposite side. Secure the end and stitch up the openings.
Repeat at the opposite end of the sheet.

Materials required
1 pair sheets and pillowcases, single size.
Clark's Anchor Stranded Cotton (used with three strands throughout):
3 skeins each Kingfisher 0160, Buttercup 0298, Flame 0334, and White 0402; 2 skeins grey 0398
Alternatively, use 1 × 10 gram ball Clark's Anchor Pearl Cotton in each of these colours.
1 crewel needle No. 7.
Tracing paper.
Transfer pencil.

Tracing the design

1 Trace the design onto the paper with the transfer pencil, making two copies for each sheet and one for each pillowcase.

2 Fold each sheet in half lengthwise and place with the top edge towards you.

Place on the tracing paper, with the design, side down, 6.5cm ($2\frac{1}{2}$in) from the edge of the sheet and 4cm ($1\frac{1}{2}$in) from the fold. Iron off, using a medium-to-hot temperature. Repeat for the other half of the sheet to match.

3 Fold each pillowcase in half withwise and crease lightly. Place on the design centrally to the fold and 7.5cm (3in) from the top edge of the pillowcase. Iron off as before.

The embroidery

Work the embroidery, using the key and numbered diagram as a guide to the stitches and colours. Press the finished embroidery on the wrong side.

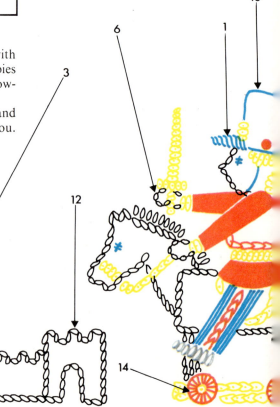

70

Key to Diagram

1 – 0160		
2 – 0298	}	Satin Stitch
3 – 0334	}	
4 – 0398	}	
5 – 0298	}	Back Stitch
6 – 0402	}	
7 – 0298	}	
8 – 0334	}	Chain Stitch
9 – 0402	}	
10 – 0160	}	
11 – 0398	}	Stem Stitch
12 – 0402	}	
13 – 0160		Stem Stitch Filling
14 – 0334		Buttonhole Stitch
15 – 0160	}	French Knots
16 – 0298	}	
17 – 0402		Straight Stitch

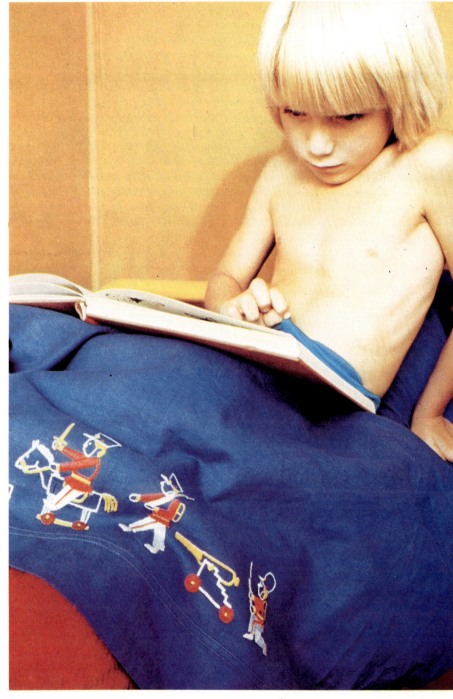

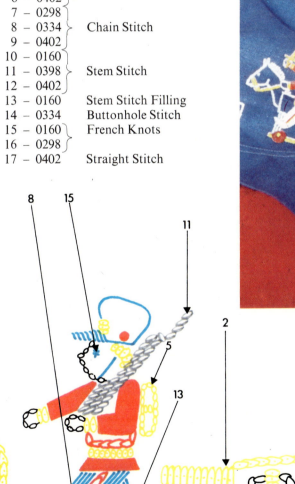

Pillowcases

Pillowcases are cheap and easy to make, whether plain or with a decorative edging. Choose a fabric to match, tone or contrast with sheets and bedroom décor to make an interesting and unusual focal point.

Plain pillowcases with a 'housewife' flap are very straightforward and easy to make. The flap is cut in one with one side of the pillowcase.

To make a pair of plain pillowcases, finished size 47cm (18½in) by 72.5cm (28½in), you will need: 1.1m (1¼yd) of 178cm (70in) wide cotton sheeting.

Cut the piece of cotton sheeting into two so that each piece measures 178cm (70in) by 57cm (22½in). Each piece makes one pillowcase.

Making a plain pillowcase

Cut each piece of cotton sheeting as follows:

One piece measuring 89cm (35in) wide by 49.5cm (19½in) deep (piece A).

One piece measuring 80cm (31½in) wide by 49.3cm (19½in) deep (piece B).

1 Make a narrow hem on one short side of piece A.

2 Make a 2.5cm (1in) hem on one short side of piece B.

3 Place piece A on piece B, right sides facing and matching corners x and y (fig. 1).

4 Fold the flap of piece A over B (fig. 2).

Stitch all around three sides of the pillowcase through all thicknesses, leaving the entire top edge unstitched. Trim corners, turn to right side and press.

Plain edged pillowcases

These are a little more complicated to make and require more fabric. To make a pair of pillowcases, finished size including edge 80cm (31½in) wide by 57cm (22½in) deep, you will need 2.6m (2⅝yd) of 115cm (45in) wide fabric. Cut the fabric as shown in fig. 3.

1 Turn a narrow hem on one short side of piece B. Fold this side 15.3cm (6in) to the wrong side and press (fig. 4).

2 Place piece B, wrong sides of fabric facing, on top of piece A, centring it exactly (fig. 5).

3 Fold sides and bottom of piece A along fold lines, turn a narrow hem and tack to piece B, mitring corners (fig. 6a and b). Machine stitch.

Fold down top edge, turning under a narrow hem so that the hem just meets the fold of the flap piece. Mitre the corners, tack and machine stitch, making sure that the stitches do not catch the flap of B.

Trim corners, turn to right side and press.

Finish off the edge of the pillowcase by working two rows of zig-zag machine stitching with the machine set to satin stitch, placing the rows 1.5cm (½in) apart (fig. 7).

Right: Make these fine pillowcases in a bold mix and match colour contrast.

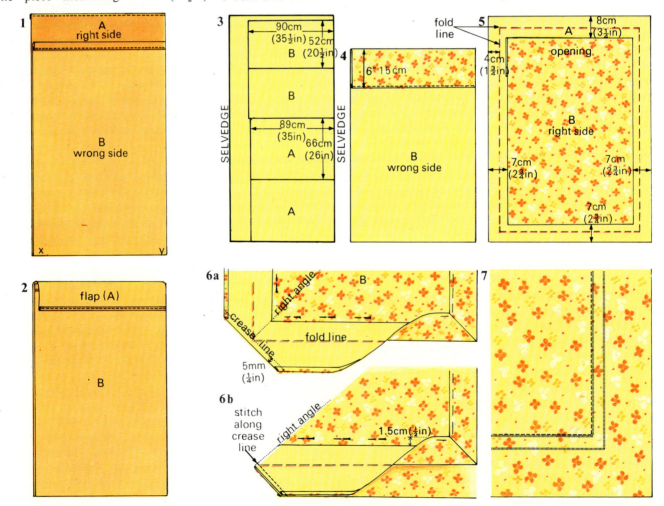

Woven quilt

Making a conventional quilt on an ordinary sewing machine is often impossible because there's a limit to the amount of bulk you can feed through. This woven quilt does not involve machining through wadding and is simply made up from lots of separate tubes, filled with strips of wadding and woven together to give a luxuriously padded quilt.

Choose two colourways of the same print to accentuate the texture.

To make 9 crosswise (red) tubes.
Following the cutting layout (fig.1) cut the 4.1m (4½yd) length of fabric into 9 strips each 91cm × 45.5cm (36in × 18in). With right sides facing, fold each 45.5cm (18in) wide strip in half along the length and machine down long sides, taking a 1.5cm (½in) seam allowance which is given throughout. Be sure to fold strips along straight of grain.

You now have 9 tubes 91cm (36in) long and 21.5cm (8½in) wide. Press the seams open and, with the seam along one side, close one end of each tube by machine. Turn the tubes to the right side.

To make 4 lengthwise (blue) tubes.
Following the cutting layout (fig.2) cut the fabric into 2 equal lengths and cut each piece in half lengthwise to give 4 strips 183cm (72in) by 45.5cm (18in). Fold along the length and make up as crosswise (red) tubes.

Making up the quilt. Cut length of wadding 183cm × 96.5cm (72in × 38in). Cut this into 4 strips 183cm × 24cm (72in × 9½in).

Cut the remaining wadding into 9 strips 90cm × 24cm (36in × 9½in).

Insert a length of wadding into each tube, feeding it in carefully so as not to pull it apart. Turn in the raw edges of each tube and close either with slip stitching or machine. If machining, stitch very close to the edge to give a neat finish.

Weaving together involves assembling

Opposite: An ingenious idea, derived from the principles of weaving, this colourful wadded quilt is easy to make. Choose colourways that make an attractive contrast as shown here.

the quilt on the floor, so start by marking out a right angle.

First lay a lengthwise (blue) tube and then a crosswise (red) tube on top of it, following the lines of the right angle.

Pin down the ends of each tube securely using long glass-headed pins (fig.3).

Line up the other 3 lengthwise tubes side by side, going over and under the crosswise strip alternately. Pin down in position.

Take each remaining crosswise tube and weave it in and out of the long tubes, overlapping the edges very slightly so no gaps appear (fig.4). Secure at each end to a lengthwise tube.

To complete, overcast tubes together all around the outside.

Double bed quilt

Cutting 9 crosswise tubes. Cut the fabric into five 183cm (2yd) lengths and cut each piece lengthwise to give 9 strips 45.5cm × 183cm (18in × 72in).

Cutting 8 lengthwise tubes. Cut the fabric into four 183cm (2yd) lengths and cut each piece lengthwise to make 8 strips 45.5cm × 183cm (18in × 72in).

To make up, cut the wadding into 17 strips each 183cm × 24cm (72in × 9½in). Make up into tubes, fill and weave together as single bed quilt.

Fig 1 / Fig 2

90cm (36")

— cut
--- fold

90cm (36")

45cm 18"

4·25m (4½ yds)

180cm (72")   3·6m (4yds)

45cm 18"

Fig 1   **Fig 2**

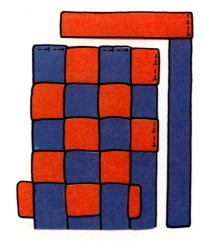

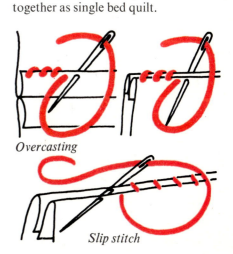

Overcasting

Slip stitch

Continental quilt

Duvets or continental quilts are an increasingly popular form of bedding, devised from the warm feather beds characteristic of Germany and Eastern European countries. These quilts not only replace the top sheet and blankets, but they are easy to handle, light to sleep under and retain heat exceptionally well. Duvets are available with a number of different stuffings: goose down, feathers and a mixture of feathers and down; also synthetics such as polyester mixtures. Of these, pure down is the most superior but all will give a warm comfortable covering. Because of their simple rectangular shape, it is very easy to make a duvet cover and less expensive than buying one. A complete matching set comprised of valance, bottom sheet, pillowcase and duvet cover can be made. There are many interesting ways of making the set attractive and individual: plain or printed fabrics can be used or appliqué worked using a motif from the curtains in the bedroom.

Duvet cover

Size: the average size of a duvet is 137cm × 198cm (54in × 78in) for a single bed and 198cm × 198cm (78in × 78in) for a small double bed. The duvet cover should be about 5cm (2in) larger all around than the duvet. This enables the duvet to move freely inside the cover.
There are various ways of fastening the cover, but the easiest and most popular are Velcro or a zip fastener.

You will need

Single duvet cover: 4.30m (4⅝yd) of 178cm (70in) wide fabric.
1m (40in) of 2cm (¾in) wide Velcro or 75cm (30in) zip fastener.
Matching thread.
Double duvet cover: 4.30m (4⅝yd) of 229cm (90in) wide fabric.
1m (40in) of 2cm (¾in) wide Velcro or 75cm (30in) zip fastener.
Matching thread.

Bed sizes

Quantities and instructions are for two standard sizes of bed.
Single bed size: 91cm × 190cm (3ft × 6ft 3in).
Small double bed size: 137cm × 190cm (4ft 6in × 6ft 3in).

Individual quantities are given for each piece of the set, made from either 178cm (70in) wide sheeting for a single size, or 229cm (90in) wide sheeting for a double size.
Sheeting in a polyester and cotton mixture is preferable as it is quick drying and requires little or no ironing. Unless otherwise stated, instructions given are the same for a single bed or double bed, the base standing 30.5cm (12in) from the floor.
1.5cm (½in) turnings have been allowed unless otherwise stated.

Cutting out

For a single cover cut two rectangles 150cm × 213cm (59in × 83in).
For a double cover cut two rectangles 213cm × 213cm (83in × 83in).

Making up

First prepare the bottom end of the cover to take the Velcro or zip.
Neaten with a zig-zag stitch the two raw edges and turn 2.5cm (1in) to the wrong side and press.
With right sides facing, stitch these two edges of the duvet cover together along this crease line leaving an opening in the centre of the seam the length of the Velcro or zip (fig.1).
Insert the zip into the opening or stitch the Velcro to each side of the opening (fig.2).
Press the turnings open for a zip or to one side if using Velcro.
With right sides facing, stitch the remaining three sides together taking 1.5cm (½in) turnings. Trim the turnings at the corners and neaten them together with a zig-zag stitch.
Turn the cover through to the right side and press lightly.

Fitted bottom sheet

A fitted bottom sheet with elastic corners will fit neatly over the mattress and will not slip out of position; it will also crease less than a plain unfitted sheet.

You will need

2.8m (3yd) of 178cm (70in) wide fabric for single and 229cm (90in) for double bed size.
1m (40in) of 1.5cm (½in) wide elastic
Matching thread

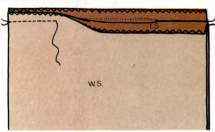

1. Leave opening for Velcro or zip

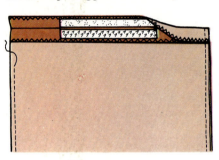

2. Stitch fastener into opening

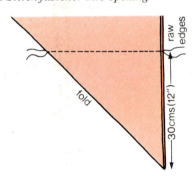

3. Stitching a fitted sheet corner

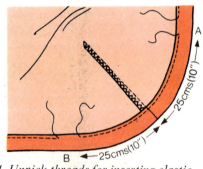

4. Unpick threads for inserting elastic

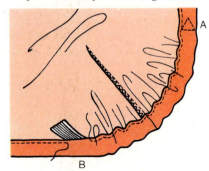

5. Stitch down elastic to gather corner

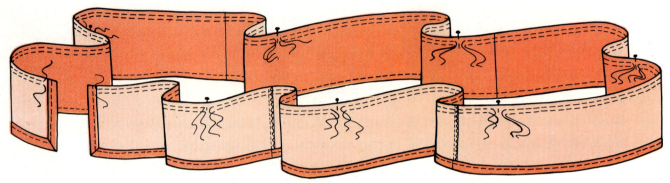

6. Divide frill into eight equal sections as shown

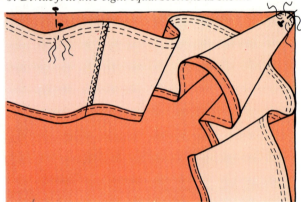

7. Connect frill to corresponding top sections

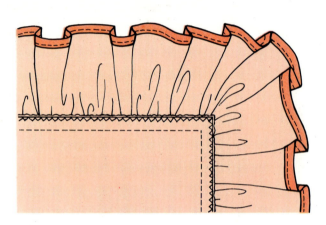

8. Press gathered seam towards frill

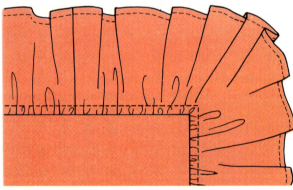

9. Topstitching through all thicknesses is optional

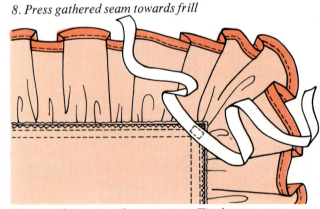

10. Attach tape to valance corners. Tie these to posts.

11. Hem top of pillowcase section

Cutting out

Cut a rectangle of fabric to the size of the mattress plus 38cm (15in) all around. The figures allow for any easy fit.

Making up

With right sides facing, fold each corner of the rectangle so that the raw edges lie together on top of each other forming a point.

Stitch across the corner 30.5cm (12in) from the point (fig.3).

Cut off the point to within 6mm ($\frac{1}{4}$in) of the stitching line and neaten the raw edges together with a zig-zag stitch.

Work a small hem all around the outside edge of the sheet; first turn under 6mm ($\frac{1}{4}$in) and then 2cm ($\frac{3}{4}$in). Machine stitch close to the fold.

At each corner measure off 25cm (10in) to each side of the dart; this section will form a channel for the elastic. Unpick a few stitches at each point, A and B (fig.4). Cut a 25cm (10in) length of elastic and thread through the channel from A to B. Secure the ends of the elastic by stitching small triangles over each end, through all thicknesses (fig.5). Stitch the opening. Press.

Repeat with the other three corners then fit the sheet over the mattress.

Valance

The valance is a frill of fabric attached to a rectangle of matching fabric or calico, and placed under the mattress so that the frill hangs to the floor, covering the base of the bed and the legs.

The length of the frill should be about double the three sides of the bed, unless you wish the frill to go all around in which case it would be double the four sides of the bed.

Above: Detail shows neatly fitted corners and completed valance.

You will need

For a valance which goes around three sides 30.5cm (12in) finished depth:
4.2m ($4\frac{1}{2}$yd) of 178cm (70in) fabric for single bed
4.2m ($4\frac{1}{2}$yd) of 229cm (90in) fabric for double bed.
2.8m (3yd) of 1.5cm ($\frac{1}{2}$in) wide tape for ties.

Cutting out

Remember that 1.5cm ($\frac{1}{2}$in) turnings are allowed throughout.

First cut a rectangle of fabric to fit the top of the bed, plus 1.5cm ($\frac{1}{2}$in) all around.

For the frill cut 6 strips of fabric each from the full width of fabric 34cm (13$\frac{1}{2}$in) deep.

With right sides facing, stitch the frill pieces together into one long strip. Neaten raw edges together with a zig-zag stitch and press to one side.

Trim fill to the required length.

Work a small double hem taking 1.5cm ($\frac{1}{2}$in) along one long edge of the frill (this is the bottom of the frill) and across the two short ends, mitring corners.

Divide the frill into eight equal parts

along the remaining long edge (fig.6). Work two rows of gathering through each section.

Attaching the frill to the base

Neaten the top end of the base cover with a small 1.5cm ($\frac{1}{2}$in) hem.

Measure and divide the remaining three sides of the base cover into eight equal parts and mark with pins.

With right sides facing, gather and pin the frill to the base cover, matching the pins on the frill to the pins on the base cover (fig.7). Pull up the gathering threads and distribute the fullness evenly. Tack and stitch. Neaten the turnings together with a zig-zag stitch and press towards the frill (fig.8).

For a strong finish and to make sure the frill hangs correctly you can add another row of stitches. Work from right side and tack the frill through seam allowance through all thicknesses. Then with one edge of the machine foot to the stitching line, stitch through all thicknesses (fig.9).

Cut the tape into four equal lengths and stitch the centre of each piece to a corner of the valance on the wrong side as indicated (fig.10).

Place the completed valance on the base under the mattress and tie the tapes around the legs of the bed, under the frill.

Pillowcase

For a pillow about 69cm × 48cm (27in × 19in)

You will need

70cm ($\frac{3}{4}$yd) of 178cm (70in) wide fabric

Cutting out

Cut out two rectangles, one measuring 88cm × 53.5cm (34$\frac{1}{2}$in × 21in) and in the other 73.5cm × 53.5cm (29in × 21in).

Making up

First neaten one short edge of the larger rectangle by stitching a small double hem, taking 1.5cm ($\frac{1}{2}$in) turnings.

Make a 1.5cm ($\frac{1}{2}$in) double hem on one short edge of the smaller rectangle.

With right sides facing, place the two rectangles together with raw edges level. Fold the extending flap on the larger piece down over the smaller piece as shown (fig.11).

With right sides facing, stitch the two rectangles together on three sides, leaving the finished ends open.

Trim the turnings at the corners and neaten the raw edges together.

Turn the pillowcase to the right side and fold flap to the inside.

Throwover bedspread

The quickest and easiest type of bedspread to make is the trimmed oblong piece of fabric you throw over the bed. For this type of bedspread choose a fabric that is crease-resistant and has a pattern or a texture, as a plain smooth fabric will appear crumpled – even with care.

If you prefer a soft, feminine room, a flounced bedspread is ideal. Light- or medium-weight fabrics, including dress and lacy fabrics, can be used, but do not use a heavy fabric because it will not gather easily. Also avoid large patterns which need careful matching at seams so causing a lot of fabric wastage.

You will need
The calculated quantity of fabric
The calculated quantity of braid or fringing (optional)
Matching thread
Tape measure and pins

Throw-over bedspreads

Throw-over bedspreads are easy to make and can be finished with either round or square corners.

Taking measurements

For the width, measure from the floor on one side, up and across the bed to the floor on the other side. Add 2.5cm (1in) at each side for hem.

For the length, measure from the top of the pillow to the floor at the foot of the bed (fig.1). If you wish to tuck the bedspread under the front of the pillows, add an extra 30.5cm (12in) to the length. Add 2.5cm (1in) to each end for hem.

If a deep fringe is to be added to sides and foot, shorten measurements accordingly when cutting out.

Fabric requirements

As furnishing fabrics are usually 122cm or 137cm (48in or 54in) wide plus selvedges, you will normally need to join widths of fabric. Therefore double the length measurement to calculate how many metres (yards) to buy. Six metres (6⅝yd) is usually ample for an average single or double bed 190cm (6ft 3in) long.

As there will be some wastage when making a single bedspread, a 91cm (36in) dress fabric might be more economical. If the fabric you choose has a large repeated design, you will need extra fabric for matching the pattern.

Making the bedspread

Cut the fabric across from selvedge to selvedge into two equal lengths. Then, to avoid having an ugly seam down the centre of the bedspread, cut one of these pieces in half lengthways. For a single bed the seams should be along the side top edges of the bed, so cut the centre piece to that width plus 1.5cm (½in) seam allowance at each side. (If the pattern on the fabric is large, cut an equal quantity from each side of the centre piece, to keep the centre of the pattern in the centre of the bed.) For a double bed the seams are controlled by the width of the fabric, and one width will form a panel down the centre.

Joining the panels

With the pattern running in the same direction on each panel, and the pattern matching, attach the side panels. With right sides facing, pin and tack them to the centre piece taking 1.5cm (½in)

Left: One of the most versatile forms of bedcovering is a throwover bedspread such as the one shown here. Make it in a coordinating fabric with soft furnishings, and if possible with wallpaper pattern.

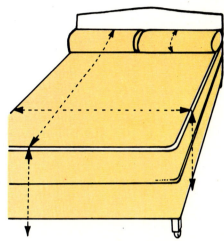

1. *Arrows indicate where to measure*

2. *Square corner on a plain bedspread*

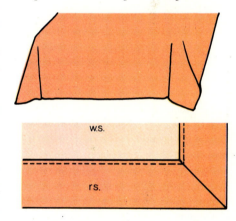

turnings all around.

Place the bedspread on the bed and check the size. Cut off any excess fabric at top and bottom leaving 2.5cm (1in) for hems.

Measure and cut the sides of the bedspread to the required depth plus 2.5cm (1in) at each side for hems.

Machine stitch the seams using a medium-length stitch, clip the selvedges at intervals and press the seams open.

Neaten raw seam edges with a zig-zag stitch, or by hand oversewing.

Square corners

Make a hem along each side of the bedspread by turning in 6mm (¼in) to the wrong side, then a further 2cm (¾in). Tack the hem in position.

Make a hem in the same way along the top and bottom of the bedspread mitring the corners (fig.2). Machine stitch along inner fold.

Remove the tacking and press hem.

Rounded corners

Put the unhemmed bedspread on the bed. Place a row of pins along the top edges on one side and along the foot to mark the depth of the overhang plus 2.5cm (1in) for hem (fig.3a).

Take off the bedspread and place flat, continue the line of pins to the edges.

Draw an arc on this corner and from one row of pins to the other.

Cut along the curved line (fig.3b).

Fold the bedspread in half lengthways, pin and cut the other corner to match.

Turn under the hem along the sides and bottom of the bedspread and tack, easing in the fullness of the fabric at the corners. Machine stitch, remove the tacking and press.

Make a straight hem at the top of the bedspread leaving the corners square.

If required, trim with braid or fringing all around the edge and press the bedspread all over.

Flounced bedspread
You will need
The calculated quantity of fabric
Matching thread
Tape measure and pins
A large sheet of paper and a pencil

Taking the measurements

This bedspread is made to go under the pillows so that the flounce will not be distorted. A throw-over flap of the same fabric can be attached to the top of the bedspread, brought forward over the pillows and tucked in. Make a note of the measurements as you take them – they will be needed to calculate the quantity of fabric required.

For the width and length of the main piece, measure across the top of the bed from edge to edge and from head to foot. Add 2.5cm (1in) to each measurement for turnings.

If the bed has a solid footboard and you do not need a flounce along that edge, add 45.5cm (18in) to the length so that it can be tucked in neatly.

For the depth of flounce, measure from the edge of the bed to the floor and add 4cm (1½in) for seam and hem.

For the length of a continuous flounce around both sides and the foot of the bed, you need one and a half times the total measurement of the two sides and one end of the bed.

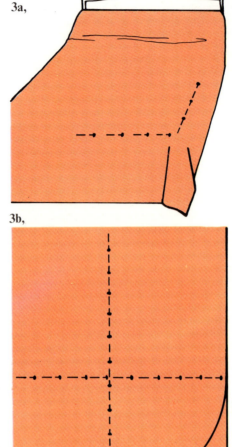

3a,

3b,

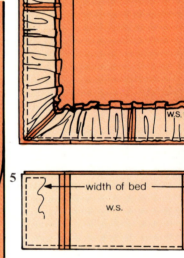

3-7. Marking rounded corners, flounce gathered and stitched on top, lined pillow flap, flap stitched to top of bedspread.

For the pillow flap put the pillows back on the bed and measure from the top of the bed over the pillow to the other side. Add 15cm (6in) for the tuck-in and seam allowances.

For the width of the pillow flap, add 30.5cm (12in) to the width of the bed so that the flap will cover the pillow easily.

Fabric requirements

To calculate the quantity of fabric required, draw a chart. Take a large piece of paper and draw an open-ended rectangle with the width representing the width of the fabric you plan to use. The simplest scale to use is 1cm to 10cm or 1in to 10in. The sample chart on

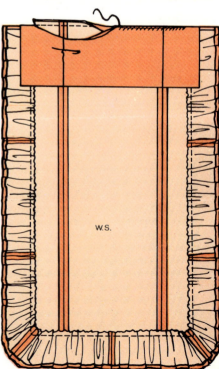

throw-over bedspread along the short ends of the flounce. This will go to the head of the bed. Press.

Make hems along the bottom of the flounce in the same way.

Divide the flounce into eight equal sections, and the sides and foot of the bedspread top into eight equal sections, marking the divisions with tacking. (If there is no flounce at the foot, divide into six sections).

Gather the top 6mm ($\frac{1}{4}$in) from the edge of the flounce, using a long machine stitch or short running stitch. Work another row of gathering 9mm ($\frac{3}{8}$in) from the edge.

Put ends of the flounce 1.5cm ($\frac{1}{2}$in) in along each side from the top of the main section and match the other divisions on the flounce to those on the top section. Pin with the right sides of the fabric together. The tuck-in is attached to the top of the main section after the flounce has been sewn to the other two sides and foot.

Draw up the gathering to fit and pin, placing the pins at right angles to the edge of the fabric so that the gathering can be adjusted easily. Tack and machine stitch the flounce to the top section taking 1.5cm ($\frac{1}{2}$in) turnings (fig.4). Press the turnings up on to the main section and overcast together.

If you are not having a flounce at the foot of the bed, make a narrow hem around the edges of the tuck-in piece.

Pillow flap

Join the pieces of the flap in the same way as for the main section. Make up pieces for lining the flap from left-over fabric or from lining.

With right sides together stitch the lining to the flap with 1.5cm ($\frac{1}{2}$in) turnings, leaving an opening of the same width as the top section in the middle of the top edge (fig.5). Turn right sides out and press.

With the right side of the flap facing the wrong side of the main section, fit the top edge of the main section to the opening and pin it to the top piece of the flap only, leaving the lining free to turn in later.

Stitch the pieces together, taking 1.5cm ($\frac{1}{2}$in) turnings. Press the seam towards the flap. Fold the lining over the seam and hem down enclosing the raw edges (fig.6). Press.

page 86 shows layout for average double bed. Draw the main section first. If the bed is wider than the fabric, measure the remaining section on either side, adding 4cm (1$\frac{1}{2}$in) to the width of each section for turnings.

Draw these panels along the selvedges so that the pattern can be matched more easily to the main piece.

For the flounce cut strips across the width of the fabric, so that the pattern, if any, will run down towards the floor. To calculate how many strips you will need for the flounce, in a plain or small-patterned fabric, draw the strips to the calculated depth. Calculate how many strips would be required to make up the required length. Allow 2.5cm (1in) on each width for turnings.

If you have chosen a fabric with a large repeated pattern, considerably more fabric may be required to match the pattern on the flounce and this will vary according to the pattern.

Draw the pieces for the pillow flap, calculating the width in the same way as for the main section.

When you have drawn in all the main pieces and marked each piece, draw a line across the bottom of the chart. Measure the length of the rectangle and convert back to give the amount of fabric required.

Cutting out

Cut out all the pieces to the size shown on your cutting chart, matching the pattern where necessary.

Making up

Taking 1.5cm ($\frac{1}{2}$in) turnings throughout, join any side panels to the main section as described in making the throw-over bedspread.

Join the pieces for the flounce and press. Make a 2.5cm (1in) hem as for the

Lace bedspread

The bedspread is made with a straight piece of fabric for the top of the bed and has a gathered flounce around the sides and foot. The flounce is made in a continuous piece for divans or it can be in three sections – one for each side and one at the foot – so that it can be fitted around bedposts. Alternatively, for beds with solid footboards the flounce is attached along the sides of the main section only. At the head of the bedspread you can add a throwover flap – sometimes called a pillow flap – which is a separate piece of fabric stitched back to front to the top edge of the straight section to cover the pillows. The bedspread is first put on to the bed without the pillows, which are then put in position on top of it. The flap is folded back over them and tucked underneath. This helps the bedspread to keep its shape because if it were put over the pillows they would pull up the flounce.

The fabric
Lace can be bought from the roll the same way as other fabrics. It comes in widths from 69cm–152cm (27–60in). It can be made from rayon, nylon, wool, terylene or cotton, and some lace can be bought with a scalloped border. As with ordinary patterned fabrics, try to match up the pattern at the seams.

Measuring the bed
Measure the bed with its bedclothes but without the pillows. Make a note of the measurements as you take them and then draw the pieces onto a cutting chart (see over) to estimate the total amount of fabric required.
1 For the width of the main section, measure from edge to edge across the bed and add 2.5cm (1in) for turnings.
2 For the length of the main section, measure from the head of the bed to the foot and add 2.5cm (1in) for turnings. If the bed has a solid footboard and you do not need a flounce along the edge, add 45.5cm (18in) to the length so that it can be tucked in neatly.
3 For the depth of the flounce, measure from the edge of the bed to the floor and add 5cm (2in) allowance for turnings

Left: An utterly feminine bedspread, made up in a simple throwover pattern, using lace as the fabric. Today's synthetic laces are easy to launder.

and hems.
4 For the length of a continuous flounce for divans, allowing fullness and a half for the gathering, multiply the length of the bed by three (i.e. a length and a half for each side) and add one one and a half times the width of the bed. For other beds, simply allow one and a half times the length of each section (excluding any extra for the tuck-in at the foot).
5 Put the pillows back onto the bed and measure for the depth of the throwover flap from the top of the bed over the pillows to the other side. Add 15cm (6in) so that it can be tucked under. For the width of the flap, add 15cm (6in) to the width of the bed so that it will cover the pillows easily at the sides.

Making a cutting chart
1 On a large piece of paper draw an open-ended rectangle with its width representing the width of the fabric you are using. The simplest scale to use is either 1cm × 10cm, or 1in × 12in. The sample cutting chart shows a layout for an average double divan.
2 Draw on the piece for the main section first. If this is wider than the fabric used, you will have to add strips onto the sides of the main section to make up the width. To calculate the width of the strips, subtract the width of the fabric less 2.5cm (1in) seam allowance from the width of the section. Add 2.5cm (1in) for turnings to the remaining measurement and divide by two.
3 Draw in the width of the strips from the selvedges (see the sample cutting chart), so that the pattern can be matched to the main piece.
4 The flounce is made up from strips cut across the width of the fabric so that the warp threads (those running parallel to the selvedge), and the pattern if any, run down the flounce to the floor. To calculate how many strips you need, divide the length of the flounce by the width of the fabric, taking it to the width above (the extra amount will be used up in turnings and gathering).
5 If you are using plain lace in a pattern which does not need careful matching, draw on the strips to the calculated depth. Some of the pieces could be taken from the waste left from cutting the side strips of the main section. If you are using patterned lace which must be carefully matched, compare the

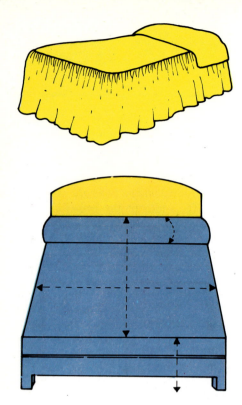

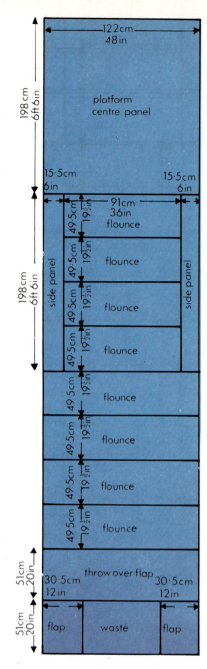

Within the diagram (image 2) labels:
122cm / 48in
198cm / 6ft 6in
platform centre panel
15·5cm 6in (left) · 15·5cm 6in (right)
91cm / 36in flounce
198cm / 6ft 6in
side panel (left) · side panel (right)
49·5cm / 19½in flounce (repeated)
flounce (×8)
51cm / 20in
throw over flap
30·5cm 12in (left) · 30·5cm 12in (right)
51cm / 20in
flap · waste · flap

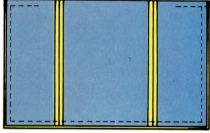

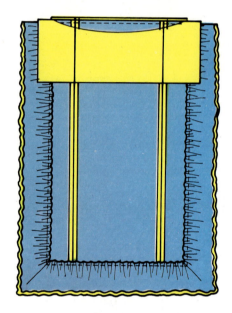

depth of the flounce with the pattern repeat (your retailer can tell you this), and draw on the strips increasing their depth to the nearest repeat above.

6 Draw on the pieces for the throwover flap, calculating the width of the side strips in the same way as for the main section. The flap can be lined with some of the leftover fabric.

7 When all the pieces are drawn on, draw a line to complete the rectangle. Measure the length of the rectangle to give the amount of fabric required.

Cutting out

Cut out all the pieces to the size shown on your cutting chart, matching the pattern on necessary pieces.

Making up

1 If you have to join strips for the top section, do this first.

2 Join the pieces for the flounce in a similar way, but making plain seams. Press the turnings open.

3 Make 2.5cm (1in) hems along the short ends of the flounce. Press.

4 Make a 2.5cm (1in) hem along the bottom edge of the flounce. Press.

5 Divide the flounce into sections for the sides and foot of the bed, marking the divisions with tacking. Then divide the sections into quarters and mark them in the same way.

6 Divide the sides and foot of the main section into quarters and mark them.

7 Gather the top edge of the flounce, using a long machine stitch or short running stitch 1.5cm (½in) from the edge.

Work another row of gathering 9mm (⅜in) from the edge.

8 Place the top ends of the flounce 1.5cm (½in) in from the top edge of the main section and match the other divisions on the flounce to those on the top section with the right sides of the fabric together.

9 Draw up the gathering evenly to fit and pin, placing the pins at right angles to the edge of the fabric so that the gathering can be adjusted easily. Tack and machine stitch the flounce to the top section, taking 1.5cm (½in) turnings. Press the turnings onto the top section and then overcast the edges together.

Throwover flap

1 Join the pieces for the flap in the same way as for the main section. Make up pieces for the lining from the leftover

fabric (mis-matching the pattern will not matter because it will not show).

2 With right sides together stitch the lining to the flap with 1.5cm (½in) turnings, leaving an opening of the same width as the top section in the middle of the top edge. Turn right side out and press.

3 With the right side of the flap facing the wrong side of the main section, fit the top edge of the main section into the opening and pin it to the right side of the flap only, leaving the lining free.

4 Stitch the pieces together, taking 1.5cm (½in) turnings. Press the seam towards the flap, fold the lining over the seam and hem down enclosing the raw edges.

Right: Make this fun eiderdown cover for a teenager's room – it's easy to do.

Frilled eiderdown cover

This beautiful frilled eiderdown cover would make a fascinating project for someone wanting to use up oddments of fine fabric, who also wants to create something really original. Made up here in shades of blue terylene lawn the result is feminine and pretty, but a mixture of patterns and colours would make an equally attractive alternative, although crease resistant fabrics are recommended.

You will need
Materials needed to cover a single divan
2.1m (2¼yd) patterned fabric, A
1.8m (2yd) plain fabric, B
1.8m (2yd) plain fabric, C
1.6m (1¾yd) patterned fabric, D
1.4m (1½yd) plain fabric, E
0.9m (1yd) patterned fabric, F
0.9m (1yd) patterned fabric, G
0.5m (½yd) plain fabric, H
2.8m (3yd) plain sheeting 229cm (90in) wide

To make the frilled cover
Lay out the sheeting singly and cut it into three as shown in (fig. 1).
Make a small hem at the top edge of piece A, either by hand or by machine. Either tear or cut each of the fabric pieces from selvedge to selvedge, into strips 23cm (9in) wide and 91cm (36in) long (fig.2).
Keeping the different fabrics separate, join the strips together, taking a 6mm (¼in) seam. On the wrong side, fold the seam flat to one side, fold over a further 6mm (¼in) and stitch. This gives a neat enclosed seam (fig.3a). Make a small double hem along one long side of each strip.
Join the ends of the long strips to form circles of varying sizes (fig.3b). Pleat the strips on the unhemmed edge, making 2.5cm (1in) pleats at approximately 10cm (4in) intervals, and making several pleats where the strips form a corner.
Pin the pleated frills onto the sheeting piece A, beginning with strip A and positioning it 13cm (5in) in from the edge (fig.4). Adjust the pleats so that they are evenly spaced all around. Pleat and pin the rest of the strips to the cover at equal intervals of approximately 13cm (5in) (fig.5).
Make a small double hem at the top

edge of the sheeting piece B and with right sides together, place the frilled cover on top of piece B (fig.6a).
Fold over the flap on piece B (fig.6b) and

stitch all around three sides of the cover through all thicknesses, leaving the top edge unstitched (fig.6c). Trim the corners and turn to the right side.

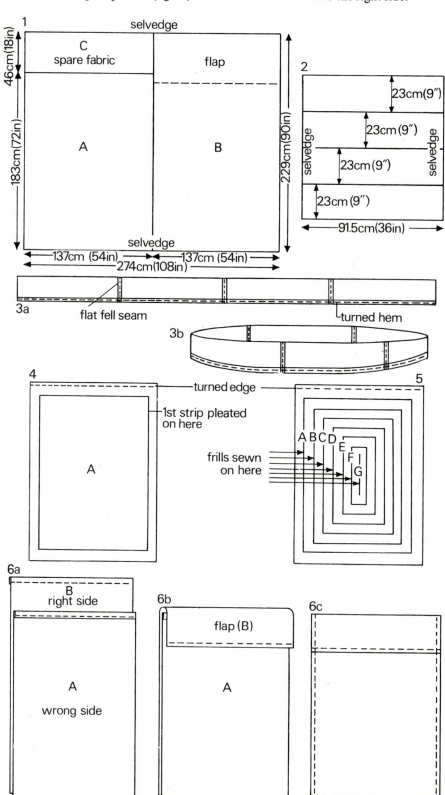

Smocked gingham bedspread

Cutting out the bedspread
Cut out the gingham and backing fabric as for a bedspread with a gathered flounce.

Making up
1 Mount each piece of gingham with a plain piece of fabric. Tack around edge.
2 Join the pieces for the flounce, matching the checks of the gingham carefully.

Working the smocking
The smocking is different from regular smocking in that the fabric is not gathered first. The stitches are worked on the corners of the gingham squares and form a honeycomb pattern.
1 Working from right to left on the right side of the fabric, leave a complete gingham square along the top and right hand edge of the flounce. Using three strands of embroidery thread, knot the end of the cotton and make a small stitch at the bottom right hand corner of the first square.
2 Pass the thread along the front of the fabric and make another small stitch at the bottom right hand corner of the next square. Pull the thread tight, thus drawing the first and second stitches together. Make another half back stitch and pass the needle onto the wrong side of the fabric. This completes the first honeycomb stitch.
3 Still with the needle on the wrong side, bring it out at the corner of the next square.
4 Keep the fabric flat between the previous stitch and this point and make a small back stitch to secure the front of the fabric and make a small stitch at the corner of the next square.
Pull the thread tight to draw the third and fourth squares together.
5 Continue like this until six honeycomb stitches have been made.

6 Move to the row below and work five honeycomb stitches in the alternate spaces to the row above so you are joining the second square to the third, the fourth to the fifth and so on.
7 Work four honeycomb stitches centrally in the third row so you are omitting the first and sixth stitches of the first row.
8 Work three honeycomb stitches in the fourth row, two stitches in the fifth row and one stitch in the sixth row to complete the V shape.
9 Work the next blocks of stitches in the same way all along the length of the flounce. You will now see how the space between the blocks forms an inverted 'V' shape.

Attaching the flounce
1 When all the smocking has been worked, it will form into pleats automatically along the top edge of the flounce. Pin these down and secure with tacking.
2 Make narrow hems along the side edges of the flounce.
3 Pin the top edge of the flounce around the edge of the main section of the bedspread and machine stitch taking 1.5cm (½in) turnings. Neaten the turnings and press them onto the main section.
4 Make a hem along the top edge of the main section.
5 Try the bedspread on the bed and mark the hem line so that it just clears the floor.
6 Stitch the hem and press the finished bedspread.

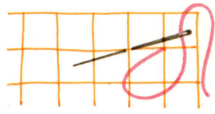
Making the first honeycomb stitch

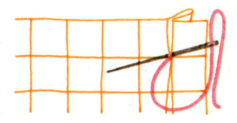

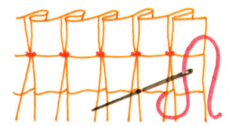
Working row of five stitches

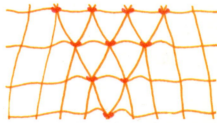
Above: Completing the 'V' shape
Below: Detail of design on bedspread.

Quilted cot warmer

By lining an ordinary cot with this pretty quilted warmer, it can be transformed into a cradle for a new baby. Remove the lining when the baby is a little older and the quilt will provide sufficient warmth.

You will need
To fit a cot 56cm (22in) by 117cm (46in), with sides 61cm (24in) high
4.10m (4½yd) patterned cotton fabric 122cm (48in) wide (A)
1.8m (2yd) contrast patterned fabric 122cm (48in) wide (B)
4.10m (4½yd) striped cotton fabric 122cm (48in) wide (C)
4.10m (4½yd) terylene wadding 122cm (48in) wide
matching sewing threads
3.2m (3½yd) piping cord
1.4m (1½yd) iron-on vilene 91cm (36in) wide
6.9m (7½yd) straight tape to match striped fabric
3.2m (3½yd) bias binding 2.5cm (1in) wide to match both patterned fabrics

To make the cot warmer
Wash and pre-shrink all the cotton fabrics and the straight tape.
Cut the patterned fabric (A) and the striped fabric (C) to measure 331cm × 61cm (131in × 24in).
Cut the terylene wadding to measure 330cm × 58.5cm (130in × 23in).
Trace off the tulip shapes from the trace pattern given, and cut four flowers and four leaves from the vilene.
The fabric shapes are cut with a 1.5cm (½in) seam allowance all around.
Place the vilene shapes on the wrong side of the cotton fabrics and iron in position. Cut four flower shapes from each of the fabrics (B) and (C) and four leaf shapes from each of the fabrics (C) and (A), remembering to include the seam allowances.
Fold the seam allowances over the vilene shapes and tack in place.
Position the fabric shapes on both the large fabric pieces (fig.1), placing the flowers on the contrasting fabrics.
Tack in place and machine stitch all around each shape, close to the edge.
The tulip stems are formed from the

Left: A padded cot warmer makes a snug haven for baby, and gives protection from banging against the sides too.

matching straight tape. Cut eight 23cm (9in) lengths, turn under 1.5cm (½in) at each end, and machine stitch in position. Place the two pieces of quilted fabric together with right sides facing, and tack in place.
Machine stitch around three sides, taking a 1.5cm (½in) seam allowance, leaving one short side open.
Turn to the right side and insert the terylene wadding, pre-cut to the correct size.
Close the fourth side by hand, taking small hemming stitches.
To form the sides of the cot warmer, tack and stitch through all thicknesses from T to W, S to X and R to Y.
To complete the quilting, machine stitch 1.5cm (½in) around each tulip shape and around the leaf shapes, through all thicknesses (fig.3).
To finish off, sew 45.5cm (18in) lengths of straight tape to the edges of the warmer at the positions indicated (fig.1).

To make the quilt
Cover the piping cord with the 2.5cm (1in) wide bias tape.
Cut both the striped fabric and the patterned fabric (B) to measure 91cm × 56cm (36in × 22in).
Cut the terylene wadding to measure 89cm × 53.5cm (35in × 21in).
Trace off one flower shape and one leaf shape from the vilene.
Prepare the flower and the leaf shape in the striped fabric (C). Position the tulip on the main fabric piece (B) as shown (fig.2), and tack and stitch in place.
The stem is formed as before, using the straight tape.

Making up
Tack the piping in place all around the edge of one main fabric piece, positioning it 6mm (¼in) from the edge. With right sides facing, tack the two halves of the quilt together and machine stitch around three sides, taking a 1.5cm (½in) seam allowance, leaving one short side open.
Turn to the right side and insert the terylene wadding, pre-cut to the correct size. Close the fourth side by hand, as before.
To complete the quilt, machine stitch 1.5cm (½in) around the tulip petals and around the leaf shape, through all thicknesses (fig.3).

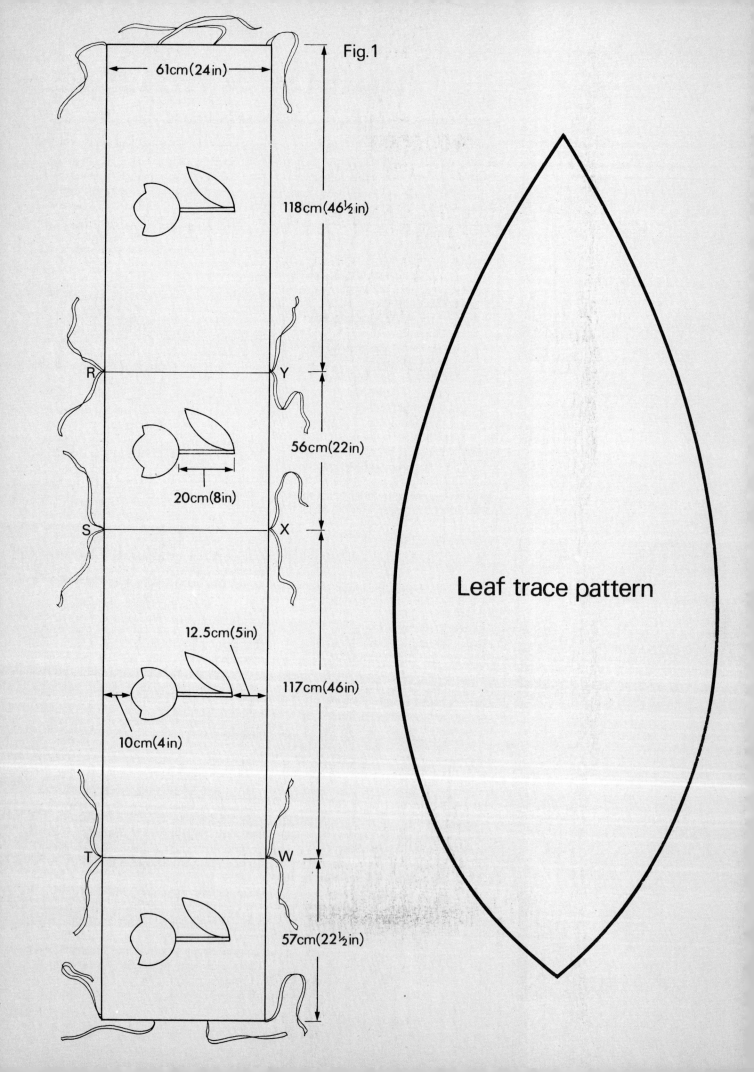

Fig. 1

61cm (24 in)

118cm (46½ in)

R   Y

56cm (22 in)

20cm (8 in)

S   X

12.5cm (5 in)

117cm (46 in)

10cm (4 in)

T   W

57cm (22½ in)

Leaf trace pattern

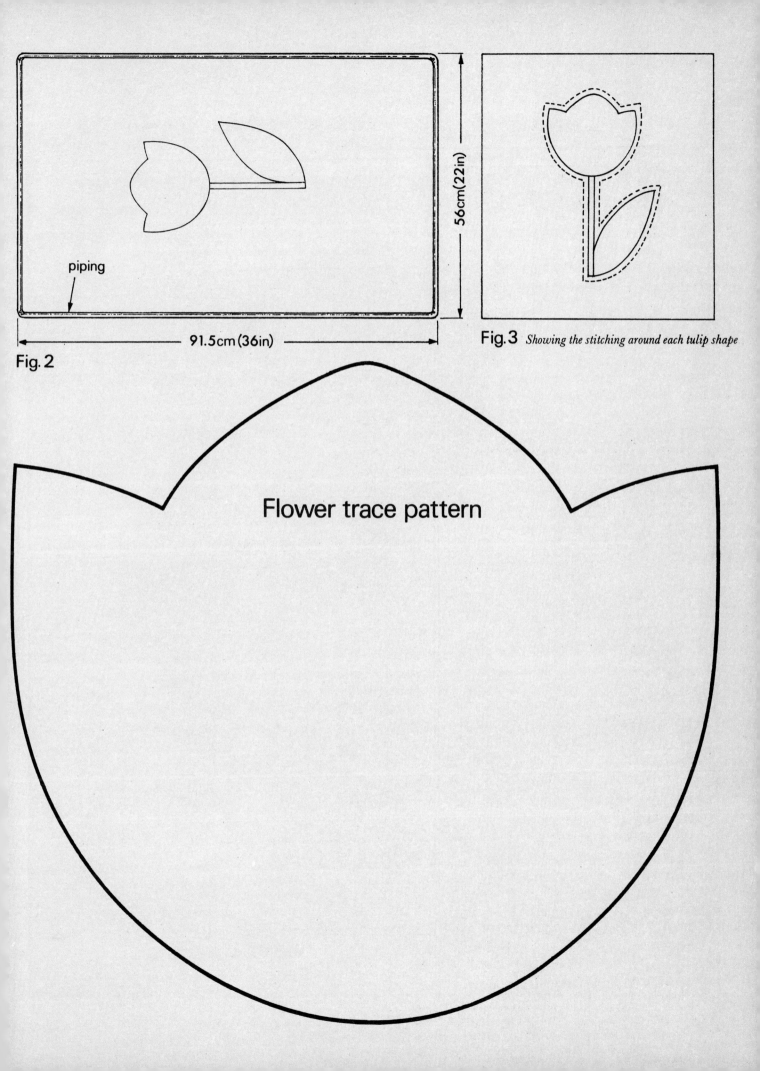

piping

91.5cm (36in)

56cm (22in)

Fig. 2

Fig. 3 *Showing the stitching around each tulip shape*

Flower trace pattern

Embroidered baby sheets

Sizes
Sheet (excluding frill) – 152.5cm × 102cm (60in × 40in)
Pillowcase (excluding frill) – 39.5cm × 35.5cm (15½in × 14in)

Fabric required
1.95m (2⅛yd) white cotton fabric 115cm (45in) wide
35cm (⅜yd) red and white gingham 115cm (45in) wide, with 3mm (⅛in) square checks
(The checks on some ginghams are not exactly square so make sure that the one you buy has square checks in order that the embroidery can be worked successfully.)

You will also need
4.60m (5yd) white broderie anglaise trimming, 4cm (1½in) wide
5 skeins white (0402) Clark's Anchor Stranded cotton (used with three strands throughout). Alternatively, use 1 ball (10 gram) white (0402) Clark's Anchor Pearl Cotton No.8.
Crewel needle No.7

Cutting out
1 For the sheet, cut a piece of white fabric 155cm × 104cm (61in × 41in). For the embroidered border, cut a piece of gingham 14cm × 104cm (5½in × 41in).
2 For the pillowcase, cut one piece of white fabric for the front 38cm × 42cm (15in × 16½in), and two for the back 38cm × 35.5cm (15in × 14in) and 38cm × 13cm (15in × 5in).
For the embroidered border, cut a piece of gingham 14cm × 42cm (5½in × 16½in).

The embroidery
1 Fold the pieces of gingham in half in both directions, crease lightly and mark the lines with tacking.
2 Leaving seven squares free on each side of the horizontal centre line, work the cross stitch borders on the long sides of the gingham. Following the diagram, start in the centre at the point indicated by the blank arrow, and work outwards in both directions. Each stitch is worked on one square of the check.
3 Trace on the motifs for the flowers so that the dotted lines correspond with the centre lines on the gingham. Repeat to left and right along the length of the border, spacing evenly.

4 Work section 1 of the motifs in back stitch, section 2 in satin and section 3 in chain stitch. Press the embroidery on the wrong side.

Making up
Sheet
1 Make 6mm (¼in) hems all around the edge of the white fabric.
2 Turn under 1.5cm (½in) onto the wrong side all around the edge of the gingham. Tack the trimming in place around the edge of the gingham with the raw edges level on the wrong side. Gather it to ease it around the corners. Overlap the short ends of the trimming so that the pattern matches, overcast the raw edges and slip stitch together.
3 Place the gingham onto the right side of the sheet at one short end so that the trimming protrudes at the top and sides. Tack and machine stitch in position.

Pillowcase
1 Turn under the lower long edge of the gingham for 1.5cm (½in). Take a piece of trimming along this side so that the raw edges are level on the wrong side.
2 Place the gingham onto the right side of the front section of the pillowcase so that the top and side raw edges are even. Tack in position and machine stitch along the trimmed edge.
3 Place the remaining trimming along the side and top edge of the right side of the gingham so that the raw edges are level and the trimming is facing in. Gather the trimming at the corners and tack in position.
4 Make 6mm (¼in) hems along one 38cm (15in) side of each back section. To form the overlap, place the larger back section to the front section with right sides facing and outer raw edges level. Place

the smaller back section to the opposite end of the front with right sides facing and outer raw edges level. Tack and machine stitch taking 1.5cm (½in) turnings. Neaten the raw edges by zig-zagging or overcasting. Turn the finished pillowcase right side out and press lightly.

Left: Make the nursery bright and gay with this embroidered gingham cot set. It's a marvellous method of giving faded covers a brand new lease of life, or else you can add a personal touch to a gift of bed linen for a child. Gingham is an ideal base for doing simple but effective embroidery, and the broderie anglaise trimming makes a crisp finish for pillows and sheets.

Stitch diagram for flower motifs

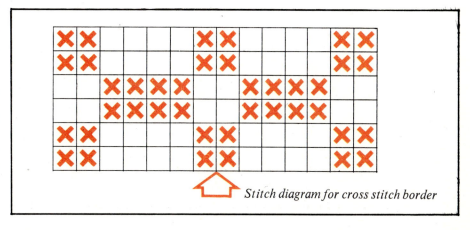

Stitch diagram for cross stitch border

PATCHWORK

As home decor becomes much more relaxed and informal, the trend towards brightly coloured patchwork for use in soft furnishings and home accessories is growing. Many homes have a country cottage atmosphere, with traditional quilts, cushion covers and tablecloths made up in exquisite designs. Patchwork creates a really happy and fresh mood in any room, and it's not a bit difficult to learn how. The following step-by-step course and the accompanying projects let you develop at your own pace, and as well as enjoying a soothing craft, you'll have the satisfaction of knowing that your patchwork furnishings are today's fashion favourites.

Patchwork techniques

Today the art of patchwork is enjoying a great revival – not only because of the real practical need for re-cycling materials, but because it provides a means of relaxation and of exercising one's artistic talent in creating unique and exciting new patchwork designs. It can be worked in a wide variety of materials and has instant effect. It is the ideal pastime while watching television or talking to friends. Nowadays, beautiful patchwork fabric can be made quite simply and quickly on any sewing machine. Oddments of material, which would otherwise be discarded, can be cut into squares or rectangles and joined together with straight machine stitching to form strong fabrics in a variety of patterns, colours and shades. Make them up into eye-catching soft furnishings for the home. Patchwork can also be appliquéd onto plain fabrics to form striking decorations or borders for such things as curtains or bedspreads.

The fabric of patchwork will often conjure up a score of memories – a scrap of the first dress you ever sewed, a piece of the blouse that never looked right with anything – reminders of friends and family. Autographed patches can be turned into a cushion or wall-hanging to make a charming memento of a special occasion.

How to find fabrics

The fabrics used in a patchwork can be gathered from many sources and it is useful to keep a bag or box in which to store them. Home dressmaking, either your own or a friend's, will yield a good supply of scraps; you can also use old clothes, provided the material is still strong, along with bargains from rummage sales. There is usually a remnant box in any store selling fabric which can provide useful offcuts at a reasonable price. The store-keeper might also be willing to part with outdated colour swatches of manufacturers' fabrics.

Part of the fun of patchwork is in collecting the right patterns and colours to create a design. The sense of achievement is even greater when one knows that a cushion or bedspread was put together from scraps that cost next to nothing!

By hand or machine

Patchwork is still mainly a home craft, sewn throughout by hand using the traditional centuries-old methods. It was inevitable that the invention of the sewing machine should inspire attempts to use it for patchwork, but until recently nothing more than modern designs in large rectangular pieces had been produced. The invention of the swing needle and machines capable of embroidery have made more complicated techniques possible.

For the great majority who want to do patchwork, hand sewing is the most convenient and pleasurable method. You can pick it up at any time, doing a few patches or a little planning as the mood takes you.

As hand sewn patchwork is likely to take some time to make, it is worth checking that you have enough patchwork pieces to complete a design before beginning the work – it may not be easy to come by a similar piece of fabric later on.

Because of the time and patience involved in making hand sewn patchwork, the item produced may be of some sentimental value and you may wish to mix different fabrics in it which are of personal significance. It is possible to mix fabrics in a patchwork but, as the stronger fabrics will tend to pull out the weaker ones, it is better to confine these mixtures to items which will not receive hard wear.

Sewing

Patchwork is within the scope of anyone who can sew by hand and knows how to stitch evenly and neatly.

Tools

You probably have most of the things that are needed already in your sewing equipment, but since the sewing must be fine and fairly close, needles and threads must be fine too. Use the finest needles and sewing thread that are available. Pins must also be very fine. You could use dressmakers' pins, but tiny short pins are better because they do not get in the way so much. They are particularly useful for stabbing through a patch to hold it in place on a board when planning. A board or small table is invaluable when designing the arrangement of your patchwork. You can use it to lay out patches like a jig-saw. The 'board' can be anything into which pins

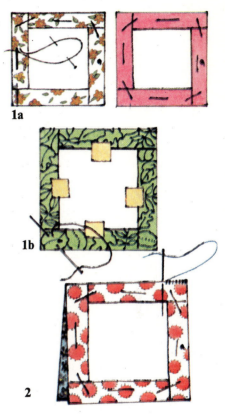

1a. Tacking the patch to the paper
1b. On fine fabrics, stick edges to paper with masking tape and tack only the corners
2. Oversewing patches together

can easily be stabbed. Cork squares thick cardboard, insulation board or a card table are all good.

Paper

The patches are generally constructed over paper shapes which are cut out from templates to help make the patches exact. They act as linings and hold the patches out firmly so they may be joined together conveniently. Both tacking and lining are removed when patchwork is completed. Paper for this purpose can be of any colour but must be of good quality – standard note-paper would do, crisp enough for the edges to be felt within the folds as the edges of the patches are turned. Here again you can be thrifty and use up envelopes, letters, Christmas cards, etc. When heavier types of material are used, then a thin cardboard is necessary. Vilene can be used as an alternative and is usually left in, to add firmness.

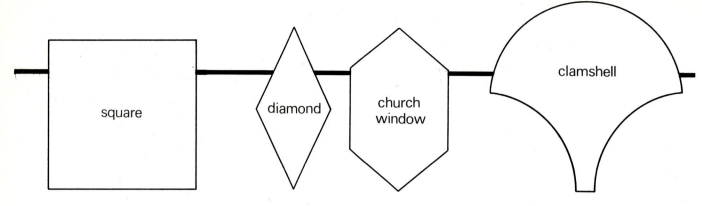

square · diamond · church window · clamshell

Templates

The word 'template' means pattern and in patchwork these are the patterns for the patches. There is a variety of shapes. The most popular come in a great assortment of sizes, of which the hexagon, diamond and square are certainly most common. The church window (long hexagon in most catalogues) is another alternative shape. The octagon is not so frequently used and has to be combined with a square of the same size. The clamshell is the usual name given to the mushroom-like shape which creates attractive scalloped lines when the patches are joined. It is also called 'shell' or 'scale'. You will find the basic template shapes appearing in many other crafts and in unsuspected places, such as glazing, mosaics and parquetting. In modern architecture the hexagonal shape is frequently used as a room shape as it is attractive and space-saving. In fact, once you are interested, you will discover patchwork patterns in everything. Templates may be home-made from cardboard, plastic or metal or they can be bought from craft suppliers. Either way it is essential that they are accurate otherwise the patches will never fit together precisely. Plastic or metal templates are best because they keep their rigidity. Cardboard templates will not last very long and soon lose their accuracy.

The size of the shape is usually given as the length of one of its sides. For example a 1.5cm ($\frac{1}{2}$in) diamond or hexagon has sides of that measurement. Beginners could practise with a 2.2cm ($\frac{7}{8}$in) or 2.5cm (1in) hexagon. The square is also comparatively easy, but the turnings which lie alongside the corners can be tiresome. Only the top edges are stitched when joined up and these turnings can sometimes get in the way. Templates bought from a craft store are often pre-packaged. The kits contain usually a solid metal shape, together with a slightly larger plastic one with a frosted band around the clear area. The latter is the 'window' from which the patch is cut; the solid is the pattern for the papers. If the solid shape can be bought separately, then the window may be home-made. Draw the solid shape very accurately onto card. Measure 6mm ($\frac{1}{4}$in) all around the outline to make a larger replica of the shape. Finally cut out both outlines with a scalpel or modelling knife and you will find that you have your own window template.

Using the templates

The solid template represents the size of the patch when it has been made. Use it to cut out the paper backings.

Trim off a strip of paper a little wider than the template, fold it two or three times into a pad and place the metal in the centre. Hold it firmly in one hand, then cut around with sharp scissors, placing the blades close to the metal edges, to be sure of accuracy.

Cut the fabric to size with the window template. Place the window on the fabric then draw around the outer edge with a pencil or chalk. Cut out the patch along the pencilled line.

Pin the paper shape to the wrong side of the patch. Turn in the 6mm ($\frac{1}{4}$in) overlap of material all around and tack down with neatly folded corners until the shape is completed. Pinch the folds in to make sure the material fits the paper lining exactly.

The sharp points of a diamond patch need a double fold because of the extra material. The clamshell has a different technique, more complicated than the other shapes. Clamshells are usually joined by hem-stitching, rarely with oversewing. The scallop arrangements are very attractive but because they are difficult to make and assemble they are less popular than the more usual patches. The resulting effect, however, is worth the trouble.

Fabrics for patchwork

Generally speaking the best fabrics for patchwork are those which are firm in weave and texture and therefore do not fray or stretch. Good cottons are best from all points of view. Man-made materials are not as easy to use as those made from natural fibres, because of their crease resistance.

Mixing fabrics

Always observe two important rules when selecting materials for a piece of work. Never mix silks and cottons, and only combine materials of equal weight and thickness. Remember the story of the unfortunate lady who made herself a patchwork bedspread and mixed cotton print and corduroy together. The finished patchwork would never lie flat as the fabrics were of such different weights and to add to the disastrous consequences the colour ran when the cover was washed! If you are in any doubt, test for colour fastness before beginning the work. Patchwork is often made into things which need to be washed and if the colours run they could ruin something into which you have put a great deal of effort. Silks and drip dry cottons are marked permanently by pin and needle marks. To avoid this, the paper must be held in the middle of the wrong side and the tacking stitched only into the paper, not right through the patch. Practise this on materials which do not need this care.

Top and Opposite top: Samples of some familiar templates. The word 'template' means pattern, and in patchwork it creates the shape of each patch. From left to right the shapes are square, diamond, church window, clamshell, hexagon, octagon. The final two shapes are a solid template for cutting paper, and a window template for cutting fabric.

Right: A variety of effects
1. Rectangles arranged in a 'brick wall'
2. Diagonally running squares with triangle edges
3. A border of diagonal squares

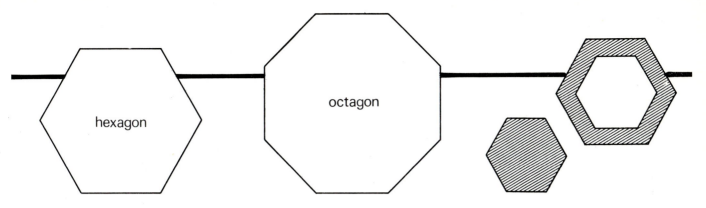

hexagon

octagon

Designing in patchwork

The excellence of any piece of patchwork depends equally on good technique and good colour and design. This is true of even the smallest piece of work. A window template is particularly useful when using a patterned material. It means you can select the exact units you need to make your own arrangement.

When you have assembled your oddments of fabric, decide on the size of patches to be used in the patchwork, bearing in mind the size of the finished article and how it is to be used. It is pointless to use very large patches on a small item which will not show them off to advantage. When you have cut the patches, take time over planning the design – this can be an absorbing and enjoyable stage. A good design is generally a simple one and it's fun to work it out in shades and tints. Random schemes can be very pretty too, especially if some sort of colour grouping is attempted. If you are using a fabric with a nap or pile, carefully consider the direction of each patch to ensure that the final product looks both even and consistent.

Colour schemes

Because colour plays such a vital role in the design of patchwork, it is useful to understand the principles of colour relationship. Red, yellow and blue are the primary colours from which all other colours are combined.

Secondary colours are made by mixing primary colours. For example, if blue and yellow are mixed in equal parts, the resulting colour is green, and variations of green can be achieved according to the balance of the primary colours. Blue and red make purple, and finally, red and yellow make orange. The tone of a colour is its lightness or darkness.

Using colour

Before planning a design, consider all the factors involved. For example, if you are making a cushion cover, look at all the colours in the room, the carpet, curtains, walls and upholstery. If all or most of these are patterned, then it is a good idea to use plain materials in your patchwork. If the room is full of different colours, then pick out the most striking of these and use shades of them in your design. If you have only one main colour in your room, then use a contrasting colour to make a striking focal point. Closely related colours can make a very effective design. By using, say, blue and green only, you will have all the tones of blue from pale blue to navy, and all the tones of green plus the

4

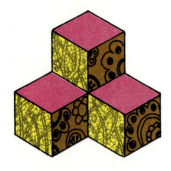

5

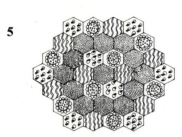

6

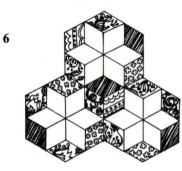

7

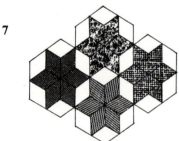

8

9

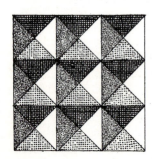

turquoise colours made from mixing blue and green together.

If you use contrasting colours, it is worth keeping to one dominant colour, one less dominant colour and one or two accent colours. If, for example, your main colour is pink and you wish to use tan as a second, less dominant colour, then small quantities of yellow and charcoal used as accent colours will help to co-ordinate the design. Accent colours often look best if they are combined in a patterned patch as shown in fig.1.

If, however, the only materials available are a motley of different colours, then pick out and use those featuring the dominant colour which will help to give the design some shape. Unless the colour demands it, try not to mix naturalistic and stylized patterns because, on the whole, they do not combine well.

Using texture

Patchwork is very effective when textures are mixed. Although it is inadvisable to mix materials of different weights for patchwork which will be taking a lot of wear, it is possible to do this with textured patchwork which is intended to be more decorative than hard wearing. If some of the patches are very lightweight, you can use a bonded fibre fabric lining to strengthen them.

The texture of a material often alters its colour. For example, a patch in red velvet will look glowing and jewel-like whereas a patch in exactly the same colour, but in a shiny material, will seem much lighter and brighter. Mixing silks, velvet, corduroy, satin, knobbly tweed and corded silk in approximately the same colours can make a most exciting design. Textural patchwork works best when you limit the number of colours you use and let the structure of the materials create the interest.

Three dimensional patchwork

Colour alone can be very exciting when it is used to create a three dimensional

4. Patterns highlight an accent colour
5. Effectively mixed textures
6, 7. 'Star' structures
8. Patterns used as light and shade
9. Four triangles meet to form blocks giving an overall 3-D look.

effect. Sets of three diamonds joined together can be made to look like boxes piled on top of one another. Use the different patterns and colours as light and shade, highlighting the top of the boxes and shading the sides (fig.8).

Alternatively, as shown in fig.9, four triangles meeting in a point in the middle and adding up to a square can be highlighted on one side more strongly than the other and so make the surface look as though it is coming towards you in points.

Completing the patchwork

The final stage has been reached when the patches have been joined – edges may need to be straightened by inserting half patches, or strips may be placed behind to fill spaces or strengthen curves. Here you must use common sense and choose the best method for the particular job in hand. The work needs to be lined to strengthen the fabric; once straightened, edges must be bound or piped to give a good finish. Pads or fillings for cushion covers and tea or coffee cosies should be thought about in the early stages and planned beforehand. Choose whatever method seems most suitable – remembering shape and practical use.

When all is done, when you have made something you can look on with pride, you can derive a good deal of satisfaction from knowing that you have used scraps which might never have otherwise been used: yet out of them you will have created something beautiful and useful. For in patchwork, you not only develop a certain amount of technical skill but also have the unique experience of expressing your own personality in colour and design.

Machine patchwork

Machine patchwork is a speedy alternative to hand stitching, especially if you are working with patches of 4cm (1½in) and over in length. Smaller patches are better sewn by hand. Fabrics suitable for machine-made patchwork are cottons and wools, silks, needlecord and velvets and fine tweeds. Very densely woven fabrics are not suitable for machine patchwork if you are making patches with acute angles, like diamonds, as the needle has to cope with several thicknesses of fabric. Leather,

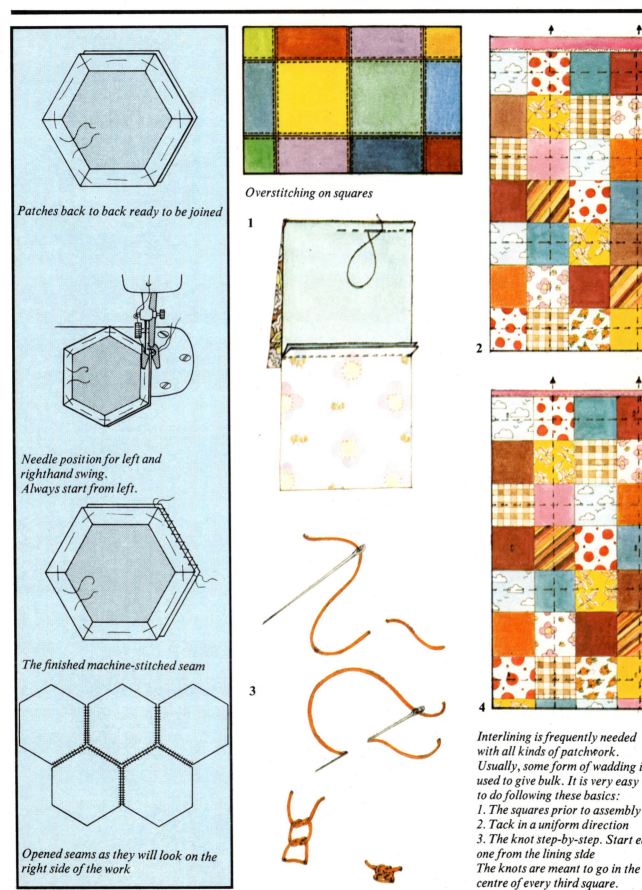

Patches back to back ready to be joined

Needle position for left and righthand swing.
Always start from left.

The finished machine-stitched seam

Opened seams as they will look on the
right side of the work

Overstitching on squares

1

2

3

4

Interlining is frequently needed
with all kinds of patchwork.
Usually, some form of wadding is
used to give bulk. It is very easy
to do following these basics:
1. The squares prior to assembly
2. Tack in a uniform direction
3. The knot step-by-step. Start each
one from the lining side
The knots are meant to go in the
centre of every third square.

suede and PVC (vinyl) coated fabrics are particularly good as they will not fray and do not need turnings. You simply cut the patches to size without the usual allowance for seams, match the edges of the patches together and swing stitch them on the right side.

Sewing the patches together

Prepare the patches as for hand sewing. If the patchwork is for fashion appliqué use bonded fibre fabric instead of papers and leave them in the finished work.

Needles, threads and stitches

Use a No.14 machine needle (continental No.90) and change to a new needle more often, as patchwork papers tend to blunt the point. Stitch with a fine thread, No.50 or 60, and use a mercerized or synthetic thread according to the material you are using.

A swing needle swings from left to right and back again. Left is the starting point and you must always start the needle ready to swing to the left. Turn the balance wheel by hand to discover which way the needle is going to swing and set it ready to swing to the left.

Place the patches, right sides together, under the machine needle and turn the balance wheel towards you so that the needle pierces the top right hand corner of the pair of patches. Lower the presser foot, and stitch, not too quickly at first. At the left hand swing the needle should pierce the fabric and papers of the two patches and at the right hand swing the needle should pass just beyond the side of the patches.

When you come to the end of the working edge, make sure that the needle swings to the right for the last stitch – you will then be ready to swing back to the starting point when you begin the next seam. Give the balance wheel a half turn toward you, lift the presser foot and draw out the patch, leaving at least 5cm (2in) of thread before cutting off. This is essential as the ends must be tied off to secure the stitching. It is best to tie off with a double knot as this prevents the threads becoming tangled. If you prefer, instead of tying off each pair of patches separately, you can stitch a whole series of pairs of patches together in sequence so long as you leave enough thread between them for tying off. The threads are cut afterwards.

When stitching diamond patches it may be necessary with some fabric to 'help' the machine over the points as there can be up to eight layers of material to penetrate. Open out each seam and you will see that the patches are joined together with firm, even stitches straight at the front and crisscrossed at the back.

1. The cut and stagger technique. First cut and arrange the strips, then join the pieces together using a machine.
2. Having joined the strips together horizontally, cut them vertically, so that each strip is composed of squares.
3. Next join the squares together so that a staggered pattern is achieved.

Add as many patches as you need, keeping the grain of the material running as straight as possible. When the work is large enough, take out the tacking threads and remove the papers. (This will also make it easier to work if the patchwork becomes cumbersome.) The papers may have been caught by the needle but will pull away easily, and often can be used again.

The running stitch
If you are using the standard running stitch, follow the same principles as just described for the swing stitch. The only thing which is different is the seam itself, which is straight, not zig-zag, and which is sewn about 9mm ($\frac{3}{8}$in) in from the working edge.

Pressing
Machine patchwork should be pressed well, with a steam iron and a pressing cloth. If there is velvet in the patchwork use a padded board. Press as if it were hand sewn patchwork and pay particular attention to the edges of the piece if the patchwork is for fashion appliqué.

Lining and interlining
Patchwork, unless it is to be used for appliqué, should always be lined. If the piece of patchwork is to be made into a bedcover it is advisable to place a piece of interlining between the patchwork and the lining.

Lining
Use a firmly-woven cotton or other lining material. If edges are not bound with lining, the work can be bagged. To do this trim the lining to 6mm–9mm ($\frac{1}{4}$in–$\frac{3}{8}$in) (the width of the patchwork turnings) larger all around than the patchwork. Unfold the turning on the edges of the patchwork. Place the lining and patchwork with right sides together, tack around three sides and part of the fourth to the width of the patch turning from the edge. Machine or hand sew along the line of tacking on three sides. Clip the corners, then turn the 'bag' right side out. Slip stitch the opening. Make a line of even running stitches all around the 'bag', 3mm ($\frac{1}{8}$in) from the edge, to hold the edges firm. If the patchwork is fairly large, knot it to the lining at regular intervals, placing each knot in the centre of a patch. Alter-

natively the lining and patchwork can be knotted together as for interlined patchwork and the edges completed as mentioned below.

Interlining
Synthetic wadding is ideal for interlining patchwork items as it is washable, quick-drying and available in a variety of weights. It is possible to use flannelette as interlining but this is not quick-drying and gives a flatter result than synthetic wadding. Lay a piece of lining fabric 5cm (2in) larger all around than the patchwork, wrong side up on a large flat surface. Place the wadding on top and then the patchwork, right side up, on the top of that.
Tack the three layers together with regular parallel lines of tacking stitches worked from side to side and from top to bottom. It is important that all the lines of tacking, which are parallel to each other, are worked in the same direction (fig.3). · This avoids puckers. Work knots as shown (fig.3) through all thicknesses at regular intervals across the whole piece of work (fig.4). The knots should be made on the lining side in the centre of every fourth patch, when small patches are used, and every third patch, when larger patches are used. Trim lining 6mm–9mm ($\frac{1}{4}$in–$\frac{3}{8}$in) larger all around than the patchwork, unless the edges are bound with lining. Remove tacking.

Alternative methods for edges
The interlined or lined work can be finished with piping, bound with bias strips or mitred. Otherwise, trim interlining, if used, to 3mm ($\frac{1}{8}$in) less all around than the finished size of work. Trim 6mm–9mm ($\frac{1}{4}$in–$\frac{3}{8}$in) all around the edge of the lining and press the turnings carefully. Oversew the lining to the patchwork with small stitches.

Strengthening the fabric
To give extra strength to the patchwork you can carefully topstitch up and down the lines of patches on the right side of the fabric, 3mm ($\frac{1}{8}$in) from either side of the seams. This will help to keep the seam allowances in place and is particularly advisable for items that will need regular washing. Without this re-inforcement, patches made from heavy fabrics are in danger of pulling loose.

Quilting patchwork
There are two reasons for working quilting on a patchwork or appliquéd fabric: firstly, to add warmth and, secondly, to throw the design into relief. One of the traditional methods is to outline the patchwork patterns with small running stitches worked in two movements. It is quite feasible to work small pieces in the hand working from the centre outwards. Large quilts are best worked in a frame. A rectangular embroidery frame (slate frame) is suitable. Move the frame across the work as you complete each section. It is always essential to tack the three layers of patchwork fabric, wadding and lining together before quilting.

Patchwork cushions

Use the prettiest left-over pieces in your sewing box to make these simple cushions. They are made in the simplest and quickest form of patchwork where the fabric is cut into squares or oblongs.

The fabric
It is normally best not to mix old and new fabrics in a piece of work because they will wear unevenly. For the same reason, it is advisable not to mix fabrics of different fibres, nylon and cotton for example, or of different weights, such as denim and lawn.

The design
The squares can all be cut to the same size and joined in strips, or you can combine squares and oblongs in different sizes. If you choose the former method, the sewing must be accurate so that all the joins meet. With the latter method, you should plan your design carefully on paper first as this will simplify cutting the patches. To plan your design, use graph paper marked with 2.5cm (1in) squares, and draw on the overall shape of the finished item.
For square patches, anything between 5cm–15.5cm (2in–6in) is a practical size. For oblong patches, it is normally most effective if you make the short sides between 5cm–10cm (2in–4in) and the longer sides between 10cm–15.5cm (4in–6in).

Making the patches
Cut or tear the patches on the straight grain of the fabric, allowing 6mm ($\frac{1}{4}$in) all around for turnings. If you are making all oblong patches they can be joined in a brick pattern, so that the vertical seams on each alternate row come to the centre of the patches in the row on each side. For this, you will also have to cut half-width patches to fill in the spaces at each end of alternate rows.

Joining the patches
Where possible, join the patches into strips for the vertical rows. If you are practised at using a machine, there is no need to tack the patches together first, if you put the pins at right-angles to the edge so that the machine foot can ride over them. Where it is essential to have accurate joins, pin these first and then put in the intermediate pins. Press the turnings open after completing each

Left: These delightful, fresh looking cushions are an easy way of starting on patchwork projects, since they are designed for the simplest technique – joining up squares and oblongs.

Below: Detailed patterns of motifs.

strip. For cushion covers, the patchwork need not be bound in any special way because the turnings of the seams will be hidden inside.

Estimating covers
For a good fit, the cover should be slightly smaller all around than the cushion pad. For a 45.5cm (18in) square cushion with piped edges you would need 103cm (1$\frac{1}{8}$yd) of 91cm (36in) fabric or 57cm ($\frac{5}{8}$yd) of 121.9cm (48in) fabric. This estimate includes fabric for bias strips for piping and 1.5cm ($\frac{1}{2}$in) seams, so allow correspondingly less for an unpiped cover. Measure perimeter of cushion to determine the amount of piping cord (pre-shrunk) needed.

Designing with hexagons

Hexagon possibilities

The regular hexagon, known as the honeycomb, with all its sides equal in length, is probably the best known of all patchwork shapes. It is extremely simple to use and the wide angles at the corners mean that there is no difficulty in making a neat fold when turning the hem around the patchwork paper.

Seven hexagons joined together make a single rosette which can be used for a decorative motif. Or you could join several rosettes together to make up a larger piece.

When using a patchwork shape for the first time it is wise to choose something small and quick to make. You will need to use templates for the hexagons and these are obtainable pre-packaged in a wide range of sizes, from most good craft stores.

The rosette

This is a good basic design as well as an attractive way of using up small quantities of fabric. A single rosette is made up of seven hexagons (fig.1). The surrounding patches are usually made from one colour and if they are varied it is important that the colours or patterns of the patches combine to form a well-balanced shape. Single rosettes can be linked quite simply by making each centre patch of the same colour. A second row of hexagons in another tone or colour can be added to make a double rosette (fig.2), and yet another row of patches makes a triple rosette.

Grandmother's flower garden

This attractive, traditional design is made by using double rosettes in a rather special way. The central patch is surrounded by patches cut from a floral fabric and the second row of patches is cut from plain or printed green fabric, giving the effect of a large flower surrounded by foliage. The double rosettes are separated by lines of white or natural hexagons, which represent garden paths.

This is a good design to use on a quilt, because it makes such a restful cover for the fortunate recipient.

More ideas

A few basic pattern designs using hexagons are illustrated here (figs.3–10) but the possibilities are endless. Experi-

ment with your patches and their colours to make many more.

Border designs

Hexagons can be used to make border decorations and motifs for items such as curtains, valances and bedspreads and tablecloths.

Ocean waves (fig.7) is a traditional border design and for the best results the fabrics should be of different tonal values, shading from light to dark.

All the designs illustrated, except the festoon (fig.10), can be worked as part of a whole patchwork fabric. Or, for a quicker effect, borders, motifs or even single hexagons can be appliquéd onto background fabric.

Above: An unusual but thoroughly practical way of using patchwork.

Right: Traditional block quilt

Variations on the regular hexagon

The 'church window' and the 'coffin' are both variations of the regular 'honeycomb' hexagon. They are formed by elongating the basic shape as shown.

Many people do not venture further than the hexagon in patchwork as this shape has the advantage of being the simplest to turn under and join neatly. But because of their flexibility in shape, there is more to designing with hexagons than first meets the eye. It is amazing how useful they are.

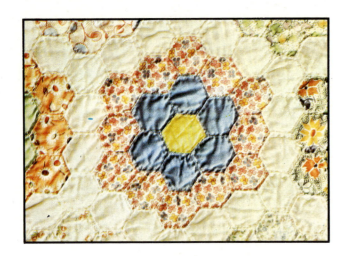

Left: Detail of a quilt made up from a pattern of double rosettes.

Right: The 'church window' and 'coffin' are variations from the 'honeycomb'.

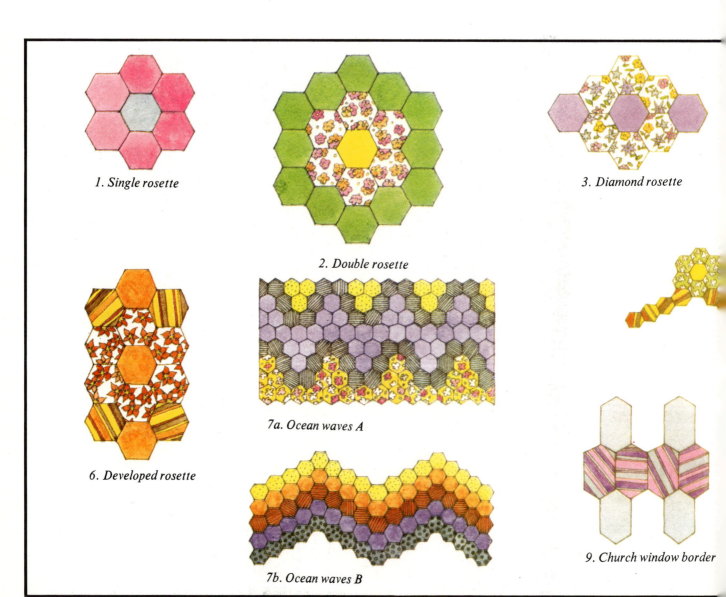

1. Single rosette

2. Double rosette

3. Diamond rosette

6. Developed rosette

7a. Ocean waves A

7b. Ocean waves B

9. Church window border

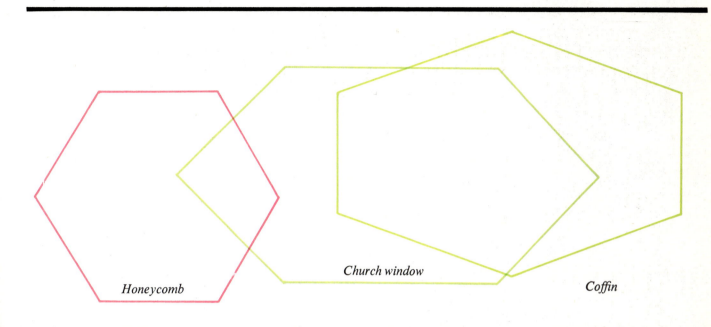

Honeycomb

Church window

Coffin

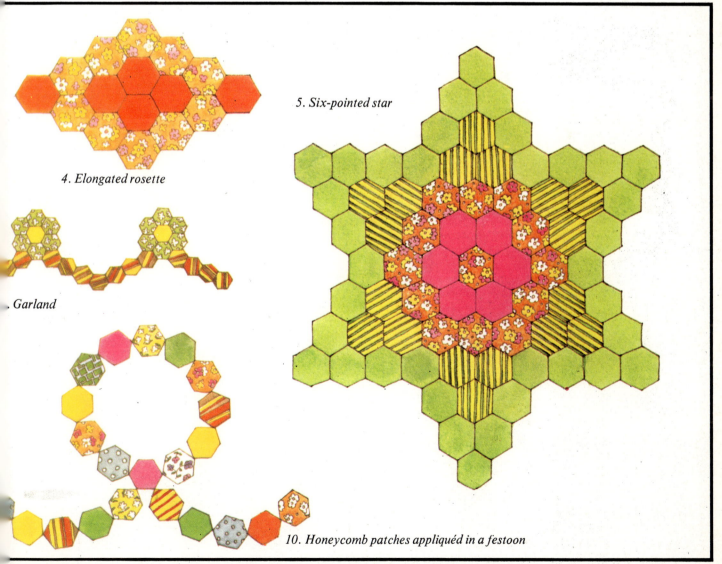

4. *Elongated rosette*

5. Six-pointed star

Garland

10. *Honeycomb patches appliquéd in a festoon*

Silk patchwork cushions

These beautiful silk cushions are an exquisite example of how patchwork can be worked to look both subtle and delicate. They are made up of traditional hexagonal shapes and the colours have been arranged to form a pattern of subtle pastel shades. Alternatively, brightly coloured patches can be arranged at random.

You will need
Cushion pads
Large bag of silk fabric scraps in different plain colours
Silk fabric in harmonizing colour to cover the cushion
Pre-shrunk piping cord
Stiff cardboard
Paper

Stop to think
It is important to select the colours for each cushion carefully. Use either three different colours in equal proportions, or four different colours, making one predominant to tone in with the colour scheme of the room.
For a really elegant effect, select the silk fabric in shades that are close to each other in tone. If using slubbed or grained silk, work the patches so that they lie with the grain running in opposite ways to reflect the light in different directions.

To make the patches
The fabric shapes are cut out using a template, and then backed with paper to keep them firm while they are being stitched.
Templates can be purchased, but they can also be made quite satisfactorily from stiff cardboard. To make patches the same size as those illustrated, trace off the hexagonal shape given here and cut it out from cardboard. Make two templates, one exactly to the size given and the other 6mm ($\frac{1}{4}$in) larger all around. The smaller is for cutting the paper shapes, the larger for cutting the fabric pieces, with a seam allowance all around. The backing used for the patches should be fairly stiff paper, to keep them firm while working. Magazine covers or old greeting cards are suitable for this.

To prepare the patches
Cut out paper and fabric shapes.
There are approximately 8–10 hexagons along each edge of the patchwork square, but this can be varied according to the size of the cushion.
It is advisable to work out both the size and the colour arrangement beforehand on a sheet of graph paper. In this way it is possible to work out exactly how many shapes of each colour are required, remembering that the template shape given here is the exact size of the finished patch. Pin a paper shape to the wrong side of a fabric patch, placing the paper so that the turnings are exactly equal on all sides. Fold the turnings over the paper, pulling the fabric to the patch. Do not tie a knot in the thread, but simply tack the paper in place and remove the pins (fig.1). Prepare the required number of patches in the same way.

Joining the patches
Patches can be joined by straight machine stitching (fig.2a) or by hand. To join patches by hand, place two backed patches together, right sides facing, with edges carefully matched. Stitch along one edge, using a fine needle and matching thread (fig.3b). Never pull an edge to fit if it does not match up, but unpick the patch and begin again. When all the patches are stitched together, press the work lightly on the wrong side. Snip the tacking threads, pull them out, then remove the paper backing.

To make up
Make a piped cushion cover from plain silk fabric in one of the colours used to make the patchwork. Cover the cushion and either stitch together the final seam or insert a zipper. Lay the finished patchwork on one side of the cushion and stitch neatly in place.

1. Tack the turnings over the paper
2a. Join patches by machine
2b. Hand sew patches if preferred
3. Open the patches out flat and press.

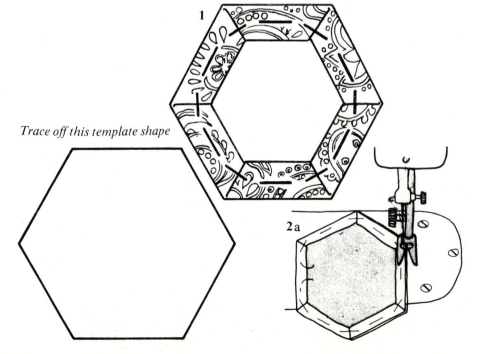

Trace off this template shape

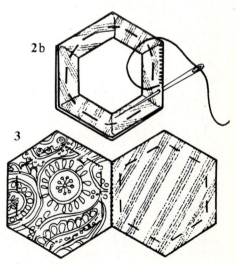

Triangle and diamond designs

The triangle and the diamond, whether used alone, together, or combined with other shapes, are almost as popular for patchwork as the hexagon. Triangles in particular are to be found in many early patchwork designs because they were easy to cut from a square (manufactured templates were not available). So try experimenting with these shapes and see what you can produce.

You will find there are numerous ways of joining them to form exciting geometric designs. If you do not want to make a large expanse of patchwork, consider them for filling in or for making a straight border.

If you have plenty of scraps of plain fabric, triangles and diamonds are good shapes to use as the dramatic, geometric shapes formed lend themselves to the use of plain fabrics.

Triangles and diamonds are slightly more difficult to handle than hexagons because the sharp points are more tricky to cope with. But with practice this becomes easier. Triangles and diamonds are much used in traditional American patchwork.

Templates and papers

Both solid and window templates for both types of diamond and equilateral pyramid triangle can be purchased. If you buy just the solid shape, make a window template in the way described in the introductory section on templates. 'Papers' are best cut from thin cardboard as this is stronger and will be a more accurate guide than paper when folding fabric over the points. It is a good idea to cut fabric patches using the window template as you can see what the finished patch will look like.

Cut triangular patches with one edge on the straight of grain. When cutting diamonds make sure either that two sides are on the straight of grain or that the axes are on the straight of grain. With some designs, such as box and star patterns, it is not possible to join the patches with the straight grain matching. Make each patch by pinning the paper to the wrong side of the fabric patch. Fold over the turnings and trim, if necessary, as shown and tack (fig.1). Remove the pin and join as for hand or machine sewn hexagons.

The triangle

There are two basic kinds of triangle used in patchwork, the 'pyramid' and the 'long triangle'.

The pyramid

This triangle (fig.2) has a short base line and the two other sides equal (these can be the same length or longer than the base line). This shape can be made by halving a diamond widthwise. 'Streak of lightning' and 'Dog's tooth' (figs.3 and 4) are designs made from this shape. These designs can be made up into large areas of patchwork or into strips and used as borders. The illustrations on these pages will give some ideas.

Opposite: The name chosen for the pattern of these two cushions is 'Basket of scraps'. The resulting design is very effective.

Above left: This beautiful tablecloth has been created from long triangles.

Below left: This cushion is simply the 'Star of Bethlehem' design, made up of long diamonds.

Below: The soft, subtle shades used in this quilt of 'baby blocks' make it ideal for use as a child's blanket.

The long triangle
This triangle has its base line longer than the two equal sides. This shape can be made by halving a diamond lengthwise or by dividing a square diagonally (fig.5).
'Cotton reels' and 'Whirlwind' (figs.6 and 7) are two designs which can be made from this shape.
An effective way of using the long triangle in traditional patchwork is to make the triangles into separate 'basket' shapes and then to appliqué them to a plain background, adding a matching base and handle to each one (fig.8).

The diamond
Again there are two basic variations of the diamond shape, the 'lozenge' and the 'long' diamond.

The lozenge
This shape (fig.9) can be made from a hexagon and is made up of two equilateral triangles.

113

The box (or 'baby blocks') is another old and striking favourite.

It can be made from three different fabrics by sewing the diamonds in groups of three, taking one fabric as the 'lid' and the other two for the 'sides'. The three-dimensional effect will become obvious as you work.

Although ideal for a cot quilt, this pattern can become a bit tiring on the eyes if used over a large area so it is sometimes used as a border.

The 'six-point' star is also made from the lozenge shape (fig.10).

The long diamond

It is a simple matter to draw your own long diamond shape using a protractor and a pair of compasses (fig.11).

Decide on the length of the sides (they are all the same); draw a line A–B to this length.

Place the protractor at B and mark 45° with a dot, C. Draw a line through this dot to B.

Set the compasses to the length of A–B and keep this setting throughout.

With the point of the compasses on B, mark the length on B–C at E.

With the point at E and then at A mark the arcs to cross at F.

Join E–F and A–F.

Finally check the accuracy of your work by making sure that the angles FEB and FAB are 135° and that AFE and ABE are 45°.

The figure AEB is one of eight identical triangles which when fitted together form an octagon.

The 'eight-point star' design is made from long diamonds (fig.12).

The 'Star of Bethlehem' is another design made from this shape. It has been a favourite with American women for generations and on some quilts the star is so enormous that it covers the whole quilt.

The trick in making a successful Star of Bethlehem is, like so much else in patchwork, the planning. The cushion in the photograph is an exquisite example of how careful consideration can yield both an interesting design and pleasing colour scheme. A cushion like this is a good place to start too.

The cushion shown in the photograph is made up on a white background. You will find instructions for making up on page 111 and 154-157.

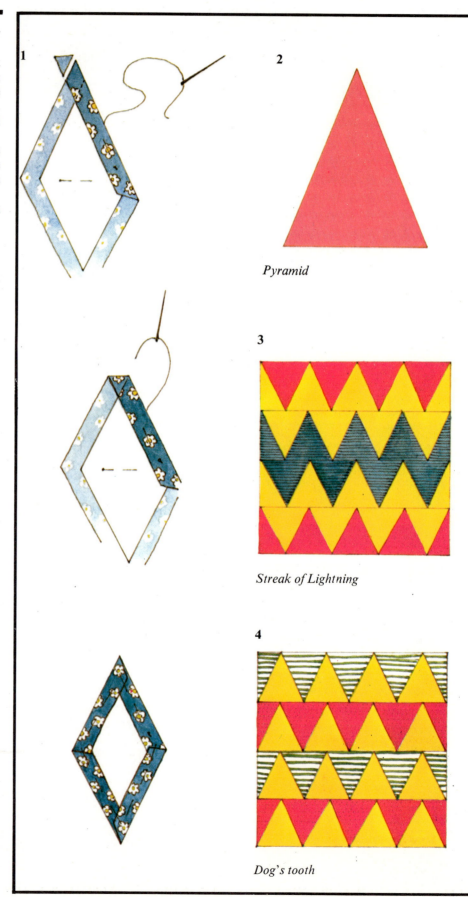

2 Pyramid

3 Streak of Lightning

4 Dog's tooth

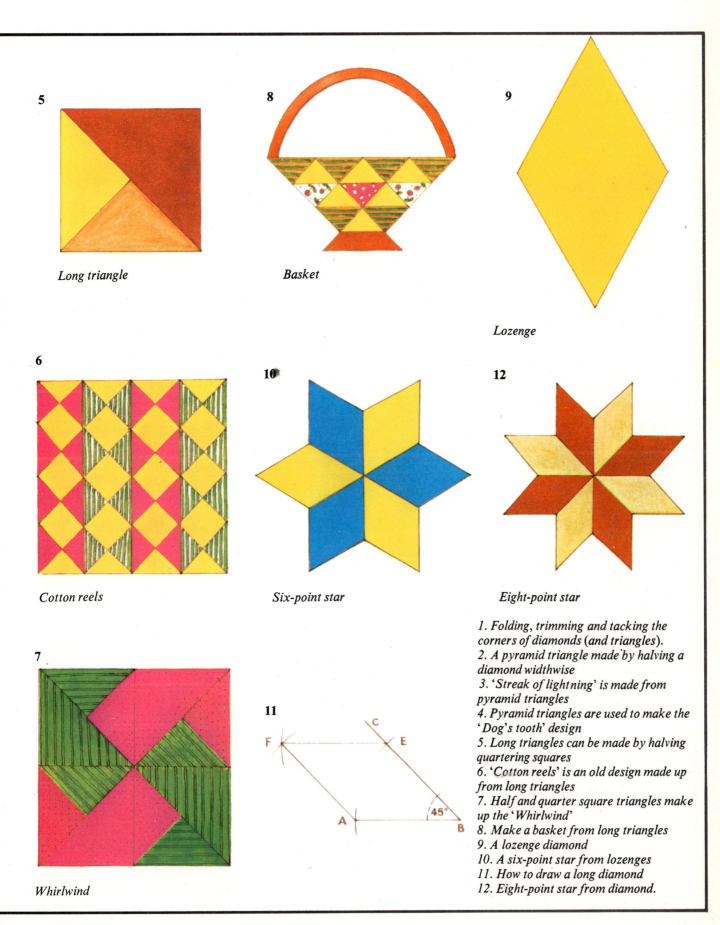

5

Long triangle

8

Basket

9

Lozenge

6

Cotton reels

10

Six-point star

12

Eight-point star

7

Whirlwind

11

1. Folding, trimming and tacking the corners of diamonds (and triangles).
2. A pyramid triangle made by halving a diamond widthwise
3. 'Streak of lightning' is made from pyramid triangles
4. Pyramid triangles are used to make the 'Dog's tooth' design
5. Long triangles can be made by halving quartering squares
6. 'Cotton reels' is an old design made up from long triangles
7. Half and quarter square triangles make up the 'Whirlwind'
8. Make a basket from long triangles
9. A lozenge diamond
10. A six-point star from lozenges
11. How to draw a long diamond
12. Eight-point star from diamond.

115

Combination shapes

You will need
Scraps of plain cotton fabrics in five colours
Sewing thread
Thin cardboard
50cm (20in) square cushion pad
Zip fastener (optional)

Previous chapters have dealt with some of the more common patchwork shapes and how to handle them. There are many exciting ways in which these can be combined to create unusual effects,

a few of which are shown here (figs. 1–3). There are specific instructions for making a cushion like two of those in the photograph (the centre one and the one at the front right). The design appears to be complicated but is simple. This chapter also covers some of the less common patchwork shapes and shows how they can be used alone or combined with more familiar shapes.

The cushions
Both cushions have been made in the same way by using a basic long triangle

of diminishing size.
The pattern is drawn straight on to thin cardboard which is then used for the 'papers', although you could make a template first from thick cardboard.
The instructions are for a 50cm (20in) square cushion.

To make up
On thin cardboard draw a square with side of 19cm (7½in). Mark the centre of each line and join the centre of one line to the centre of the adjacent side. Repeat all around the square.

Find the centres of the lines in the new square (these lie on the diagonals of the original square) and join them in the same way. Continue this process until six squares in all have been drawn (fig.4). Cut along the cardboard carefully to separate the triangles and the square. Using these pieces as patterns, cut out the fabric allowing turnings all around. Cut two of the largest triangles from the first colour and the remaining two from a contrasting colour.

Use two more colours for the next size of triangle.

Alternate this colour sequence until the other three sizes of the triangle have been cut out. Use the fifth colour for the centre square.

Tack the fabric to the papers folding the turnings to the wrong side. When all the patches have been tacked, assemble the design on a flat surface and, starting at the centre and working outward, stitch the patches together with tiny over-sewing stitches.

Below: A selection of attractive cushions made from combined patchwork shapes.

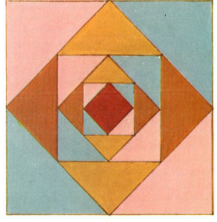

1, 2. The different effects obtainable from squares and church windows
3. Honeycombs and lozenge diamonds
4. Pattern for block of cushion which shows the precise colour scheme.

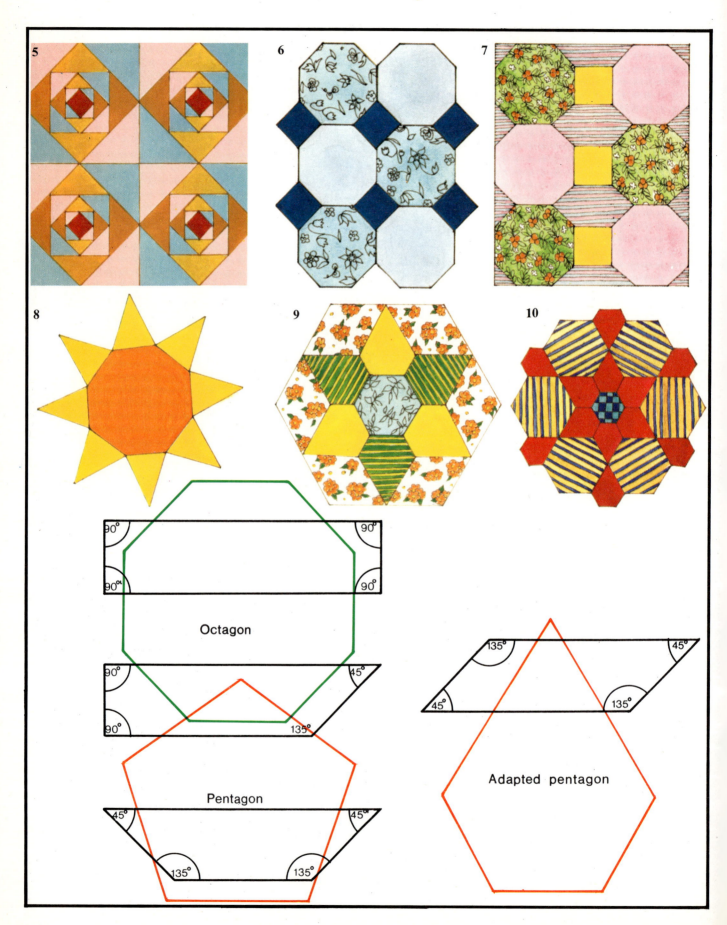

Octagon

Pentagon

Adapted pentagon

Make seven more square blocks in the same way.

Stitch four square blocks together so that opposite triangles match in the centre. Press work on the wrong side before removing the papers.

Repeat with the other four blocks.

For the outside border, cut from thin cardboard, eight 2.5cm (1in) deep trapeziums with longer parallel side of each 43cm (17in) and the shorter parallel side of each 38cm (15in).

Use these shapes as papers for fabric of the same colour as the central square in each block. Cut out, making seam allowances all around. Tack, then stitch four trapeziums to each square to make a larger square (fig.5).

From thin cardboard cut eight more 2.5cm (1in) deep trapeziums, but make the longer parallel side of each 48cm (19in) and the shorter one 43cm (17in). Use these as papers for a contrasting fabric. Cut out allowing 1.5cm (½in) turnings on longer parallel sides (these are essential for making up patchwork into a cushion). Make normal allowances on other sides of the trapeziums. Tack and stitch four to the outside edge of each square in the same way as before.

Make up the two large squares into a cushion.

Above right: This intricate and subtly coloured quilt and bolster set has been made largely from blocks using squares and long triangles.

5. Four trapeziums stitched to each square to make a larger square
6. Octagons are combined here with slightly inverted squares
7. The same principle is used by combining church window and squares
8. By combining a central octagon with long and pyramid triangles you can create this 'sunburst' design
9. The box and the star design, made up of a hexagon, adapted pentagons and lozenge diamonds
10. A central small hexagon surrounded by adapted pentagons and larger hexagons results in this attractive variation on the box and star design

Below opposite: Outlines of some of the more unusual shapes with angles drawn in for accurate reproduction

The octagon

Templates of various sizes can be bought for this shape. Alternatively make your own templates from strong cardboard, using the tracing above for your pattern, if you like.

This shape has eight equal sides and all its angles equal (fig.A). It is as easy to make up as the hexagon because of its wide angles.

Octagons cannot be joined together on all sides, but with the addition of a square an attractive continuous fabric can be made. Try combining octagons in a variety of printed fabrics with squares in a constant, plain, dark colour (fig.6). Or combine octagons, squares and church window hexagons (fig.7).

An octagon combined with pyramids (made by halving a long diamond widthwise) and long triangles and squares makes an attractive 'sunburst' pattern (fig.8). This could be repeated across a quilt, alternated with large plain squares or used as a border.

The strip or extended rectangle (fig.B), the adapted rectangle (fig.C), the trapezium (fig.D) and the rhomboid (fig.E) are useful fill-in shapes.

The pentagon (fig.F) with five equal sides and angles is impossible to use alone for a flat patchwork fabric. Twelve of these pentagons, however, will make up into a ball which could be filled and could be used as a pin cushion, for example.

The adapted pentagon (fig.G), a more versatile type of pentagon, is made from a lozenge diamond with one point cut off.

An attractive box and star design can be made from a hexagon, adapted pentagons and lozenge diamonds (fig.9). A variation is made from a small hexagon, adapted pentagons and large hexagons (fig.10).

There are many other ways to combine shapes. When you have tried the ones shown here, experiment with ideas of your own.

American patchwork quilts

More importance is attached to the art of patchwork quilts in America than in any other country. Traditionally, the neighbourly custom of 'quilting bees' – parties at which women gathered to help in the final work in making quilts – lent social significance to this craft. No bride's bottom drawer was considered complete without thirteen quilts. The first twelve were made throughout a girl's adolescence, and the last was the marriage quilt itself, adorned with a heart and completed at a quilting bee during which the betrothal was formally announced.

The block method of quilt construction which evolved in the nineteenth century and which was greatly aided by the invention of the sewing machine in about 1885 is not the only form of patchwork practised in America, It is, however, the most common method, probably by virtue of its being so economical in terms of time and material.

Basically, the block method consists of piecing scraps of fabric together in a geometric pattern to form a square section or block. (The term 'piecing' simply means the sewing together, edge to edge, of small pieces of cloth.)

When enough blocks have been worked to make up a complete quilt, they are sewn or 'set' together, either directly adjacent to each other or separated by strips or blocks of plain fabric.

This method obviously reduces the sewing time, particularly as no paper patterns are required and the straight seams involved lend themselves especially well to machine sewing.

Although it is possible to piece and set the blocks by hand in back stitch and using papers, this is a much more laborious process than machine stitching which enables you to run up blocks at a speed unknown to many other forms of patchwork.

In addition to these practical advantages, the block method permits enormous scope for design and invention. There are two stages of design – that of the blocks themselves and that of the arrangement of the blocks.

There are hundreds of traditional patterns to follow. The importance given to their colourful names is another characteristic of American patchwork. The possible combinations of geometrical shapes are innumerable and constitute a refreshing change from the popular English hexagon.

It is advisable to start by following a traditional pattern. First master piecing – then create your own designs.

Planning

Before you embark on constructing a quilt, it is important to plan your design if the end result is not to be confused or messy. Indeed, simple patterns are often the most successful. Measure the bed you intend covering from top to bottom and from side to side. If you wish your quilt to reach the floor on three or all four sides of the bed, add this measurement – from the top of the bed to the floor – to your calculations where appropriate.

If you are to obtain a regular design all over the quilt, rather than a random effect, it is obviously important to check that you have enough of each fabric to be used. It is safer to over-estimate your requirements, especially if you are using scraps of old material which you will not be able to match up if you run out.

Experiment first with a few sample blocks. This may help you choose a design, and will give you practice in sewing straight seams. It will also enable you to calculate the area of cloth that a given block takes and to estimate roughly how much of each fabric is needed for the total number of blocks required.

Building blocks

There is no correct size for blocks. They can vary from 15cm (6in) to 60cm (24in) square. The most common size, how-

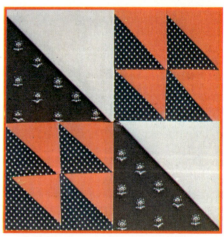

Above: Reading clockwise patterns are: Double Four-patch, Road to California or Jacob's ladder from the nine-patch family, Saw-tooth Star and Flock of Geese.

Right above: A detail of the Shoo Fly bedspread incorporating a fascinating variety of American blocks in vivid contrasting colours.

ever, and probably the most manageable is 25.5cm (10in) to 30.5cm (12in) square. Whatever design and size you choose, accuracy is of the utmost importance. The secret of success is to use window templates, allowing 6mm ($\frac{1}{4}$in) for seams.

On the wrong side of fabrics chosen for the block, pencil along both outer and inner lines of the template. Cut along the outer line – the inner line will act as a seam guide. In this way, you will obtain accuracy both in cutting the patches to be pieced together and in seaming. Quilt piecing is a craft of precision; tiny inaccuracies may throw your pattern out – blocks will not be exact squares, corners will not match up with each other.

Start constructing your block according to the design you have chosen, being careful to follow seam guides. Open up and press each seam flat as you go. Spraying the assembled patches lightly with spray starch is a quick and efficient way of obtaining flat units.

The actual piecing of blocks will obviously vary slightly according to the pattern chosen. A general rule, however, is to join any triangles first to form squares, and then to build up the squares to form bigger and bigger units. A good example of this is the construction of the Windmill block.

It is a good idea to pin the points at which the seams meet, as you go, to ensure that the lines of the pattern match. If these basic principles are followed, there are no patterns based on squares and triangles that cannot be assembled.

Most pieced blocks belong either to the four-patch (fig.2) or to the nine-patch (fig.3) family. As their names imply, they involve either four or nine basic units, which can be subdivided in any number of ways.

Other blocks can be made up by using

1. Sew triangles together

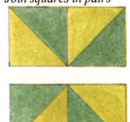

Join squares in pairs

Make up first square patch

Final four-patch block

2. Simple four-patch block

Old Maid's Puzzle

Broken Dishes

Indian Hatchet

3. Basic nine-patch block

Bear's tracks or Bear's Paw

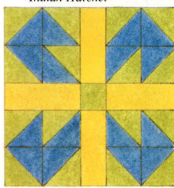
Jack in the Box

4. Alternate pieced and plain blocks

5. Alternate blocks diagonally

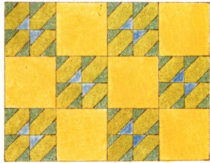

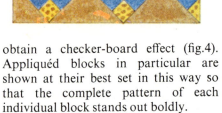

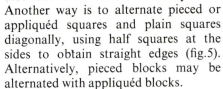

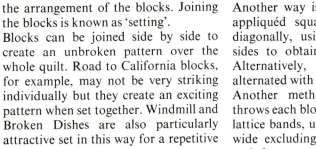

6. Blocks separated by lattice bands

7. Diagonal lattice strips

a combination of piecing and appliqué, or by using appliqué alone.

Setting

The final design of the quilt depends on the arrangement of the blocks. Joining the blocks is known as 'setting'.

Blocks can be joined side by side to create an unbroken pattern over the whole quilt. Road to California blocks, for example, may not be very striking individually but they create an exciting pattern when set together. Windmill and Broken Dishes are also particularly attractive set in this way for a repetitive all-over result.

This way of setting can create a messy effect, however, particularly as the finished article is to be quilted. Quilting tends to be confused or concealed on all-patchwork quilts.

It is often advisable, therefore, to set each block beside a square of plain material – using a window template to cut it out exactly the same size – to obtain a checker-board effect (fig.4). Appliquéd blocks in particular are shown at their best set in this way so that the complete pattern of each individual block stands out boldly.

Another way is to alternate pieced or appliquéd squares and plain squares diagonally, using half squares at the sides to obtain straight edges (fig.5). Alternatively, pieced blocks may be alternated with appliquéd blocks.

Another method setting which also throws each block into relief is the use of lattice bands, usually about 7.5cm (3in) wide excluding seams, which separate and frame each block (fig.6). This is sometimes known as sash work. Lattice strips cut on the straight of the fabric can also be set diagonally, again using half blocks at the sides (fig.7).

Finishing

When sufficient blocks have been set to make the required quilt, they can be bordered with a simple frame of plain material, bound with bias tape or even decorated with a pieced border – made up in a similar way to the blocks.

The finished article can then be lined and quilted. Quilting by blocks should be done by hand. No frame is necessary.

Right: This superb bedspread is made up of 'Winged square' blocks.

Log cabin patchwork

Above: An extravagant but effective use of log cabin patchwork is shown here. Indeed, the designs are so magnificent that it is worth making a display of them as wall hangings as well as cushions and bedspreads.

Opposite below: A detail of log cabin patchwork showing very clearly the subtle gradation of the shades of colours to achieve the 'firelight' effect so typical of the tradition.

1. Card templates to use as a guide for cutting strips. Also shown is a foundation square.
2. Centre square tacked to the foundation material
3. First, second and third strips laid down in position
4. Fourth strip sew in position
5. Thirteenth strip in position
6. Completed square.

'Log Cabin' was a popular form of patchwork both in England and America during the second half of the nineteenth century. Strips of material are built out from a central square, their edges overlapping. The square is divided diagonally by the light and dark shading of the strips. Traditionally the central square represents the fire, the light half of the square is the firelit side of the room and the dark side is the shadows.

Like crazy patchwork, 'Log Cabin' is sewn onto a foundation material so a mixture of fabrics is possible, but the design relies for its effect on the light and dark shading of the patches. Variations of this form such as 'Straight Furrow' and 'Barn Raising' depend on the placing of the light and shade patches when they are joined together. 'Pineapple' pattern is made in the same way as 'Log Cabin' except a strip is sewn diagonally across the corners on alternative rows.

To make a 'Log Cabin'

You will need a square of fabric to use as a foundation – a 30.5cm (12in) square is a good size if you are making a bedcover, a 15cm (6in) if you are making

pieces to make a cushion or handbag. Take a square of fabric for the centre and tack it to the foundation (see diagram). The other fabrics in light and dark shades should be cut into strips of 2.5cm (1in) wide. For each square of the design you will need two light and two dark strips.

It is helpful in placing the patches if a light pencil line is drawn diagonally from each corner of the foundation piece, crossing in the centre of the square, before sewing centre square.

The first short strip of light materials is placed right side down on the centre square and stitched 6mm ($\frac{1}{4}$in) from the edge, covering one side of the square. It is then folded back and pressed down. A second strip of light material is sewn along the second side of the centre square, overlapping the first strip at one end. The third and fourth sides of the square are covered with strips of dark material, each one overlapping the previous one at the end. By using two strips of light fabric and then two strips of dark you will end up with all the dark 'logs' on side one of the square and all the light 'logs' on the opposite.

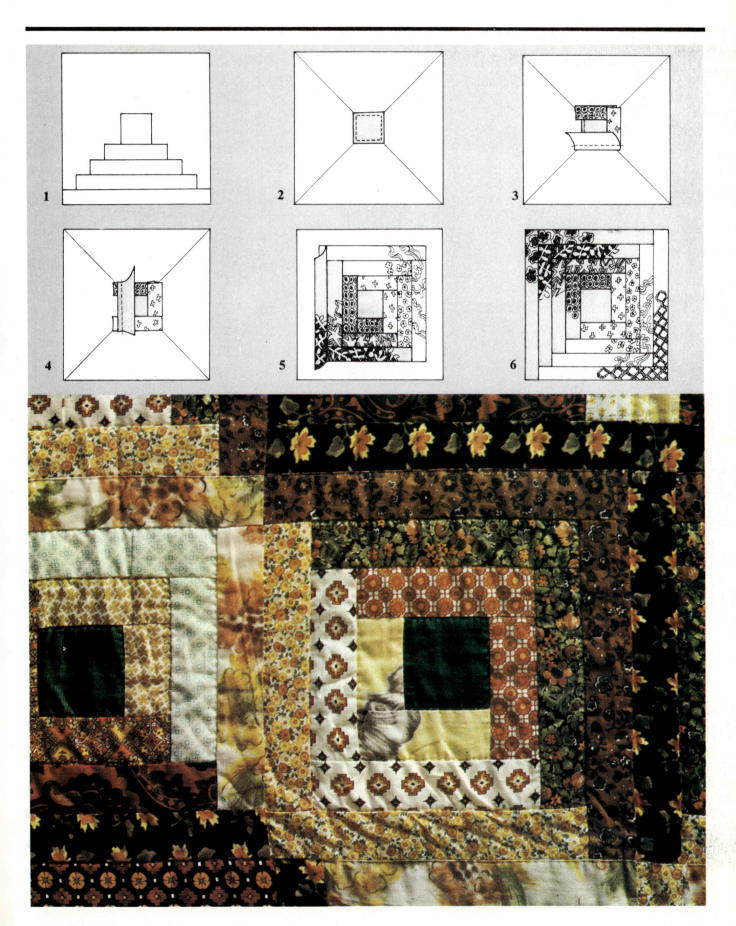

APPLIQUÉ

Soft furnishings decorated with appliqué can be really exciting and colourful. Like patchwork, this is a craft which makes use of scraps of materials, and is therefore a super money-saver for the budget conscious household. Use appliqué boldly, as in the ribbon technique to provide a dramatic trim to cushions and curtains. Alternatively you can explore the more whimsical styles like the Polly Pinafore motif, with its studied naivete. The range of effects that can be achieved with appliqué is amazing – compare the cheerfully inexpensive sunrise table mats with the sophistication of Victorian style lace curtains – you'll find delightful ideas to use in every room.

Appliqué techniques

Making a start with appliqué

Like patchwork, appliqué is a craft which makes use of scraps of material. The pieces are cut and then applied to another material with stitches. In its simplest form appliqué can be tackled by any beginner; results are quick and satisfactory and the easiest stitches can be used.

Appliqué can be left plain or richly decorated and can be worked in coarse or delicate fabrics. Its uses extend to decorating curtains, bedspreads, cushions and, of course, to building up pictures.

Fabric choice

Choice of fabrics and surface decoration will depend upon whether or not the article is intended for hard wear and laundering.

It is easiest to begin with non-fraying fabrics. Felt is particularly easy to work with, is fun for quickly-made objects and ideal for creating pictures, when anything from string to sequins can be added.

Design inspiration

Start by thinking about pattern making and by working out designs with scissors and some folded paper, like those made by children.

Fold a piece of paper into quarters and then triangles, experiment with cutting out various shapes, then open out the paper to see the effect you have produced.

As you grow more skilled you can experiment with fruit shapes, stars, initials, the outlines of familiar domestic objects like a vase or teapot, or the silhouettes of flowers and leaves. Remember when you draw a symmetrical shape to fold the pattern paper in half, so that both sides are exactly equal when you open the paper. Children's book illustrations are full of adaptable possibilities from fairytale animals to supermen. Trace a favourite character and enlarge or reduce the scale to the size you need. Birds or animals, cars or trains, clowns, cartoons, even dinosaurs, can all be adapted in this way as long as the basic shapes are sufficiently simple to be easily cut out and applied.

When you progress to more sophisticated designs, go to your local museum or library for inspiration. The flam-

Above: Useful and decorative, appliqué pincushions are good for beginners.

boyant shapes Art of Nouveau are ideal for appliqué, so are many oriental designs and the work of some primitive artists. Study the earliest forms of appliqué; you can find examples of the beautiful counterchanged designs that were used in ecclesiastical banners centuries ago, where two colours were intricately fitted together and used alternately for background and motif.

Preparing felt motifs

Using thick paper, cut a template of the shape you have chosen. If there are several parts to the chosen motif cut a template of the complete silhouette, then cut separate templates for each of the various parts.

Place the templates on the appropriate felt pieces and draw around them with a well-sharpened, soft pencil on the wrong side, so that pencil marks do not show on the finished work.

Cut out the motifs, using small sharp scissors.

Positioning motifs

Carefully position the motifs on the right side of the background fabric, remembering to allow sufficient margin on the background fabric for any seams. If the appliqué is to be centrally placed on a square of fabric, fold two diagonal lines from corner to corner of the square; the centre will be where they cross. Match this with the central point of the motif.

Joining methods
Bonding

For quick results appliqué shapes can be bonded to the background. The bonding material consists of a non-woven adhesive web which is prepared with a special paper backing. Cut a piece of bonding slightly larger than the motif, draw the outline of the shape required onto the paper backing and iron onto the wrong side of the motif material (fig.1a).

1a. Bonding a motif 1b. Removing backing

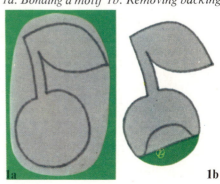

Allow to cool and cut out the motif shape. The non-woven adhesive web is now fused to the back of the motif.

Peel off paper (fig.1b), place motif right side up onto the background fabric and iron into place. Use a steam iron or a dry iron and damp cloth. Fabric bonded in this way can then have decorative stitching added around the edge.

This method is suitable for most fabrics except delicate ones and others, like velvet, which need special care.

Another simple technique is to use a little fabric adhesive on the back of the motif, taking care not to go to the edges. Then add decorative hand or machine stitching for the finishing touch.

Stitching felt motifs

Small motifs can be easily stitched in the hand so long as care is taken to keep the surface flat, but it is advisable to use an embroidery hoop, slate or tapestry frame to hold the fabric taut on larger projects. Tack the motif in place and sew to the background, making tiny stab stitches in exactly matching thread. If the stitching is not intended to be part of the decoration, it should be unobtrusive. Alternatively, you can use a spaced blanket stitch, worked with embroidery thread to produce a strong decorative edge on the motif.

Basic stitches
Stab stitch

Bring needle up through background fabric and motif, close to the edge of

Top: Oversew motif Centre: Blanket stitch a. Stab stitch b. Stab reversed

Below: Cut out small circles, squares or triangles from coloured, gummed paper and arrange in groups.

motif, then, making a very small stitch, take needle down again through the two thicknesses (fig.a). An alternative method is to bring needle up from background fabric immediately outside the edge of the motif, then take it down again a fraction inside the edge (fig.b).

Blanket (simple buttonhole) stitch
This can be worked close for securing edges of motifs cut in woven fabrics, or spaced out for motifs cut in felt.

Outline stitches
Details can be picked out with simple embroidery stitches, such as satin stitch or French knots. If you wish to emphasize the outlines you can add couching or chain stitch in a contrasting embroidery thread. Consult the stitch library at the beginning of the book.

Non-fraying woven fabrics
You can cut out motifs in most firmly woven fabrics and apply them successfully without turning under the edges. Choose a fabric of the same or a lighter weight than that used for the background and keep the shapes simple. When cutting the motif, make sure where possible that the grain on the motif matches that of the background fabric. Cut out the motif and work oversewing close to the edge. Find the right position for the motif and tack it onto the background fabric. Stitch into place with closely worked blanket stitch, covering the oversewing completely.

Using appliqué motifs
The patterns given in this chapter, enlarged if necessary, can be used in a number of ways.

Start with something small; make a pot holder for the kitchen from two squares of felt. Stab stitch the plump chicken motif to one square, place the two pieces of felt together with a piece of wadding sandwiched in between, then machine stitch the layers together and pink the edges to finish.

Child's bed cover
Multiply the motifs to make a child's bed-cover. Alternate the colours of the background squares to make a chequerboard effect and join them together by hand or machine. Line the cover and interline it with synthetic wadding as described previously.

Below left: Trace diagrams for the motif patterns.
Below: Felt motifs on corduroy

Polly Pinafore cushion

After experimenting with some of the ideas already given, you will probably want to progress to more complicated designs.

This chapter introduces the preparation of more complicated designs and methods of hand stitching fabrics which fray. (The methods are also suitable for non-fraying fabrics.)

Preparing a design

You will need to work from a paper pattern unless you are sufficiently confident to cut out motifs directly from the fabric.

Make a full-scale drawing of the design on paper, marking in the various sections which are to be cut from different fabrics and noting where sections are to overlap. Ears, wings or paws, for instance, can be cut out separately and positioned with one edge under the main part of the motif, which makes sewing easier by avoiding difficult angles.

Trace the outlines of each section separately onto another piece of paper and cut them out to use as patterns. Outline the complete design lightly in pencil on the background fabric or use dressmaker's carbon paper on a transfer pencil.

Another method is to draw the design on tissue paper, pin this to the background fabric, tack around the design lines, then tear away the paper.

Fabrics which fray

It is not difficult to apply motifs cut in fabrics which fray, if a little extra time and trouble is taken in working with one of the methods described here.

Stitch and cut

This is a good method to use on thin fabrics. Cut out a larger area than you need and mark in the shape of the motif with a pencil. Tack motif to background fabric and work close blanket stitch through both thicknesses around this outline (fig.1). Then carefully cut away the surplus motif fabric.

Another method of dealing with fraying or flimsy fabrics is to reinforce them with iron-on, nonwoven interfacing before cutting out the exact shape of the motif. This will provide a firm edge on which to work. The motif can then be tacked and closely blanket stitched to the background fabric.

Alternatively, cut out the exact shape in the interfacing. Iron it onto a larger piece of the motif fabric, cut out with seam allowance and apply as for turned-under method.

Turned under method

Motifs cut from most woven fabrics can have their edges turned under before they are applied. Here are some techniques to help you achieve good results.

Closely woven cotton fabrics are the easiest to handle. Remnants of other dressmaking fabrics can also be used, but when selecting patterns bear in mind the purpose for which the design is intended and never add a non-washable fabric to a washable article. Careful cutting and placing helps the appliquéd design to lie flat. Find the straight of grain before cutting each section if there is no selvedge to guide you. Match the straight of grain of the applied fabric to the straight of grain of the background, except for small curved motifs which can be cut on the cross.

Cut out each piece of the motif, adding a hem allowance of 6mm ($\frac{1}{4}$in) all around each section. Turn in and tack down all raw edges except those which join other parts of the motif, i.e. the pinafore and bonnet edges on the Polly Pinafore motif on the cushion. One edge (the pinafore edge) is left without its hem allowance turned in and the other has its allowance turned in.

If the shape is curved make snips in the hem allowance at frequent intervals, just less than 6mm ($\frac{1}{4}$in) deep, then turn in the edges. The snips will overlap on a convex curve and open out on a concave one.

Below: Pieces of motif are tacked separately onto the interfacing.

To mitre a right-angled, or wider, corner, first fold in one edge (fig.2a), then fold over the other (fig.2b) and tack. To mitre a sharper point, first fold in the point (fig.3b), fold one side over this (fig.3b), then the other (fig.3c) and tack to secure.

The edges can be pressed lightly before applying but take care to press only the edge so you do not mark right side.

Alternatively tack the shape to the paper pattern and then press the whole piece (the paper will prevent the turnings from marking the right side). Remove tacking and paper.

Position the motif onto the background fabric so that adjoining sections have the edge with hem allowance turned in placed over the one which is left raw (fig.4). Tack, and stitch the motif neatly in place with small slip stitches in a matching thread, or with neat running stitches worked in matching or contrasting thread.

Adjoining edges can be stitched to the background in one operation.

Flowers in relief
A pretty variation of appliqué can be achieved by leaving the edges of motifs unattached to the background. Flower petals can be attached at the bottom only. Cover the stitches with a separate flower centre, slip-stitched in place. Edges can be bound with close blanket stitches or the petals can be cut double, the edges stitched with right sides together, then turned to the outside through a small opening which is then stitched up. The second method takes a

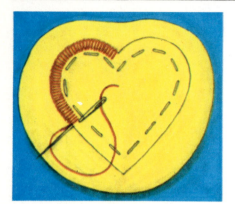

1. Buttonhole stitch motif to fabric

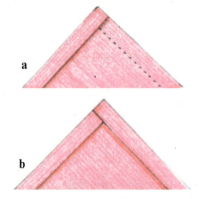

2. Mitring a right-angled corner

4. Joining different fabrics

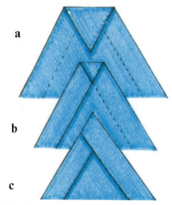

3. Mitring an acute corner

5. Flower and leaf motif

little longer to work, but results are sufficiently sturdy to be used on children's garments.

Leaves can be made in the same way, but stitch these in position with a stem stitched spine, to about two-thirds of the length of the leaf.

The petticoat frill of Polly Pinafore is attached in a similar way. In this case the frill is cut slightly wider than the bottom of the skirt and pinafore, and a small hem made on one long and the two short sides of the frill. The fourth side is then gathered and this edge is covered by the skirt and pinafore.

Polly Pinafore cushion

The Polly Pinafore cushion is made in plain cotton with an appliqué motif made from printed cotton fabrics. The edges of the various parts of the motif are turned under and slip stitched into place. The finished cushion is 48cm (19in) square and the motif is 41cm (16in) high but the motif could be made to fit a cushion of any size.

You will need

For the cushion: 1.15m (1¼yd) of 91cm (36in) wide plain cotton fabric Cushion pad, 51cm (20in) square For the appliqué: bonnet and petticoat frill – 20.5cm × 28cm (8in × 11in) piece of broderie anglaise; pinafore – 25.5 × 18cm (10in × 7in) cotton fabric; dress – 20.5cm × 10cm (8in × 4in) piece of fabric for ribbons, hands, basket, sleeve, boot.

To make the cushion

Cut two pieces of plain fabric 51cm (20in) square and put one aside for the

cushion back.

Take the remaining square of fabric (the cushion front) and find the centre of the square.

Enlarge the motif (fig.5), make paper patterns and outline the design centrally on the cushion front as described in this article.

Cut out the various parts of motif (except the petticoat frill) in appropriate fabrics, allowing 6mm (¼in) all around each piece for the hems.

Cut a piece of broderie Anglaise for the petticoat frill, 28cm × 4cm (11in × 1⅝in). Narrowly hem one long edge and two short edges.

Work a row of gathering 3mm (⅛in) from the fourth edge and pull up the gathers to fit the bottom of the skirt. Back stitch the frill into position on the cushion along the gathering line (fig.6). Work the rest of the appliqué by the slip stitch method as described in this chapter. Make sure that the bottoms of skirt and pinafore are slip stitched securely on the gathering line of the frill enclosing the raw edge (fig.7).

Make up the cushion. Instructions are given on pages 154-157.

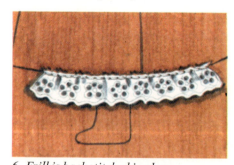

6. Frill is back stitched in place

7. Skirt stitched over frill edge

133

Machine-stitched appliqué

Another similarity between patchwork and appliqué is that both can be either hand or machine sewn. Machine-stitched appliqué has the advantages of being hard-wearing, practical for most fabrics and time-saving. Motifs can be reinforced with iron-on, non-woven interfacing in the same way as for hand sewn appliqué. A fusible web, such as Bondaweb Vilene can be used similarly.

Zig-zag stitch

If your machine can work a zigzag stitch you will find this invaluable. An open zig-zag stitch can be worked around the raw edges of any closely woven fabric or felt motif.

Satin stitch by machine

If you close up the zig-zag stitch sufficiently you can achieve an effect like fine, smooth satin. The satin stitch is worked in half the time taken to achieve the same effect by hand, and is ideal for securing and decorating the edges of motifs in one operation. The satin stitch is best worked with a No.59 sewing thread. Either use a frame to keep the fabric taut, or place the work on two sheets of thin paper when machine stitching to avoid puckering (fig.1) – the paper can be easily torn away.

It is worth spending some time experimenting with stitch lengths and widths and learning how to sew accurately around angles and curves, which can be tricky. The stitch-and-cut method can be worked in machined satin stitch.

Straight stitch

Alternatively, appliqué can be sewn to the background with straight machine stitching. In this case, unless you are using felt, leather or PVC, a small turned-under hem must first be tacked around the edges of the various parts of a motif. Treat corners and curves as you would hand sewn appliqué when using the turned-under method.

Ric-rac braid provides a quickly-produced decorative edge on simple appliquéd shapes. Complete edges of the shape with open zig-zag stitch or oversew edges by hand and tack to the background. Tack the ric-rac into position and secure with straight or zig-zag machine stitching.

Where ric-rac is used to cover adjacent edges of a motif, these edges should be overlapped by 3mm ($\frac{1}{8}$in) before the ric-rac is tacked into place.

Russian braid, a narrow braid made up of two adjoining cords, makes an alternative decorative edge for motifs. Complete the edges of the shapes as for applying with ric-rac braid, and secure braid with straight stitch worked between the cords (fig. 2a) or with open zig-zag stitch worked across (fig.2b).

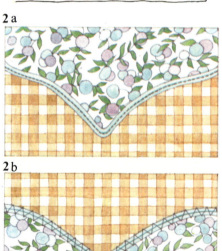

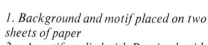

1. Background and motif placed on two sheets of paper
2a. A motif applied with Russian braid using a straight stitch
2b. Russian braid stitched around a motif with a zig-zag machine stitch

Using printed fabric

Small motifs can be cut from spare pieces of printed fabric and applied to a plain fabric. You can cut individual flowers from the fabric used for a floral tablecloth and apply them to a set of plain napkins. You can also make appealing trimmings for soft furnishings in this way.

Try to make a printed fabric work for

you in a witty and imaginative way. First cut out your motif shape in tracing paper and move this around on the motif fabric until the details of the pattern are in the best position for cutting out. A spot can become the eye of a bird or animal, or a line of stylized daisies can march down the back of a seated cat.

Choose a print to harmonize with the subject of the motif – see how the designer of the cushion has chosen fabrics – a small all-over print for the tablecloth and an embossed one for the doily. She has used a leafy fabric for the leaves on the wall hanging and has made her lizards look more reptilian by the use of a fabric with an exotic design. Notice too, how well she has used good colour contrast.

Ribbon appliqué

Applying ribbon to soft furnishings is a very effective way of adding a luxury look. A plain curtain can be given a dramatic border of ribbons of different widths and textures in toning colours; an ordinary tablecloth can be decorated with three-dimensional ribbon-flowers; or a cushion can be trimmed with a 'lightning flash' as shown in the illustration.

There are basically two ways of applying ribbon – flat onto the background or by folding and knotting to make a three-dimensional pattern.

Work ribbon on a closely woven fabric or on felt, since this kind of backing holds the work firmly in place.

Applying ribbon flat

Choose a simple design based on straight lines. This will be relatively easy to work and will look most effective. The two cushions shown here will illustrate this point: the lightning flash on one gets its impact from the use of different textures and widths of ribbon, and the basket effect on the other is achieved by stitching three ribbons together and then interweaving them before stitching into position. The latter method could be continued across the whole cushion.

Plan your design on paper first and when you are satisfied with it transfer it to the background fabric with dress-makers' carbon paper or a transfer pencil. Pin and tack the ribbon onto the lines marked, making a fold where necessary.

Work a line of straight or zig-zag machine stitch along each edge of the ribbon, or back stitch by hand.

The folds can be slip stitched or back stitched by hand with small stitches.

Ribbons can be applied one on top of another, using a narrower ribbon each time, to add another dimension.

The ideas that are discussed here are intended to provide you with projects to start with. Then, when you have mastered these, you'll be in a good position to experiment.

Appliqué sunflower quilt

An appliquéd cover for a continental quilt can be the ideal solution to the common problem of choosing between a completely plain fabric or one with an all-over pattern which may not fit into your decorative scheme.

You could copy the sunflower shown in the photograph or, if you have a flower pattern elsewhere in the room, you could make up your own flower to match. The main factor for success with this sort of appliqué is to keep the shapes simple and bold, with clean, rounded outlines which are easy to sew. Because the cover is to be washed frequently, all the edges of the appliqué are turned under for extra strength. And for this reason also, the appliqué fabric should be the same as the duvet cover. It is easiest to appliqué the flower onto a cover which you are making yourself, but you can also work the motif on a ready-made cover although you may find it more bulky to hold.

Sunflower motif

The fabric amounts and instructions are given for one large motif 61cm (24in) square but you could also make smaller flowers and put them in the corners of your cover.

Fabric required
0.45 metre ($\frac{1}{2}$yd) each of three contrasting colours in polyester cotton.

You will also need
Tracing paper.
Matching thread for all fabrics.
1.40 metres ($1\frac{1}{2}$yd) of lightweight iron-on interfacing.

Making the pattern

Using tracing paper, trace off each shape individually from the pattern and number them as indicated. Cut out each shape.

Cutting out

Pin the pieces of the pattern onto the interfacing and cut out. Write the number of each piece on to the interfacing. Place the interfacing pieces on to the fabric according to the colour required and iron on. Cut out, leaving an extra 3mm ($\frac{1}{8}$in) all around for turnings.

Making up

1 Place one side of the quilt cover flat with the right side facing up. Decide where you want to place the flower and indicate a 61cm (24in) square in tacking, making sure that the tacking lines follow the straight grain line.
2 Arrange the stiffened pieces of fabric within the square and pin into place. Fold under the turnings with the point of a needle. Hem in place.
3 Finish making up cover.

Below: A super sunflower quilt makes cheerful splash of colour in the room.

Trace pattern for Sunflower motif

Appliqué table mats and napkins

Sunrise mat and napkin
You will need
(quantities given for one mat and one napkin in each case).

For mat: 45.5cm × 35.5cm (18in × 14in) piece of linen cut on the straight of grain

For mat appliqué: 41cm × 20.5cm (16in × 8in) piece of pink cotton; 35.5cm × 18cm (14in × 7in) piece of red cotton; 30.5cm × 16cm (12in × 6½in) piece of gingham; 24cm × 14cm (9½in × 5½in) piece of peach cotton; 16.5cm × 10cm (6½in × 4in) piece of striped cotton. All pieces to be cut on the straight of grain

Ric-rac braid: 1.8m (2yd) red, 90cm (1yd) peach, 45cm (½yd) yellow.

For napkin: 45cm (½yd) square of linen

For napkin appliqué: 20.5cm × 12cm (8in × 5in) piece of pink cotton; 16.5cm × 10cm (6½in × 4in) piece of striped cotton, cut on the straight of grain

Ric-rac braid: 60cm (⅝yd) red, 40cm (⅜yd) yellow

Matching thread

To make the mat. Enlarge the sunrise graph pattern so that the outer sunrise is 18.5cm (7¼in) high. Make a pattern for the complete shape and patterns for each colour used.

Fold linen for mat in half vertically and mark this central fold with a line of tacking.

Cut out appliqué pieces for mat in the colours shown in the illustration, placing lower edge of each piece on the straight of grain of fabric. Mark centre of each piece with a line of tacking as for the mat itself.

Neaten the edges of each section to make an even line.

Matching central lines, tack sunrise sections together, superimposing one piece on the next (fig.1).

Tack appropriate coloured ric-rac braid around all but outer band of sunrise so that raw edges of fabric are covered. Turn under 1cm (⅜in) of braid at ends to neaten. Sew in place with straight or zig-zag machine stitching.

Position appliqué on mat, matching central lines, with lower edge about 5cm (2in) up from lower edge of mat. Beginning at lower left hand corner and

folding under end of braid diagonally, pin, tack and stitch ric-rac braid around outer edge and base of sunrise, making a folded mitre at the right hand corner. and fold left hand end diagonally under to neaten.

Make a 2.5cm (1in) fringe all around mat to finish.

To make the napkin. Adapt the sunrise graph pattern so that the sunrise is 10.5cm (4⅛in) high.

Fold linen for napkin in half vertically and then horizontally and mark folds with lines of tacking.

Make patterns and apply sunrise to napkin on lower left hand corner of napkin about 4cm (2in) from the edge, working the appliqué in the same way and applying it as for the mat.

Make a 2cm (¾in) fringe on all edges of the napkin.

Heart mat and napkin
You will need
(quantities given for one mat and one napkin in each case).

For mat: 48cm × 38cm (19in × 15in) piece of linen cut on the straight of grain

For appliqué: 41cm × 32cm (16in × 12½in) piece of gingham cotton; 35.5cm × 28cm (14in × 11in) piece of paisley cotton.

Ric-rac braid: 1.4m (1½yd) red, 1.2m (1¼yd) yellow

For napkin: 45.5cm (½yd) square of linen

For appliqué: 18cm × 15cm (7in × 6in) piece of paisley cotton; 15cm × 13cm (6in × 5in) piece of gingham

Ric-rac braid: 70cm (¾yd) orange, 45.5cm (½yd) yellow.

To make the mat. Enlarge the heart graph pattern so that the overall height of the heart is 30cm (11¾in).

Make centre of mat in the same way as for sunrise mat.

Make a narrow plain hem around the edge of the mat, mitring the corners.

Cut out appliqué pieces for mat in colours shown in the illustration.

Neaten edges of each section.

Work appliqué and apply as for sunrise motif. When applying ric-rac braid begin at lower point.

To make the napkin, adapt the heart

graph pattern so that the overall height of the outer heart is 14cm (5½in).

Make a narrow plain hem all around the napkin, mitring the corners.

Fold the napkin in half vertically and then horizontally. Press in the folds. Open out napkin and refold once diagonally. Mark this line on one quarter only with a line of tacking.

Make patterns and work appliqué as for mat, positioning heart centrally on this line.

1. Sunrise shapes tacked, with each layer superimposed on the one below.
2. Graph pattern for sunrise and heart motifs used on the mats

Bottom: The two designs of table mats are shown in the photographs. Both are trimmed with ric-rac braid.

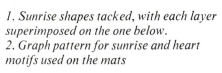

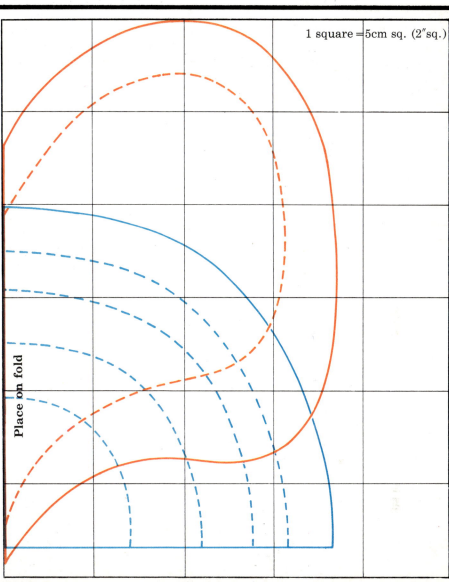

1 square = 5cm sq. (2″ sq.)

Place on fold

Appliqué quilt

It's as easy as ABC and makes an ideal gift for any child. The instructions given are for a quilt 91cm × 137cm (36in × 54in). For best results choose fabrics which will not run when the blanket is washed.

Fabric required
3m (3¼yd) of 91cm (36in) wide printed cotton (A)
0.9m (1yd) of 91cm (36in) wide printed cotton (B)
0.9m (1yd) of 91cm (36in) wide plain cotton (A)
0.9m (1yd) of 91cm (36in) wide plain cotton (B)

You will also need
Matching thread
Matching buttonhole twist
91cm × 137cm (36in × 54in) of cotton wadding
45.5cm (18in) of lightweight iron-on interfacing
If lightweight cotton has been used for the top, 2.75m (3yd) of 91cm (36in) wide medium-weight cotton
Piping cord

Cutting out and making up

1 Cut out six squares 25.5cm × 25.5cm (10in × 10in) in each of the four colours.
2 Trace the letters of the alphabet onto lightweight interfacing. Cut out. Make certain the letters will appear right side up and forward when ironed onto the fabric.
3 Iron interfacing letters onto the remainder of the fabric, making certain the printed fabric letter will go on the solid square and vice versa.
4 Cut around letters allowing 6mm (¼in) turnings.
5 Make turnings on letters and baste.
6 Centre letters on squares and appliqué by hand or zig-zag by machine into position using the buttonhole twist.
7 Pin the squares together to make four horizontal rows and six vertical rows. Sew squares together taking a 1.5cm (½in) turning on all seams. Press seams open.
8 If lightweight cotton is being used, back the top of the quilt with the medium-weight cotton lining. Repeat for the back of the quilt. Tack all around and treat as one piece.
9 Sandwich the cotton wadding between the quilt top and bottom. Pin securely and tack diagonally from corner to corner.
10 Quilt around the letters by hand or machine.
11 Cut bias strips from printed cotton A and make up piping to fit the perimeter of the quilt. Pin and machine stitch the piping in position around the edge of the quilt top. Fold under the turnings of the quilt top and bottom, and hem the fold of the bottom to the stitching line of the top.

Above: A detail of the A B C quilt shows how effective the alternation of print and plain fabric looks. The example shown gives one combination of colourways, but the possibilities are infinite. For example you could use a nursery rhyme print or animal characters rather than a floral pattern. Or you could match up the fabric to the wallpaper.

Right: As easy as ABC. Make this fun quilt for the nursery, and you'll delight any child. There are 24 squares altogether.

Appliqué cushions

Appliqué persé
Appliqué persé is the simple but effective technique of cutting out a motif from a patterned fabric and applying it to a plain background. It can be used on most kinds of soft furnishing, such as cushions, bedspreads, table linen, etc.

The pattern
The easiest patterns to apply in this way are those with a definite motif and a solid outline, such as the flowers shown in the photograph.

If the motif you are using does not have a definite outline you can still use the technique but you will have to add an outline yourself, either with embroidery stitches or paint, perhaps in a contrasting colour.

The colours
Appliqué persé normally looks best if the motif is applied to a background which matches one of its colours, although a contrasting background can also be effective if motif contains one or two colours only.

If you are applying the motif by stitching (see below), use thread in a colour to match either the background or the motif.

Applying to fabric
The motif can be applied to the fabric by hand or machine. The hand method is normally slower, but it can give a more delicate result and it is easier for a motif with an intricate shape.

Hand method
1 Cut out the motif leaving a margin round the outside of about 1.5cm ($\frac{1}{2}$in).
2 Place the motif, right side up, onto the right side of the background fabric so that the grain lines match.
3 Pin the motif in position placing the pins at right angles to the cut edge, with the pin heads facing outwards (this helps to prevent the work from puckering).
4 Tack the motif to the fabric outside the stitching line.
5 Work around the outline of the motif in neat firm backstitch.
6 Trim the surplus fabric back to the stitching, using fine sharp embroidery

Left: Appliqué persé motifs echo the flower pattern of the wallpaper.

scissors for cutting.
7 Reinforce the edge of the motif by working around it in fine buttonhole stitch or a more elaborate embroidery stitch, such as whipped chain, coral knot, Portuguese stem stitch, or with a line of couching.

Machine method
1 Cut out the fabric and pin it to the background as for the hand method.
2 Leaving the pins in position, mount the background fabric into an embroidery hoop. For machine embroidery, the fabric will wrinkle less if you place it over the outside hoop and press the inside hoop into it. Tighten all the screws.
3 Prepare your machine for embroidery, following the manufacturer's instructions. Remove the presser foot and test your tension on a spare piece of fabric
4 Insert the ring under the needle and lower the presser bar. Work around the edge of the motif in straight stitch.
5 Remove the ring from the machine and trim the excess fabric close to the stitching.
6 Insert the ring into the machine again and work several more rounds of straight stitch either side of the first line. If you prefer some of the lines can be worked in a more random style.

Applying to solid surfaces
For this technique you need some iron-on interfacing and some fabric adhesive.
1 Check that the surface to which the motif is being applied is quite clean and roughen it slightly with fine glass paper to give a key for the adhesive.
2 Lay out the fabric from which you are cutting the motif wrong side up and iron a piece of interfacing over the whole motif.
3 Cut out the motif using sharp embroidery scissors.
4 Place the motif in the required position on your surface and trace around the edge lightly in pencil.
5 Apply adhesive on to the area marked and also onto the back of the motif. Allow to dry for the time specified in the adhesive manufacturer's instructions.
6 Press the motif firmly in place onto the background, checking that it is absolutely flat and firmly glued around the edges.

Appliqué net curtains

These beautiful curtains have all the charm of old Victorian lace but are simply spotted net worked with appliqué. We photographed them here in a sitting room but they would also look enchanting in a bedroom or nursery.

The design described in this pattern is ideal for tall windows, and gives real drama. However it is only a suggestion. You may wish to make your own design, it may echo a motif from the wallpaper in the room for example.

Below: Graph pattern for tree — each square = 5cm (2in) sq.

Centre and right: Chart for the centre curtain and two side curtains.

Opposite: Romantic net curtains are given a fantasy mood. They are decorated with different patterned net motifs, which make up a fairy-tale tree for the centre curtain.

You will need

Materials required to make appliqué net curtains, one central curtain measuring 221.5cm × 150cm (87in × 60in) and two side curtains measuring 274.5cm × 76.5cm (108.5in × 30in)
5.05m (5½yd) 'Riekko' heavy net, 150cm (60in) wide
0.25m (¼yd) each of four different sized spotted nets, 150cm (60in) wide
1m (1yd 3in) net with bark-like texture 91cm (36in) wide
Small ball thick white yarn
Matching thread
Four packs of Vilene Bondaweb
8m (8¾yd) edging lace, 2.5cm (1in) wide
Ten wooden curtain rings 7.5cm (3in) in diameter
1.93cm (76in) plastic coated curtain wire

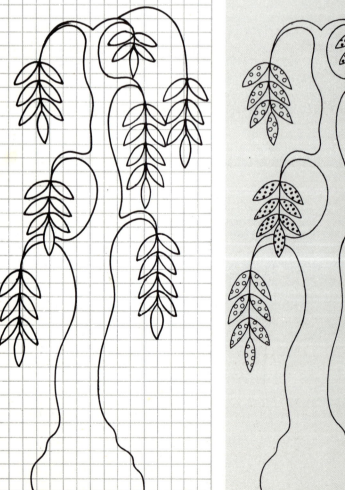

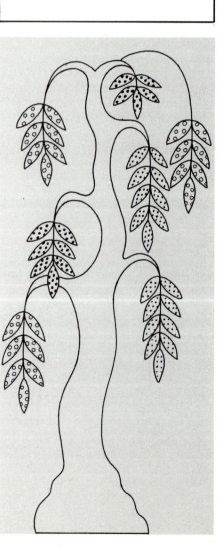

To make central curtain

Cut a piece of heavy lace 223.5cm (88in) long. Draw up the tree trunk motif to scale from the graph pattern given here. One square represents 5cm (2in) square. Cut out the trunk from the bark-like textured net. Position the tree in the centre of the curtain, the base of the trunk coming 5cm (2in) from the lower edge. Machine appliqué, using close zig-zag stitch.

Trace off the leaf shape from our pattern and cut out fifty-one leaves, using four different spotted nets. The leaves may be slightly larger or smaller than the pattern to add interest.

Using white sewing thread couch down lines and curves of white yarn to form branches. Arrange the leaves around the branches. Make all the leaves on one branch from net of the same sized spot, following chart 1 as a guide. Apply the leaves to the net by ironing on, using Bondaweb, following the manufacturer's instructions. Then machine appliqué using close zig-zag stitch.

Make a 5cm (2in) machined hem at the top of the curtain and machine lace edging along the bottom of the curtain with close zig-zag stitch. Thread the curtain wire through the hem at the top.

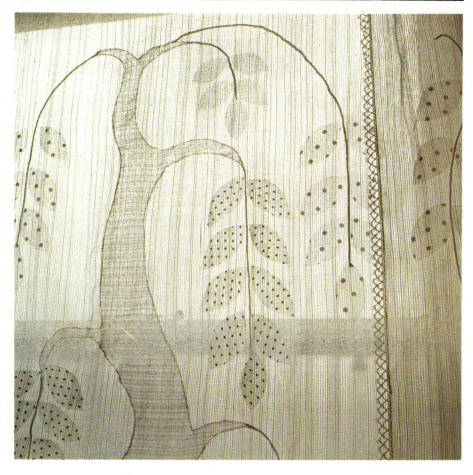

To make the side curtains

Cut a piece of heavy lace 277cm)109in) long. Cut the fabric in half lengthways to form the two curtains. From three different spotted nets cut out thirty-six leaves. For each curtain couch down the white yarn as branches and tendrils. Iron on the leaves following chart 2 as a guide. Then machine appliqué as before. The cut edges form the centre edges of the curtains and the edging lace should be machined along these and the bottom edge with close zig-zag stitch.

Make 5cm (2in) machined hems along the top of each curtain and sew on five wooden curtain rings to each one.

Arrange the curtains as in our photograph and tie back the two side curtains with some lace edging.

Above: Close-up view of the curtain showing the variety of nets used to illustrate the pattern details.

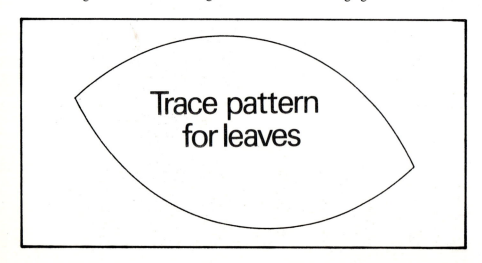

Trace pattern for leaves

CUSHIONS

Cushions are great fun to make, and are an instant way
of changing the mood in a room without spending a
fortune on expensive furnishings. Make clever use of
colour and texture, pick up the tones of the room, or
choose a bold highlight for contrast. Cushions are
available in various shapes and sizes too, round, square,
boxed and bolster are the most common, although we
have a delightful squashy cushion shaped like a sun
flower for a child's room. Every child will snuggle down
happily on our giant-sized round floor cushion, while
the expert needlewoman will want to try the super
designs for smocking and quilting techniques.

Estimating fabric amounts

Cushions can be decorative as well as useful. You can easily make an eye-catcher from a simple basic shape with clever use of fabric or trimmings. You will need some basic know-how before you actually begin.

Plain cushion cover
For a good fit, cover should be slightly smaller all around than cushion pad. For a 45.5cm (18in) square cushion with piped edges you would need 103cm (1$\frac{1}{8}$yd) of 91cm (36in) fabric or 57cm ($\frac{5}{8}$yd) of 122cm (48in) fabric. The cutting diagrams include fabric for bias, strips for piping and 1.5cm ($\frac{1}{2}$in) seams, so allow correspondingly less for an un-piped cover. Measure perimeter of cushion to find amount of piping cord (pre-shrunk).

Boxed cushion covers
First make pattern for top and bottom. Lay cushion flat on a sheet of brown paper and draw around it accurately. For the gusset measure depth of cushion to find depth, then measure all around cushion to find length required. If using piping, double this length to find amount of pre-shrunk piping needed. Add 1.5cm ($\frac{1}{2}$in) seam allowance all around cushion and gusset sections. Plan any joins in gusset strip at corners of cushion. If you wish to insert a zip at the back of cushion, cut back gusset section 2.5cm (1in) deeper.
Strong upholstery zips are available

Bolster cushion
The body piece is made from a rectangle of fabric with two circular ends which can be piped if you wish. For dimensions of rectangle, measure length of bolster, then measure circumference of round end to give you width needed. Cut two circles, each the diameter of bolster for ends, with 1.5cm ($\frac{1}{2}$in) seam allowance all around. Also cut out the rectangle with 1.5cm ($\frac{1}{2}$in) seam allowance.
For a bolster 66cm × 20.5cm (26in × 8in) you will need 91cm (1yd) of 91cm (36in) wide fabric, 137cm (1$\frac{1}{2}$yd) pre-shrunk piping cord, 45cm (18in) zip.

Squash cushion cover
Measure the cushion pad and estimate fabric requirements in same way as the box cushion. About 69cm ($\frac{3}{4}$yd) is

Above: A bold use of striking colour contrast is employed here. Massed cushions of different shapes are fun.

Right: Squab cushions are used here on traditional dining chairs.

Below right: An informal couch can be built up from plain cushions.

Opposite: Crazy patchwork was a favourite of the Victorians. Here it is made up into a bright cushion in glowing jewel colours.

sufficient for an average kitchen chair, without piping.

Piping
Piping cord can be bought in six thicknesses, depending on the purpose for which it is intended. Numbers 1 and 2 are fine cords used mainly for eiderdowns and cushions made of finer fabrics such as silk. Bias strips to cover these should be 3.5cm (1$\frac{1}{4}$in) wide; numbers 3 and 4 are for loose covers and cushions; bias strips for these should be 4cm (1$\frac{1}{2}$in) wide; numbers 5 and 6

are used for thicker materials where a bolder edge is required, bias strips for these should be 4.5cm (1¾in) wide. Measure length of piping required; then cut bias strips of the appropriate width to the length required, joining as shown in fig.1. As piping cord can shrink it is advisable to boil cord before using. Cover piping cord with bias strip (fig.2) using piping foot on your sewing machine or just tack if you prefer. 23cm (¼yd) of 122cm (48in) wide fabric will make about 6.4m (7yd) of 4cm (1½in) wide bias strip. Here is a very quick method of joining lengths of bias strips which will give about 4.8m (5¼yd) of 3.8cm (1½in) bias strips from 23cm (¼yd) 91cm (36in) size fabric (fig.3). To apply piping, tack the covered cord to right side of fabric, with stitching lines of piping matching stitching lines of fabric section. Clip outside edges of bias strip at corners and curves (fig.4). With right sides together stitch other section which is being joined using the piping foot on your machine.

Piped Bolster Cushions
When choosing fabric for a bolster cover, avoid large patterns which might prove difficult to match at seams. Cut out body section and two round ends to required size, plus bias strips for piping. With right sides together, stitch long sides of rectangle at each end, leaving space in centre for zip. Tack this opening together and press seam. Tack zip in position, turn fabric tube right side out and back stitch zip firmly in place. Turn cover to wrong side again. Prepare piping and stitch to right side of bolster ends. Snip seam allowances of tube and piping end at intervals and stitch circles to tube, right sides together. Turn to right side through zip opening. If making your own pad, use down-proof cambric for feather and down fillings. Otherwise, make as bolster cover, omitting piping and zip. Fill through opening in side, then slipstitch opening to close.

Boxed cushions
Cut out top and bottom cover sections, gusset and bias strips if required for piping. Cut back gusset strip 2.5cm (1in) deeper in inserting zip. Pin all pieces together around cushion to check fit. Prepare piping.

Cut back gusset in half along the length if using zip. Stitch seams at each end, leaving space for zipper in centre. Insert zip. Otherwise, cushion can be fastened with press studs or cover can simply be slipped on cushion through a gap left in gusset seam which is then slip stitched together (see diagram). Stitch piping to top and bottom cushion sections snipping piping seam allowance at corners. Stitch gusset seams then stitch gusset section to the piped top section with right sides together. Snip gusset turning at corners. Attach bottom of cushion cover similarly.

Covering foam cushion shapes

These can be bought ready-made in various shapes and sizes. Before making top cover, make an inner cover from strong cambric or sheeting using same method.

Buttoned cushions

To make covered buttons, cut circle of fabric 6mm ($\frac{1}{4}$in) larger than button mould. Sew a running stitch around edge of fabric and place mould in centre. Gather until fabric is pulled taut and fasten securely at back. Cover back of button with another smaller circle of fabric with edges turned in and slip stitch in place.

To attach buttons, mark exact positions on top of cushions with crossed pins or tacking thread. Mark corresponding positions on underside where small buttons with two eyes are stitched to anchor the larger ones. Fit cover on cushion. To sew on the buttons, use four thicknesses of a strong buttonhole twist and a long darning needle. Sew through eye of small button, through cushion from back of button position, through back of covered button, back through cushion and other eye of small button. Knot threads at back, drawing threads tightly so that the top button sinks into cushion. Knot firmly.

Above right: The diagrams show the method for inserting a zip into the side of a bolster, and also how to attach the circles to the sides.

Below right: This is a sample cutting chart for an average sized boxed cushion, plus diagrams showing how to make the cushion up.

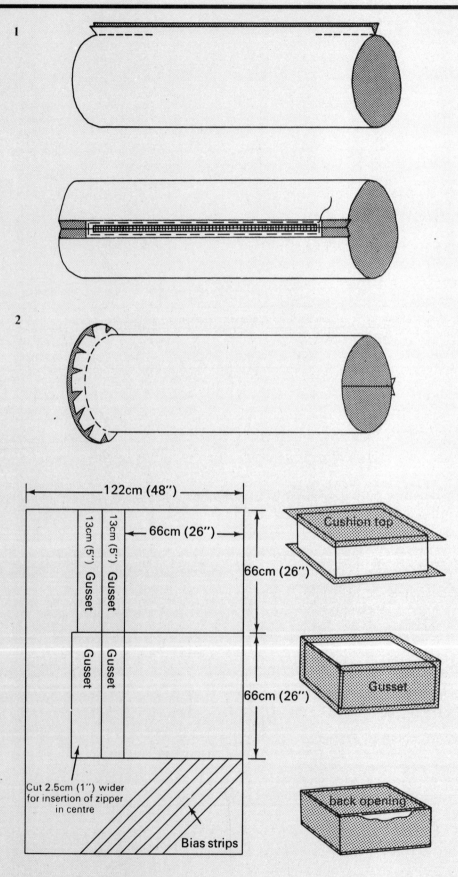

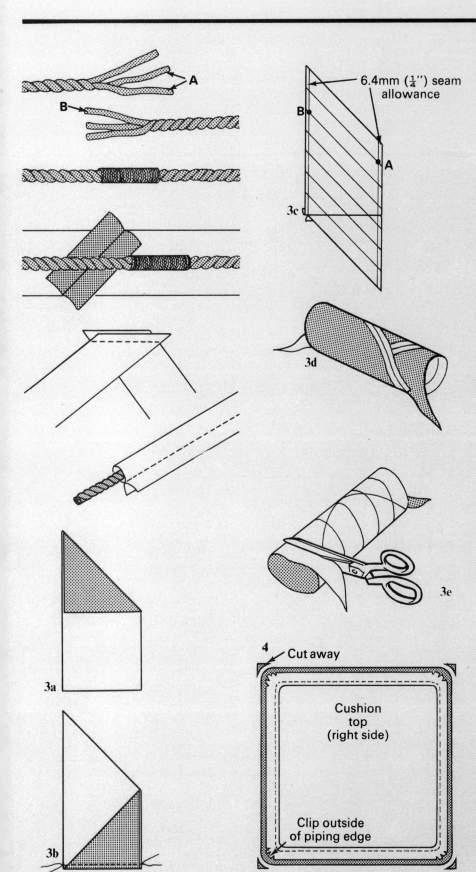

A

B

6.4mm (¼") seam allowance

B

A

3c

3d

3a

3b

4 Cut away

Cushion top (right side)

Clip outside of piping edge

3e

1. Joining piping cord. Cut cord to overlap 2.5cm (1in) and unravel and cut away two strands A. Cut away strand B. Twist remaining ends and stitch together. Then join in crosswise strip and cord.
2. Cover cord with bias strip.
3. Joining lengths of bias strips. Take a strip of fabric — length of the strip should be at least twice the width. Fold over the top right hand corner as shown to obtain the crosswise grain. Press (3a). Cut off this corner and join to lower edge with right sides facing. After stitching the pieces together press seam open (3b). Trim off any selvedges. Make a ruler in cardboard to the required width of the strips to be used as a guide. Mark the crosswise lines on the right side of the fabric in tailor's chalk, parallel to the top edge. Also mark seam allowances down each side. Mark points A and B carefully as shown (3c). Take a pin through the wrong side of the fabric at point A and through to point B and pin very accurately with right sides together. Continue pinning along seam (3d). Tack, checking that the lines are matching up exactly. Stitch, then press seam open. Turn to the right and start cutting around the spiral at the projecting strip at the top (3e).
4. Applying piping.

Below: Covering a button

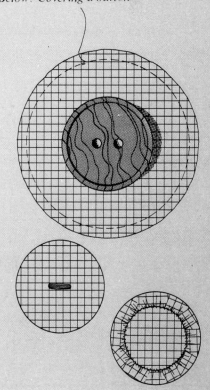

Basic cushions

Add an individual character to any room with cushions sewn by you in your own choice of fabric. Make them in a variety of shapes, sizes and textures, in colours to blend with your decor. Cushions also make a useful way to display other techniques.

The fabric

Most fabrics can be used for flat cushion covers (those without welts), although very fine fabrics usually need backing and can be difficult to work on. If you intend to pipe the edges of a cushion do not use a loosely woven fabric as the cord will show through. How much fabric? For a plain (unpiped) flat cushion decide on the size of your cushion cover and allow at least twice this amount, plus 1.5cm (½in) extra all around for turnings. For a 30.5cm (12in) flat square or round finished cover you

will need a piece of fabric at least 33cm × 66cm (13in × 26in). Allow an extra 45.5cm ($\frac{1}{2}$yd) of fabric if you intend to pipe the edge of the cover. This amount of fabric, although rather excessive in amount, avoids too many joins in the casing strip.

For a well-filled, professional looking cushion make the cover 1.5cm ($\frac{1}{2}$in) smaller all around than its pad.

Below: All these cushions are simple to make, and use fabrics with skill and imagination. Make lots for your home.

Keeping the grain straight, cut two pieces of fabric to the calculated size.
With right sides together, tack and machine stitch around three sides.
On the fourth side fold down the seam allowances onto the wrong side of each section and press. Trim the stitched corners (fig.1). Make the turnings neat and turn right side out. Press.
Insert the pad and slip stitch the opening neatly by hand. These stitches can be easily removed when the cover is washed. Rectangular cushions are made in the same way.

Plain flat round cushion

It is necessary to make a paper pattern to make sure of an accurate curve. Draw a semicircle on a large sheet of paper. To do this, attach a piece of string to a pin, and a pencil to the other end. Pierce paper firmly with pin, and draw your circle, adjusting the radius to different sizes of circles. Make the distance between pin and pencil equal to the radius of the finished cover, plus 1.5cm ($\frac{1}{2}$in).

You will need
A cushion pad
Fabric as above
Matching thread

Fold fabric in half lengthwise along the grain. Place the pattern with the straight straight edge on the fold. Pin into place and cut along the curved line only. Mark grain line along fold with tacking Cut another piece of fabric in the same way.
With right sides together, grain lines matching, place the two sections together. Tack and machine stitch 1.5cm ($\frac{1}{2}$in) from the edge all around the cover, leaving an opening of about one quarter of the circumference.
Clip small V-shapes to within 3mm ($\frac{1}{8}$in) from the stitching at 2.5cm (1in) intervals all around (fig.2).
Finish off as for a square cover.

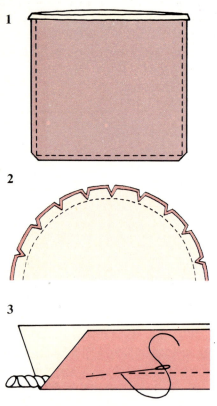

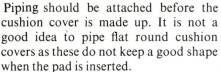

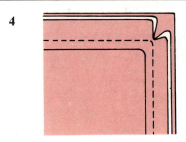

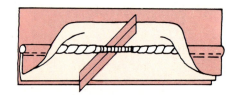

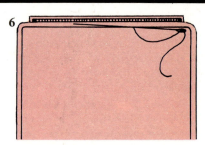

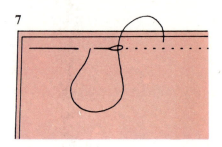

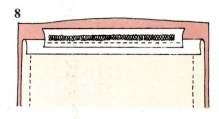

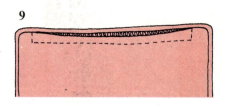

Piping should be attached before the cushion cover is made up. It is not a good idea to pipe flat round cushion covers as these do not keep a good shape when the pad is inserted.

In order to attach piping successfully by machine it is necessary to use a piping foot on your sewing machine. This is made in one piece, instead of split as with the standard foot, enabling the stitching to be worked close to the piping.

The cushion cover is usually inserted into the machine with its bulk on the left and the turnings of the seam under the foot. The needle should be to the left of the foot which is pressed up hard against the piping cord. Keep the foot in this position throughout the sewing. At the corners, leave the needle down, lift the foot and turn the fabric around to the new position. Lower foot and continue sewing.

Piping consists of a cord covered with bias-cut strips of fabric and is stitched into a seam.

Piping cord is usually cotton and made up of three strands. It comes in a range of thicknesses and number 2 or 3 is most suitable for cushion covers. As the cord is liable to shrink, buy about 23cm ($\frac{1}{4}$yd) extra. Boil the cord for about 5 minutes

and dry it thoroughly before use to ensure that it is fully shrunk.

Cut and join enough 4cm ($1\frac{1}{2}$in) wide bias strips to fit the perimeter of the cover, plus 10cm (4in).

Lay piping cord, slightly longer than the strip, centrally along the wrong side to this strip. Fold the edges together, with the cord in the middle. Tack or machine stitch casing firmly around cord to within 2.5cm (1in) of each end, keeping the stitching as close as possible to the piping (fig.3).

Starting in the middle of a side, pin the casing all around the edge on the right side of one cover piece. The raw edges of the folded casing must be level with the raw edges of the cover. At each corner, clip into the casing seam allowance to within 3mm ($\frac{1}{8}$in) of the tacking stitches of the casing. This will make the piping lie flat (fig.4).

To make a neat join in the piping unfold the untacked portion of the casing at each end and overlap them by 1.5cm ($\frac{1}{2}$in). Adjust the overlap to fit the cushion cover exactly. Join the ends as for bias strips, trimming to 6mm ($\frac{1}{4}$in). Overlap the cord for 2.5cm (1in) and trim off the excess. Unravel 2.5cm (1in) at each end and cut away two strands from one end and one strand from the

other. Overlap and twist together the remaining three ends and stitch or bind them firmly (fig.5). Fold over casing and tack around joined cord. Tack piping to cushion. Place the second cover piece on top of the piped piece, with right sides together and enclosing the piping. Tack and stitch the cover together along three sides.

Two ways to insert a zip

When a cover needs to be removed frequently for washing you may prefer to insert a permanent type of fastening such as a zip.

Zips are best kept for use on cushions with straight sides as a zip fastener is inclined to distort the shape of a round cushion.

The methods given here are for piped cushions but plain cushions can be treated un the same way.

Above: To make a bias strip, fold the fabric diagonally so that the selvedge is level with the crosswise threads. Press and cut along fold. Cut strips and join at right angles, with seams on the straight of grain. Press seam open and trim off the corners.

Above: Piping can look very effective, as shown on this patchwork cushion.

Zips stitched by hand make a very neat fastening.

Make up the cushion in the usual way but stitch along the fourth side for 2.5cm (1in) at each end. Fasten off the stitching securely. Turn the cover right side out. Press under the turning along the piped edge if piping has been used.

Place the piped edge over the right side of the closed zip so that the folded edge of the turning lies centrally along the teeth of the zip.

On the right side of the cover tack along the space between the piping and cover (fig.6).

Fold under the unpiped edge of the opening and put it onto the zip so that it meets the piped edge. Tack in position close to the edge of the zip teeth, curving the stitching into the fold at the top and bottom.

Using double sewing thread, prick stitch

the zip to the cover along the tacked line. Prick stitch is like a spaced back-stitch, but on the right side of the fabric the stitches should be extremely small (fig.7).

To stitch by machine, with the cover inside out, place the zip face downwards on the piped edge of the opening, with the teeth as close as possible to the piping cord.

Tack and machine stitch the zip to the turning and piping only, close to the teeth, using a piping foot (fig.8).

Turn the cover through to the right side and place the other folded edge over the zip to meet the piped edge.

Tack and machine stitch the cover to the zip tape 1cm (⅜in) from the fold: take the stitching across to the fold at each end (fig.9).

Undo the zip, turn cover to the wrong side and snip into the stitched-down

turning at each end.

If you prefer, the zip can be inserted before the other three sides are stitched.

Cushion pads

Many large stores sell square and oblong cushion pads in a wide range of sizes. It is, however, quite possible to make your own pads in the size and shape you want.

Down is easily the most luxurious and most expensive filling and feathers are a good alternative, but many people today prefer to use a synthetic filling which has the advantage of being washable.

Kapok, shredded foam and foam chips are cheaper fillings, but kapok can give a lumpy look and foam becomes hard after a time.

Squab cushions

Above: Squab cushions brighten up chairs

Pad covers can normally be made from sheeting, calico or any inexpensive, firmly-woven fabric, but if you choose feathers or down for the filling it is essential to buy a down proof fabric for the pad cover.

Make up the inner cover in the same way as a plain cushion cover, remembering that it should be 1.5cm (½in) larger all around than the outer cushion cover. Turn through to the right side and press. Stuff the cover with filling so that it is plump but not hard, paying particular attention to the corners. Pin, tack and stitch close to the edge.

To make the covers easy to remove for cleaning, a zip can be inserted

Fabrics for squab cushions should be firm so that they do not pull or stretch at the seams.

You must first make a pattern of the chair seat itself and cut out a cushion pad from a block of foam about 4cm (1½in) deep and a little larger than the size of your chair seat (these foam shapes can be bought from furnishing departments).

Lay a sheet of newspaper across chair seat and mark around front and side edges of seat, mark shape around struts at back of chair so seat will fit snugly. Check fit before cutting final paper pattern (fold this in half lengthwise to ensure that sides are uniform).

Mark position of back chair legs on pattern. Lay pattern on foam, draw around with a ballpoint pen and cut out shape with a bread knife. (You can make a flatter cushion without a gusset from a thinner sheet of foam which can be cut with scissors.)

Making cover

Cut top and bottom seat sections and gusset strip from fabric, allowing 1.5cm (½in) seams. Pin gusset around edge of cover to check fit. When you are sure it fits exactly, stitch seams and press. For ties, take 91cm (1yd) of 1.5cm (½in)

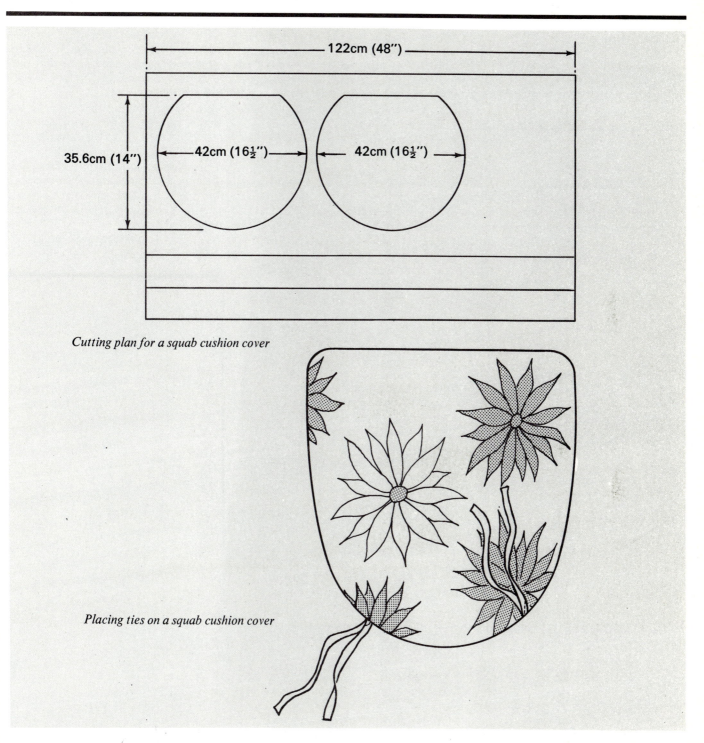

Cutting plan for a squab cushion cover

Placing ties on a squab cushion cover

wide straight tape and cut in half. Fold each piece in half and place tapes on right side of bottom cover piece to correspond with chair legs as shown. With right sides together, stitch top cover piece to gusset, clipping seams on curves. Stitch lower cover piece to gusset, taking tapes and leaving an opening in centre of back seam to insert cushion pad. Turn to right side, insert cushion pad and slip stitch opening to close.

Toggle-fastened squab
Cut cushion and cover in exactly the same way as before, but fasten to chair back with loops and wooden toggles. For loops, cut four strips of fabric, each about 21.5cm × 4cm (8½in × 1½in) (depending on thickness of fabric and chair strut). Fold in long raw edges 1cm (⅜in) and press. Fold again along the length, wrong sides together to form a rouleau. Fold two of the strips double and stitch again leaving loops at ends for toggles. Attach prepared fastenings in pairs to top of cover before stitching gusset in same way as for tape-fastened cushion. Finish cover as before, then sew on wooden toggles and slip through loops.

Round cushions and bolsters

To make a cushion, cut a circular paper pattern for the top and bottom of the cushion to the finished size.

Pin the pattern to the fabric, following the cutting chart, and cut out a top and bottom piece in fabric, not forgetting to add 1.5cm ($\frac{1}{2}$in) seam allowance all around. Cut a strip for the welt to the

1. The welt pinned onto a round cushion top with welt seam pinned in
2. Two welt strips stitched together
3. The top section of a square cushion cover stitched to the welt.

required depth, by the length of the circumference of the circular pattern, plus 1.5cm ($\frac{1}{2}$in) seam allowance all around. (If you have enough fabric it is advisable to allow a little extra on this length which can be trimmed away later in necessary.)

Fold the top and bottom pieces in half and mark the centre back of each piece with thread.

On the welt piece work a line of stitching along each long edge on the seamline. Snip into these edges at 2.5cm (1in) intervals, almost to the stitching. This ensures a good fit when the welt is attached to the top and bottom pieces.

With right sides together, pin one long edge of the welt to the top piece, 1.5cm ($\frac{1}{2}$in) from the edge. Start pinning at the centre back, matching the centre back mark with a point 1.5cm ($\frac{1}{2}$in) from one short end. Continue pinning until the welt is pinned right around the top and then pin in the welt seam (fig.1).

Stitch the welt seam and trim the seam allowance on the second short end to 1.5cm ($\frac{1}{2}$in) if necessary.

Tack and stitch the welt to the top, taking 1.5cm ($\frac{1}{2}$in) turnings.

Snip 'V'-shaped notches almost to the stitching at 2.5cm (1in) intervals in the circular piece and press the turnings onto the welt.

Pin the bottom piece to the welt, making sure that the grain runs the same way as on the top section. Tack and stitch, taking 1.5cm ($\frac{1}{2}$in) seams, leaving about one third of the edge unstitched to turn through. Notch and press turnings as before.

Turn cover to the right side, insert pad and slip stitch opening.

To make the cushion, cut out the pieces for top, bottom and welt of cushion along the grain to the finished size plus seam allowance.

Take two side strips and join them along one short **edge** taking 1.5cm ($\frac{1}{2}$in) turnings. Taper stitching into the

corners 1.5cm ($\frac{1}{2}$in) from the beginning and end of each seam (fig.2). Join the other strips to these two in the same way to make a continuous strip for the welt. Press turnings to one side.

With right sides together, pin the top section of the cover onto the welt, matching corners of the top to welt seams. Tack and stitch (fig.3).

Attach the bottom piece to the welt in the same way, but leave one side open to turn through. Make sure that the grain runs in the same direction on the top and bottom.

Turn cover to the right side, insert pad and slip stitch opening.

Bolsters

The basic bolster shape is cylindrical, and can be piped or decorated with braid, or other trimming.

The fabric should be a closely woven, medium or heavyweight fabric, such as velvet, corduroy, firm tweed, linen or heavy cotton. A loosely woven fabric like soft tweed is unsuitable as it will pull at the seams.

Before buying fabric measure the length and the diameter of the ends. You will need enough fabric to cut a piece to the length of the finished bolster, plus 2.5cm (1in) for turnings, by the length of the finished circumference of the ends plus at least 2.5cm (1in) for seams, and two circles with a diameter 2.5cm (1in) larger than that of the finished ends. Draw the pieces to scale on a cutting layout to calculate the amount of fabric required.

Piping should be first made up and attached to the ends before joining them to the body section.

If you wish to use a zip fastener you should insert this into the seam of the body section before the ends are stitched into place.

Bolster pads

Soft bolster pads can be bought ready – made in a limited size range. If you wish to make your own pad, make the cover in the same way as the outer cover but do not add piping. It should be 1.5cm (½in) larger all around than the outer cover.

Foam rubber pads for firm bolsters are sold without covers. It is advisable to make an inner cover for a foam rubber pad for the reasons described for a cushion with a welt. The same construction techniques apply.

Below: Bolster cushions look good in modern fabrics as well as in more traditional colours and textures.

Make a circular paper pattern the size of the finished ends.

Pin the pattern to the fabric, following the cutting layout, and cut out the two ends, not forgetting to add 1.5cm (½in) seam allowance all around. Cut a strip for the body section of the finished length, plus 2.5cm (1in) for seams, by the length of the circumference of the circular pattern, plus 2.5cm (1in) for the seams. (If you have enough fabric it is advisable to allow a little extra on this measurement which can be trimmed off after joining if necessary).

Fold and mark the ends as for the top and bottom of a circular cushion.

On the body section work a line of stitching on the seamlines at the sides of the bolster.

Make 'V'-shaped notches at 2.5cm (1in) intervals almost to this line of stitching. This makes it possible to ease the body section onto the ends.

Stitch the body seam, leaving an opening of half to three quarters of its length in the centre to turn through.

Pin the body section to the ends as if fitting the welt onto the top of a circular cushion (see previous page).

Tack and stitch the ends into place taking 1.5cm (½in) turnings.

Make 'V'-shaped notches at 2.5cm (1in) intervals on the circular pieces and press the turnings onto the body section.

Turn cover to the right side and insert pad. Slip stitch opening.

Box cushions

Box cushions are block-shaped cushions with squared-off edges. They are normally made from foam-rubber pads and are often used on the seats and backs of chairs in place of traditional upholstery. They also make good floor cushions.

The pad

If you are buying your own foam pad to make box cushions, check that it is of the correct quality foam for your purpose. To give the best wear, seat cushions should be of a higher density than back cushions and for comfort they should be 7.5cm-10cm (3in-4in) thick. Back cushions can be 5.5cm-7.6cm (2in-3in) thick.

The fabric

If the cushions are to be used regularly, buy a medium-weight furnishing fabric recommended by the manufacturer for loose covers. It is also advisable to make an inner cover which protects the foam and prevents the main cover from sticking to it. This inner cover can be of calico, curtain lining or any lightweight cotton. There are two methods of making a cover for a box cushion. Use method one for plain fabrics and method two for patterned or pile fabrics or if you want a piped edge.

Making a cutting chart

The simplest way of estimating the amount of fabric you need is to draw a cutting chart to scale. To do this, draw a straight line to represent the width of your fabric. Draw two more lines at right angles to each end of this. Then draw on the pieces of the cover according to which of the two following methods you are using. Complete the rectangle after the last piece. Measure the length of the rectangle to give the amount of fabric required.

Method 1

1 Measure the width and length of the top of the pad and add on twice the depth plus 2.5cm (1in) each way for

Below: Mark corners of cushion fabric to position darts for shaping.

turnings. Draw on one piece of this size for the main section of the cover.

2 Draw a second piece equal to the width by the length of the pad, plus 2.5cm (1in) each way for the bottom section of the cover.

Method 2

3 Draw two pieces equal to the width by the length of the pad plus 2.5cm (1in) each way for the top and bottom sections of the cover.

2 Measure the depth of the pad and draw strips of this width to fit the front and sides of the pad, plus 2.5cm (1in) each way. Draw a fourth strip 2.5cm (1in) wider by the length of the back of the pad, plus 2.5cm (1in). The short edges of all the strips should be parallel with the selvedges so that the pattern will be the right way up on the finished cover.

3 Allow an extra 45.5cm (18in) for the piping casing. For the piping cord, measure the perimeter of the pad and double it, allowing an extra 30.5cm (12in) for shrinkage and joining.

To make the covers easy to remove for cleaning, a zip can be inserted along the back section in both methods. Buy one which is 1.5cm (½in) shorter than the width of the pad.

Making the pattern
First method

Cut out two pieces of fabric to the sizes given in the cutting chart.

Making up

1 On the larger piece, measure in from the corners in both directions the depth of the pad plus 1.5cm (½in) and mark.

2 Make a dart at each corner by folding the adjacent edges together diagonally so that the marks match and the right sides are inside.

3 Starting 1.5cm (½in) from the raw edges, stitch up from the marks to the fold on the straight grain of the fabric. Trim off the corner to within 6mm (¼in) of the stitching. Press the turnings to one side and oversew them if the fabric is likely to fray.

4 With the wrong sides of the fabric facing out, fit the smaller piece to the edges of the larger piece, matching the corners to the darts. Stitch around taking 1.5cm (½in) turnings and leaving an opening for the zip in the back edge.

5 Press the seams and turn right side out. Finish the opening with a zip, or else you can sew it up.

Second Method

Note: cut out and make up pieces so that the design or pile runs from the back to the front on the top and bottom sections of the cover and from top to bottom on the side strips. Any motif should be placed centrally.

Cut out the pieces on the straight grain to the sizes given in the cutting chart.

3 If you are having piped edges, cut and make the casing for the cord allowing enough to fit twice around the edge of the strip. Attach it to each edge of the strip taking 1.5cm (½in) turnings. Clip into the turnings of the casing in line with each seam of the strip.

4 With the wrong side of the strip facing out, fit the top edge to the perimeter of top section, matching the seams of the strip to the corners. Tack and machine stitch as close to the piping as possible. Oversew the edges of the turnings together if the fabric is likely to fray and press the turnings down onto the strip.

5 Still with the wrong side facing out, turn the strip so that the open side is uppermost. Fit the bottom section of the cover to this edge in the same way as before. Press and turn the finished cover right side out.

1 Join the side strips to each side of the front strip along the short edges, taking 1.5cm (½in) turnings. Taper the stitching into the corners 1.5cm (½in) from the beginning and end of each seam.

2 Cut the fourth strip in half lengthwise and re-join it for 2cm (¾in) at each end, taking 1.5cm (½in) turnings. Insert a zip into the remaining opening. Attach this strip to the ends of the other strip, taking 1.5cm (½in) turnings and tapering the stitching as before. Press the turnings to one side.

1-5. Diagrams show stages in making up box cushions. The methods discussed are both easy to do.

Right: Be bold and experimental, and what's more, save money. These chic armchairs are cut from foam rubber blocks, and are covered with easy-to make duvet cushions for comfort.

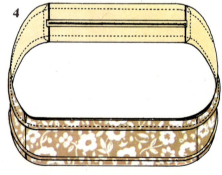
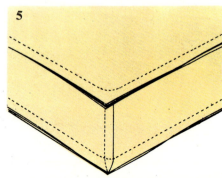

Foam seating units

Foam blocks are available in a variety of shapes and sizes so that you can cover them yourself and build up a range of co-ordinating seating units. You can also design your own shape and have it cut to size although this is a little more expensive. The seats shown in the photograph are a good basic shape and can be used without the extra duvet cushion although it adds considerably to the comfort and appearance. The instructions given below are for covering seats of this shape but they can easily be adapted for other designs.

The fabric

Choose a strong fabric suitable for loose covers for the main cover and a lighter-weight washable fabric for the duvet cushion. The simplest way of calculating how much fabric you need for the main cover is to draw a cutting chart to scale.
1 Draw a straight line to represent the width of the fabric you will be using. A simple scale is 1cm = 10cm or 1in = 12in.
2 Draw two more lines at right angles to each end of the first line.
3 Measure each rectangular section of the foam shape and add 1.5cm ($\frac{1}{2}$in) all around to allow for turnings. Draw the sections to scale onto the cutting chart. If you are using a patterned fabric, check that the design will be running from top to bottom on each piece.
4 For the shaped sections (these are the side pieces on the seats in the photograph), place the section flat onto a large sheet of paper and draw around. Draw a second line 1.5cm ($\frac{1}{2}$in) outside the first line. Draw the shape approximately to size onto the chart.
5 When all the pieces are drawn on the chart, complete the rectangle. Measure the length of the rectangle and convert it back in scale to give the amount.
6 For the duvet cushion, divide the length of the top section of the seat into equal sections approximately 15cm (6in) to 18cm (7in) long. Add four more sections plus 2.5cm (1in) seam allowance so the cushion overlaps at each end. If both sides of the cushion can be cut from the width of the fabric, buy this length. If both sides cannot be cut from the width, buy twice the amount.
7 To fill the duvet cushion, buy enough medium weight Terylene wadding to cut pieces to fit each section of the cushion.

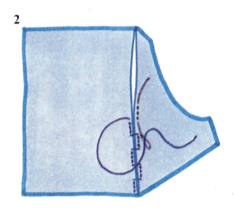

Cutting out

Cut out the pieces to the sizes shown on your cutting chart.

Making up

1 Stitch the pieces for the front along their adjoining edges taking 1.5cm ($\frac{1}{2}$in) turnings. Taper the stitching into the corners 1.5cm ($\frac{1}{2}$in) from the beginning and end of each seam so that the corner can be opened out when the sides are joined on.
2 Join on the sections for the back and base to the front but do not join them to each other.
3 Work stay stitching along the edges of the front which will join the curved edge of the side sections. Clip into edge up to the stay stitching at 1.5cm ($\frac{1}{2}$in) intervals.
4 Pin the side sections to the front and base so that the corners of the sides match the seams on the front. Do not join the sides to the back yet.
5 Press the seams and overcast the turnings together. Turn the cover right side out.
6 Insert the foam into the cover, pushing

1. Front and back sections of cover
2. Stitching on the side sections
3. Filling the sections of cushion.

Right: Giant, squashy cushions are perfect for children and make a snuggly retreat for the nursery.

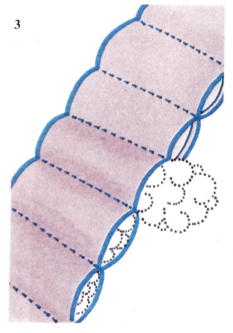

it well into the corners.
7 Fold under the turnings along the open sides and bottom, place them together so that they just meet and slip stitch using a curved needle and strong thread.

The duvet cushion

1 Mark the sections on one side of the cushion with tacking.
2 Stitch the sides together along the top, bottom and one side. Turn the cover right side out and press.
3 Fold under the turnings along the opening and press. Machine stitch along the tacked lines marking the sections through both thicknesses.
4 Insert the pieces of wadding into each section, pushing it well into the corners. Slip stitch folds of the opening together. For cleaning, the whole duvet cushion can be washed or you could unpick the slip stitching, remove the wadding and wash the cover separately. Do not dry clean the whole cushion because the fumes of the cleaning solution will be retained in the wadding and this can be dangerous.

Giant floor cushions

Giant, squashy cushions make a cheap and attractive alternative to conventional furniture. Make this huge, segmented cushion in a riot of contrasting colours for a brilliant effect, or in subtle, toning shades for a restful room.

You will need

1.5m of 1.5m (1⅔yd of 60in) wide jersey in navy

0.9m of 1.5m (1yd of 60in) wide jersey in beige

0.9m of 1.5m (1yd of 60in) wide jersey patterned in beige/brown

or

1m (1¼yd) of the same colours in 91cm (36in) wide fabric

2 × 0.34 cub m (12 cub ft) polystyrene granules

Making the cushion

Draw up a paper pattern from the graph, in which one square equals 2.5cm (1in). Cut one bottom section and one top section from the navy jersey. Cut two navy side segments, two beige side segments and two patterned side segments. With right sides together, pin one long side of a navy segment to one long side of a beige segment. Tack and machine stitch, taking 1.5cm (½in) seam allowance. Stitch a second 3mm (⅛in) in from the first, for strength. Pin the long side of patterned segment to the beige segment, and stitch in the same way. Continue alternating the segments until a circular shape is formed.

With right sides together, pin and tack the top navy section in position. Stitch the seam twice, as for the sides. Pin in the bottom section and stitch in the same way around five sides. Trim seams and press flat. Turn the cushions through to the right side.

Filling the bag

1 Insert the inner cover into the main cover so that the openings match.

2 Place a cardboard tube into the opening of the inner cover and place the opening of the bag of granules over the other end of the tube, tying it with an elastic band.

3 Pour the granules through the tube until the sag bag is two-thirds to three-quarters full.

4 Sew up the openings with small firm over-sewing stitches. Remember that you can re-use the tube again.

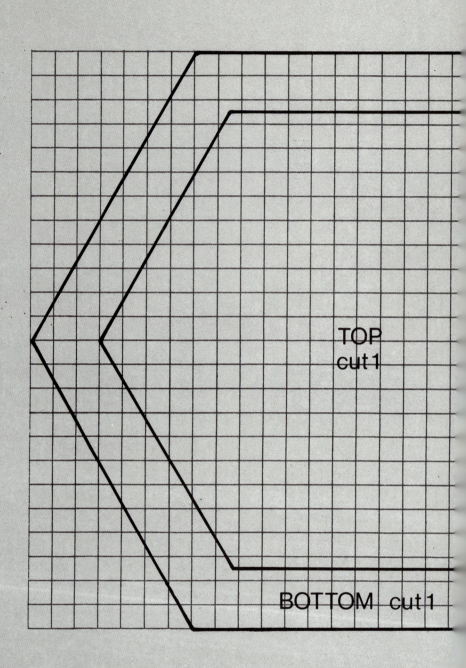

graph pattern for floor cushion

one square = 2·54 cm (1in)

seam allowance included

TOP cut 1

BOTTOM cut 1

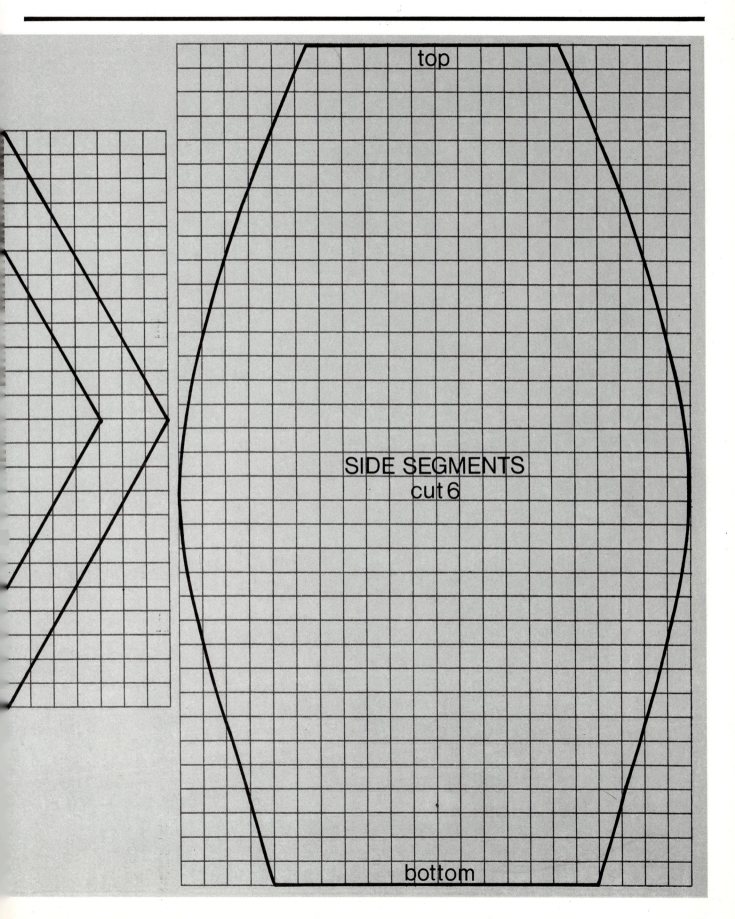

top

SIDE SEGMENTS
cut 6

bottom

Sag bag cushion

Making the pattern

1 Draw each pattern piece to the size indicated on the chart.
2 To cut the circle, simplest method is to use a 76.5cm (30in) square of paper. Fold this in half and in half again to make a 38cm (15in) square.
3 Tie one end of the string around the pencil. Measure down the string 38cm (15in) and pin it at this point to the corner of the paper where the folds intersect.
4 Holding the string taut, draw an arc from point A to point B. Cut along the arch through all thicknesses of paper. Open out the circle.

Cutting out the sag bag

1 Following the cutting layout, place the pattern pieces on the hessian. Pin into place and cut out. Cut a second circle as indicated.
2 Cut out the bias strips, 4cm (1½in) wide, from the spare fabric as shown.
3 Cut out the lining fabric for the inner cover of the sag bag as for the hessian, but without the bias strips.

Making up the cover

The inner cover of the sag bag is made in the same way as the hessian cover, but omitting the piping. For safety, stitch the seams of the inner cover twice with the second row of stitches 3mm (⅛in) inside the first.
1 Join the 30.5cm (12in) sides of the side strips taking 1.5cm (½in) turnings.

Left: Another cheerful floor cushion trimmed with contrast piping.

2 Join the 46cm (18in) sides in the same way but leave an opening of 41cm (16in) in the middle of the seam. Neaten the edges of the turnings by oversewing or zig-zag stitches.
3 Work stay stitching 1.5cm (½in) away from the top and bottom edges of the side strips.
4 Make up the piping to fit the top and bottom edges of the side strips. Stitch it to the side strips taking 1.5cm (½in) turnings.
5 Clip into the turnings of the piping and the side strips at 1.5cm (½in) intervals.
6 With right sides together, pin the top edge of the strip to the edge of one of the circles. Tack and machine stitch. Neaten the turnings together.
7 With right sides together, pin the bottom edge of the side strip to the edge of the remaining circle in the same way.

Filling the bag

1 Insert the inner cover into the main cover so that the openings match.
2 Place a cardboard tube into the opening of the inner cover and place the opening of the bag of granules over the other end of the tube, tying it with an elastic band.
3 Pour the granules through the tube until the sag bag is two-thirds to three-quarters full.
4 Sew up the openings with small firm oversewing stitches.

Below: The pin and string method of making a semi-circle; hold the string taut, and draw an arc between the points described A and B.

Below centre: Attach welt to base with tacking stitches, then machine stitch around the seam.

Bottom: Cutting layout for floor cushion includes bias casing.

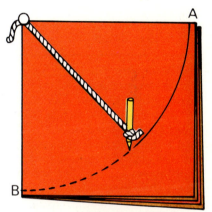

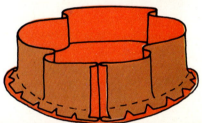

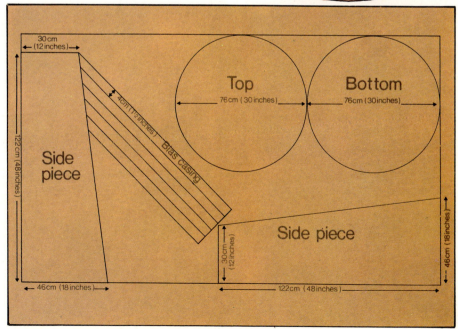

Sunflower floor cushion

Flowers are springing up in the most surprising places. This cheerful sunflower is a child-sized floor cushion for the playroom. It's fun for tea-parties and games at floor level and comfortable for watching television. Make it in fur fabric or cotton in brightly contrasting colours.

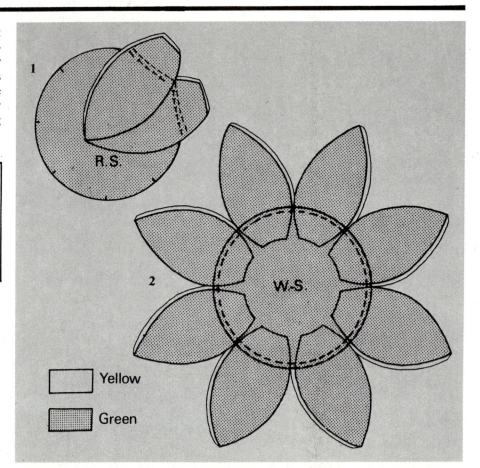

To make a cushion measuring 91cm 36in) across you will need
0.8m ($\frac{7}{8}$yd) each of yellow and green fur fabric 122cm (48in) wide
0.5m ($\frac{1}{2}$yd) calico
kapok for stuffing
Trylko terylene thread

	Yellow
	Green

The sunflower centre

Draw up the pattern pieces to size from the graph pattern. Cut out three circles for the flower centre, one each in yellow and green fur fabric and one in calico, adding a 1.5cm ($\frac{1}{2}$in) seam allowance all around. Cut out 16 petals, 8 in green and 8 in yellow, again adding a 1.5cm ($\frac{1}{2}$in) seam allowance.
Machine stitch the calico circle to the right side of the yellow circle, leaving an opening for the stuffing. Turn the right side out and press. Insert the kapok and stitch up the opening by hand.

The petals

For each petal, machine stitch one green and one yellow piece together, right sides facing, leaving the bottom end open for the stuffing. Turn the right side out and insert kapok as far as the curved seam line indicated on the pattern.
Stitch across the bottom of the petals, 1.5cm ($\frac{1}{2}$in) outside the seam line. Pin each petal, pointing inwards and yellow side down, around the right side of the green circle (fig.1). Stitch in position along the seam line and open out the petals (fig.2).

To complete

Place the green circle and petals wrong side down over the calico of the centre cushion. Oversew the two parts firmly together around the edge of the centre cushion.

Right: Close-up of sunflower cushion
Opposite: Reverse side of cushion has colours used in contrast positions.

172

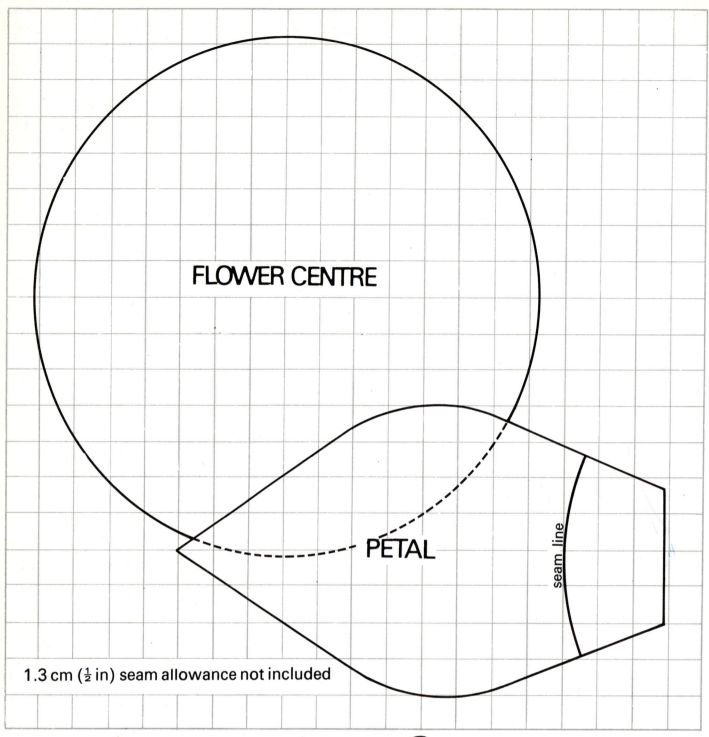

FLOWER CENTRE

PETAL

seam line

1.3 cm (½ in) seam allowance not included

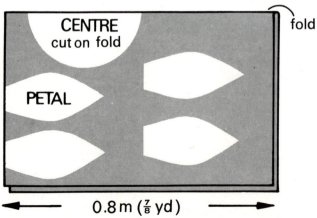

CENTRE
cut on fold

fold

PETAL

0.8 m (⅞ yd)

Above: The outline shapes for the petals and for the cushion centre are shown here on graph pattern. Each square represents 2.5cm (1in). Mark the seam lines for the sunflower petals with tailor's chalk. You will need to cut out three circles for the flower centre, and 16 of the petal shapes.

Left: Cutting layout for 122cm (48in) wide fabric. Repeat the same layout for the contrast colour. Use sharp scissors for cutting the fabric.

Smocked cushions

Sizes
Square cushion: 38cm (15in) square
Round cushion: 41cm (16in)
diameter, 10cm (4in) thick

Fabric required
For square cushion:
61cm (24in) lightweight furnishing
velvet, 122cm (48in) wide
For round cushion:
91cm (36in) lightweight furnishing
velvet, 122cm (48in) wide

You will also need
Buttonhole thread to match velvet
Graph paper for making pattern
Tacking thread in different colours
2 button moulds, 2.5cm (1in)
diameter
Cushion pads in the same sizes as the
finished covers
Transfer pencil (optional)

The pattern
Each line of smocking is worked over
three vertical rows of dots, spaced
2.5cm (1in) apart. It is possible to buy
transfers of the dots which can be ironed
onto the fabric but it is quite simple and
much less expensive – particularly if you
are making several cushions – to draw
your own pattern and transfer the dots
to the fabric with tailor's tacks.
Alternatively, you could mark the dots
on the pattern with a transfer pencil and
then iron it onto the fabric.

Making the pattern
Using graph paper, draw the pattern for
the cushion shape you are making to
scale. One square = 2.5cm square (1in
square). If you are making the square
cushion, mark the dots for each line of
smocking in different colours as shown
so you can easily see where the rows
overlap. Repeat rows two and three
until you have ten rows in all.

The square cushion
Cut the fabric in half to make two
pieces, 61cm square (24in square). Place
the pieces together and pin pattern
centrally to them. Mark the dots with
tailor's tacks, using different coloured
thread for the rows as indicated on the
pattern. Unpin the pattern, cut through
the tacks and open out the fabric. Work

the smocking on each piece separately.

Working the smocking
For ease of working the dots are
numbered to show the order of the
stitches. It may seem very confusing as
you start but after the first few smocked
pleats are formed you will soon get into
the rhythm.
1 With the wrong side of the fabric
facing up, start at dot 1 in the top left
hand corner. Using a long length of
buttonhole thread, knot the end and
make a small stitch at dot 1. Pass the
thread along the fabric and make
another small stitch at dot 2 in the line
of dots to the left.
2 Go back to dot 1, make another small
stitch over the one already there and
then pull dots 1 and 2 together. Knot
them tightly by making a loop of the
thread above the stitches and passing
the needle under the stitches and
through the loop. Be careful not to catch
the fabric as you do this or the stitch will
show on the right side.
3 Pass the thread along the fabric to dot
3 and make a small stitch. Keep the
fabric completely flat between dots 1
and 3, make a loop of the thread above
dot 3 and slip the needle under the
thread between the dots and above the
loop to make another knot. Do not
draw up the thread between the dots.
4 Pass the thread along the fabric to dot
4, make a small stitch, go back to dot 3
and make another small stitch. Pull dots
3 and 4 together and knot them as for
dots 1 and 2.
5 Move down to dot 5 and knot the
thread keeping the fabric flat, as at dot
3. Pick up a small stitch at dot 6 and join
1 to dot 5 in the same way as before.
6 Continue down the whole line in this
way, picking up a dot on the left, moving
down to the next dot in the middle row
and then picking up a dot on the right.
7 Work all the lines of smocking in the
same way, and then smock the other
side of the cushion cover.

Finishing off
1 When the smocking is complete, you
will find that pleats have formed all
around the edge. Pin these down evenly
and tack in position, checking that each
side of cover measures 38cm (15in). Pin
the pleats on the other side of the cover
in a similar way, but with the pleats

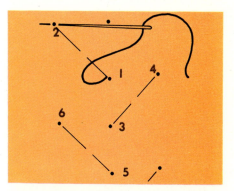
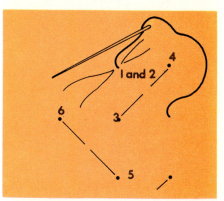
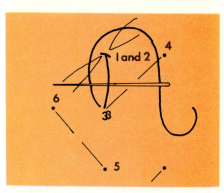
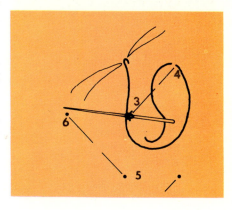

*Above and overleaf: Sequence of the
stitches for smocking the square and
round cushions is shown here. Follow the
instructions for cutting out the different
shapes.*

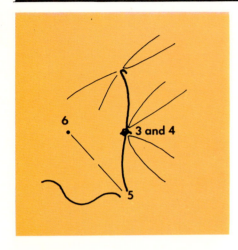

facing the opposite direction so that when the sides of the cover are put together the pleats will match.

2 Place the sides of the cover together and tack and machine stitch around three sides, taking 1.5cm ($\frac{1}{2}$in) turnings.

3 Insert the cushion pad, fold under the turnings of the opening and slip-stitch the folds together.

The round cushion
Cutting out

Cut the fabric in half to make two pieces, 91cm × 61cm (36in × 24in). Join the pieces along the longer edges, taking 1.5cm ($\frac{1}{2}$in) turnings and making sure that the pile runs the same way on both pieces. Trim the length of the fabric to 178cm × 53.5cm (70in × 21in) and use the spare piece to cover the button moulds. Fold the fabric right side out along the seam line. Place on the pattern with the line indicated to the fold. Mark all the dots with tailor's tacks. Unpin the pattern, cut through the tacks and open out the fabric.

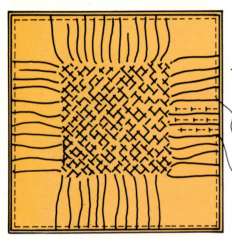

Working the smocking

1 Join the short ends of the fabric, taking 1.5cm ($\frac{1}{2}$in) turnings. The smocking is then worked in a continuous round.

2 Work the smocking in a similar way as for the square cushion. The finished effect will be less tightly plaited than the square cushion because the lines are spaced apart.

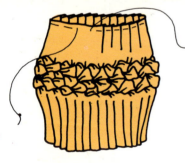

Finishing off

1 Using strong thread, attach the end securely 6mm ($\frac{1}{4}$in) from the edge of the fabric.

2 Form the nearest pleat with your fingers and make a small stitch through the fold. Draw up the thread tightly.

3 Form the next pleat, take a stitch through the fold and pull it up to meet the first pleat. Continue all around the cushion.

4 Insert pad. Repeat on other side.

5 Sew the covered buttons to the centre of each side of the cushion.

Left: Diagrams show smocking on the round and square cushions.

Right: An array of smocked cushions in sumptuous velvet adds an air of luxury to any home.

Graph for square cushion
1 Square = 2·5 cm (1 inch)

ROW 1   ROW 2   ROW 3

2		2		2	
1	4	1	4	1	
6	3	6	3	6	3
5	8	5	8	5	
10	7	10	7	10	7
9	12	9	12	9	
14	11	14	11	14	11
13	16	13	16	13	
18	15	18	15	18	15
17	20	17	20	17	
22	19	22	19	22	19
21	24	21	24	21	
26	23	26	23	26	23
25	28	25	28	25	
30	27	30	27	30	27
29	32	29	32	29	
34	31	34	31	34	31
33	36	33	36	33	
38	35	38	35	38	35
37	40	37	40	37	
39		39		39	

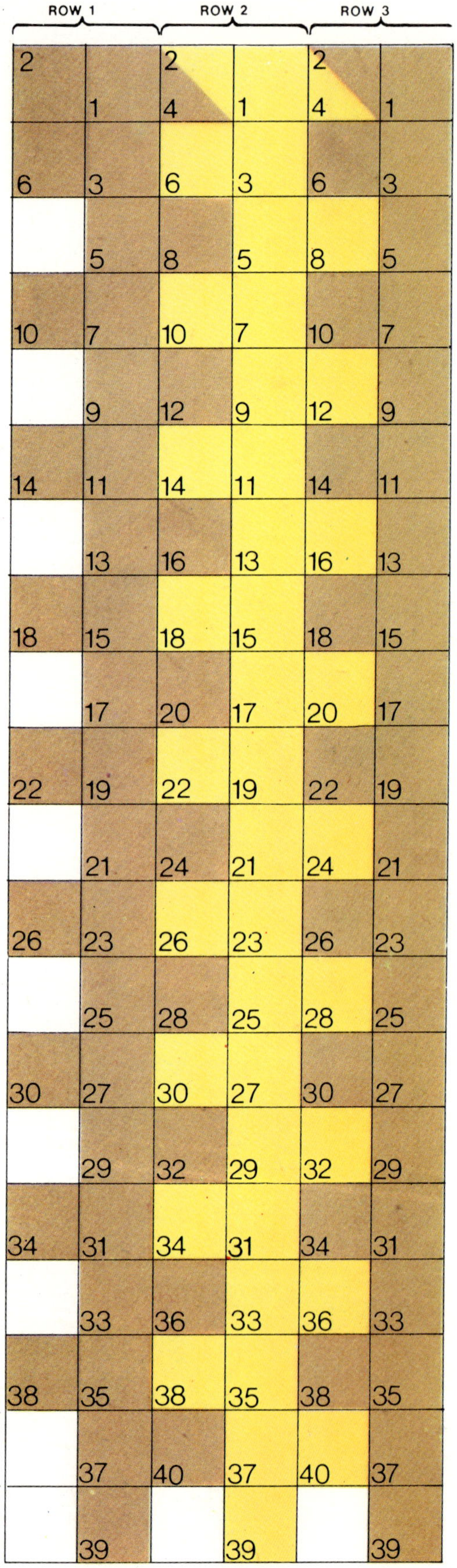

Graph for round cushion
1 Square = 2·5 cm (1 inch)

ROW 1   ROW 2   ROW 3

2	69	2	69	2	69
1	4	1	4	1	4
6	3	6	3	6	3
5	8	5	8	5	8
10	7	10	7	10	7
9	12	9	12	9	12
14	11	14	11	14	11
13	16	13	16	13	16
18	15	18	15	18	15
17	20	17	20	17	20
22	19	22	19	22	19
21	24	21	24	21	24
26	23	26	23	26	23
25	28	25	28	25	28
30	27	30	27	30	27
29	32	29	32	29	32
34	31	34	31	34	31
33	36	33	36	33	36
38	35	38	35	38	35
37	40	37	40	37	40
42	39	42	39	42	39
41	44	41	44	41	44
46	43	46	43	46	43
45	48	45	48	45	48
50	47	50	47	50	47
49	52	49	52	49	52
54	51	54	51	54	51
53	56	53	56	53	56
58	55	58	55	58	55
57	60	57	60	57	60
62	59	62	59	62	59
61	64	61	64	61	64
66	63	66	63	66	63
65	68	65	68	65	68
70	67	70	67	70	67

18cm
7 inches

18cm
7 inches

PLACE THIS LINE ON FOLD ▲

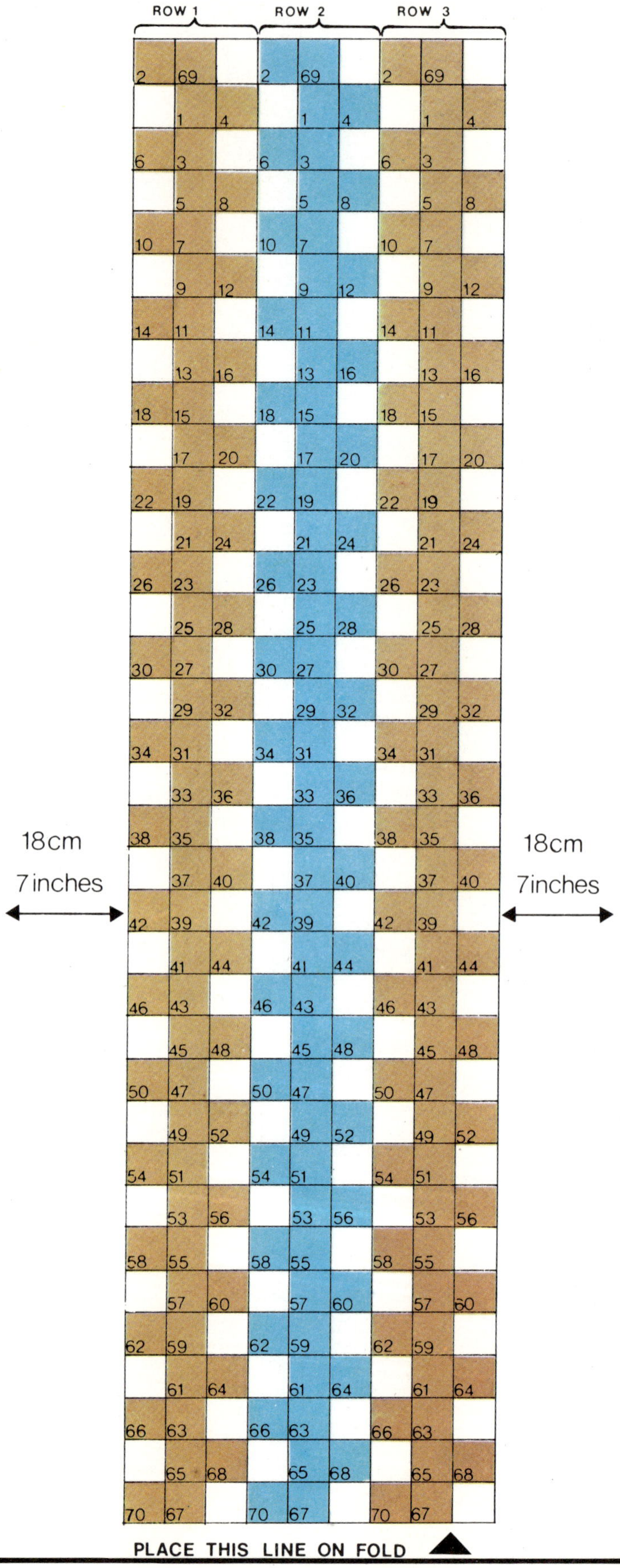

Pattern for quilting cushion on the following page
Pattern for quilting cushion at bottom left of page 182.
Right: Chart for quilting cushion at bottom right of page 182.

Quilted cushions

Quilted cushion

A quick way to add an elegant touch to a cushion cover is to decorate it with a simple, but effective quilted design. The cushion cover is made the same size as the pad – not 1.5cm (½in) smaller all around.

> ### You will need
> 40cm × 60cm (16in × 24in) cushion pad
> 1.37m (1½yd) of 90cm (36in) wide fabric
> 57cm (⅝yd) of 90cm (36in) wide muslin for backing the quilting.
> 57cm (⅝yd) of 110gm (4oz) synthetic wadding at least 71cm (28in) wide
> Matching or toning thread for quilting
> Matching thread for making up
> Dressmaker's carbon paper
> Tracing paper
> Home made quilting frame 50cm × 71cm (20in × 28in) or a slate frame.
> Drawing pins

Cut a piece of top fabric for cushion front 51cm × 71cm (20in × 28in). Cut muslin and wadding to the same size.
Note: the fabric for the cushion front, wadding and muslin are all cut 5cm (2in) bigger all around than the finished size of the cushion and then trimmed to

Below: Attach to frame with drawing pins

match the cushion back, because the quilting will probably decrease the width and depth of the fabric.
Enlarge the design for quilting (page 179) onto tracing paper until it is approximately 35cm (14in) high.
Press both pieces of fabric and lay the top fabric on a flat surface, right side up. Place carbon paper over it.
Centre the tracing on the fabric and carbon paper and, using a pencil, draw around the design.
Place the wadding over the backing fabric and the marked fabric on top.
Tack the layers together. Thread the needle with matching thread, knot it and pull knot through backing fabric to lie in the wadding.
Tack the muslin, wadding and top fabric together.
Attach the work to the home made frame with drawing pins placed about 1.5cm (½in) in from the edge (fig. 1).
Quilt by working around the outline with running stitches, beginning with the leaves; then work the petals, the flower centres and finally the stems.
Cut a piece of top fabric for the back of the cushion 43cm × 63cm (17in × 25in). Place quilted fabric and cushion back with right side facing and trim the quilted piece level with the back piece.
Make up into a cushion, remember to trim away wadding close to stitching before turning cushion through to right side.
Slip stitch opening.

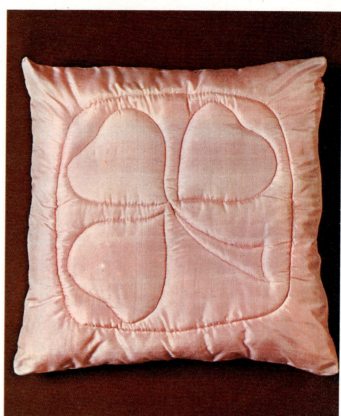

Above: Two more beautifully quilted cushions, made up as before.

Below: Patterns for these two cushions are given on page 179.

UPHOLSTERY & LOOSE COVERS

Doing your own upholstery and making your own loose covers need not be difficult. Why pay a professional when you can get a professional finish at home? Look through the following pages, and you'll be amazed at the wonderful range of styles for both traditional and modern furniture. Learn all about springs and stuffings, fabrics and foam, and also have the freedom to choose from the most up-to-date soft furnishing designs.

Upholstering dining chairs

If you have some tatty old dining chairs tucked away in the attic or picked up cheap from the junk shop, you can strip them of the old coverings and make them as good as new. In this chapter chairs are upholstered with webbing and rubber or plastic foam; of course you can use more traditional methods, such as with horse hair stuffing and springs – both good ways of bringing new life to old chairs. We show you how to do both in this and the next chapter.

Materials

Webbing. Rubber webbing takes the place of the traditional webbing and springs used in the original upholstery of the chair. It is made from two layers of bias-cut corded fabric with a rubber layer sandwiched in between. This makes it very strong and springy. It is more expensive to buy by length than traditional webbing but, since it eliminates the need for springs, it is more economical in the long run. It is also easier to use and saves a good deal of time.

Buy enough 5cm (2in) webbing for three or four strands running from the back of the seat to the front, with one strand running across it – the gaps between the the strands should be approximately 5cm (2in).

Foam biscuit, polyester or rubber 2cm (¾in) larger all around than the chair seat by 10cm (4in) deep.

Upholstery wadding to cover the foam. This material is like cotton wool and sold specially for upholstery, and gives added softness particularly along the edges. Buy enough to extend under the seat if this is where the original upholstery finished.

Cover fabric. You will not want to remove this cover frequently for cleaning, so choose fabric which will not show the dirt or can be cleaned in position. Allow enough to cover the seat, as in the original upholstery, with an extra 5cm-7.5cm (2in-3in) all around for turnings and ease of working.

Calico. A piece of this is used as an inner cover under the wadding and top cover. Allow the same amount as for the top cover plus enough for making 15cm (6in) wide strips to fit around the perimeter of the foam.

Adhesive with a latex base (such as Bostik 1 or Copydex) or general purpose glue for attaching the calico strips.

Tacks, 'improved' (with large heads), for attaching the webbing. You will need ten 1.5cm (½in) improved tacks for each strand. For attaching the main upholstery use 9mm (⅜in) fine tacks. Allow enough to make four rows around the perimeter of the seat, placed at 2.5cm (1in) intervals.

Braid, or gimp, for covering the edges and tacks of the cover fabric if this finishes part of the way down the seat frame, or around the bottom of the frame if it finishes under seat.

Gimp pins, or clear adhesive for attaching the braid. Gimp pins have a very small head and are available in several colours.

Black hessian, slightly larger than the size of the seat, to finish underneath.

Stripping the seat

Cover the work surface with newspaper, remove seat from chair base and secure the seat, upside down, to the work surface with G-clamps. Using a ripping chisel and mallet start to drive out the tacks holding the bottom hessian and cover fabric. To do this, place the tip of the chisel behind the head of the tack and drive it out, working with the grain of the wood. Use the claw side of the hammer, or a pair of pliers or pincers, to pull it out completely. It is essential to work *with* the grain to prevent it from splitting.

Next, turn the seat over and remove the cover and stuffing. Cut any twine ties with scissors. Strip off the hessian and webbing in the same way. If there is no webbing and plywood has been used as a base, remove all the nails holding this. As you work, note the way the webbing was originally placed, the side of the frame to which it was tacked, and the part of the frame which was upper-most when finished. Examine the frame carefully and remove all old tacks. If necessary treat woodworm with a proprietary brand.

If the new covering fabric is thicker than the original, the frame should be planed down a little to compensate for the extra thickness.

Webbing the seat

As the rubber webbing takes the place of the original webbing and springs, it is

1, 2. Hammer tacks on back rail and stretch to tack down at the front
3. Interlacing the webbing strands

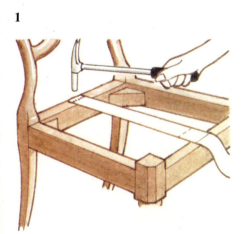
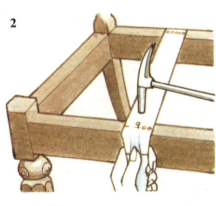
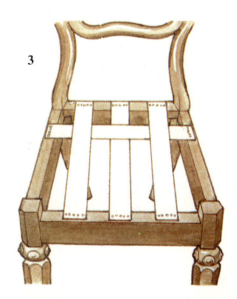

attached to the top, rather than the bottom of the seat frame. Mark the position for each strand on the back. front and side rails, and sand down the inner edges of the frame so they will not cut the webbing.

Using the webbing straight from the roll to avoid waste, place one end of the webbing in position with the cut edge just inside the outside edge of the back rail. Tack it down using five tacks placed in a straight line 6mm ($\frac{1}{4}$in) from the cut edge. Be careful to position the tacks at right angles to the frame and to tack them down so that the heads are completely flat on the webbing and cannot cut into it (fig.1). Each strand of webbing should be nine-tenths of the length of the distance it spans, and stretched to fit, so after fixing the strand at the back, mark this measurement on it and stretch it until the mark is in the middle of the front rail (fig.2). Tack in position, placing the tacks on the mark. Cut off the webbing 6mm ($\frac{1}{4}$in) outside the tacks.

Attach the other strands in the same direction then interlace the cross strip with the other strands (fig.3).

Because the cross strand has to be woven in and out you will find it is best to interlace it through the main webbing first, then tack one side. Mark the place where it reaches the opposite rail unstretched and measure one-tenth of the total measurement back from this. Stretch and tack down on the second mark.

Padding the seat

If the front legs extend higher than the seat frame and stand up above the level of the seat at the front, cut a piece of 2.5cm (1in) thick foam to size of chair and stick to frame to level the top (fig.4). Cut out the foam biscuit to the shape of the seat plus 2cm ($\frac{3}{4}$in) all around.

Mark the positions of the back uprights and cut away a piece of foam on each side, smaller than the actual size of the uprights. Mark the centre of each side of the foam and of the chair. Cut four 15cm (6in) wide calico strips to fit around the perimeter of the foam, making those for the sides and front long enough to overlap at the front corners by 7.5cm-10cm (3in-4in). The strip for the back edge should just fit between the uprights.

Fold the strips in half lengthwise and apply adhesive along them from one long edge up to the fold. Mark a 7.5cm (3in) wide border around the edge of the top of the foam, omitting the area of the uprights, and apply adhesive to it. When the adhesive is tacky, stick the calico to the foam, keeping the fold level with the edges. Do not attempt to pull down the edges until thoroughly dry.

Put the foam onto the seat, matching the centre points (fig.5). Roll the excess foam under so that it does not hang over the edge of the seat frame, and tack down the calico strips, keeping the calico smooth and taut (figs.6, 7 and 8). After the main tacks are in, more can be placed: tack in a wavy line to prevent the strips from ripping (fig.7). Try not to pull the edges down too much or the seat may become too rounded.

Wrap the calico strips around the front corners before tacking down (fig.9). Trim off excess fabric if necessary.

Place the calico inner cover over the foam and attach it by tacking down along front, back and sides in that order (fig.10). At the back uprights fold back the fabric diagonally so that the fold just touches them (fig.11).

Cut diagonally from the corner of the fabric to within 1.5cm ($\frac{1}{2}$in) of the fold (fig.12). Tuck the surplus fabric between the foam and leg, and tack down the fabric (fig.13). Finish the front corners of the calico by cutting them diagonally from corner to the edge of the foam. Fold each piece around the corner, press flat and tack down (fig.14). Cut a piece of wadding to fit over and down the sides of the calico or long enough to reach below the chair and to pad the edges if the upholstery finishes underneath (fig.15). Tack in a few places, cutting and overlapping it at the corners.

Fitting the cover

Fit the top cover in the same way as the calico, but make pleats at the front corners. If the cover finishes part-way down the frame, trim the raw edge to 6mm ($\frac{1}{4}$in) below the tacks and cover with braid or gimp.

If the cover finishes under the seat, tack it 1.5cm ($\frac{1}{2}$in) from the edge and trim off the excess fabric to within 6mm ($\frac{1}{4}$in). Finish the underneath of the seat with a piece of black hessian. Cut to exact size and tack to underneath.

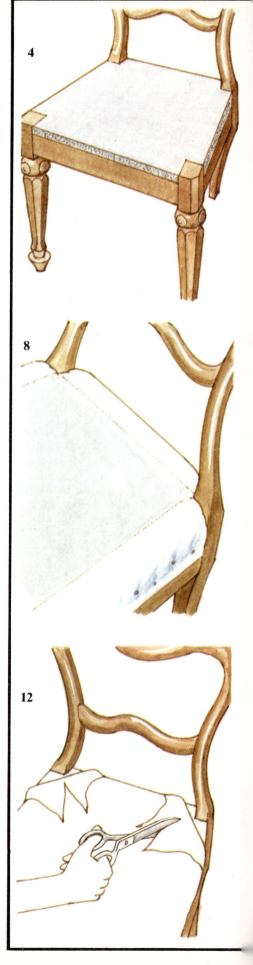

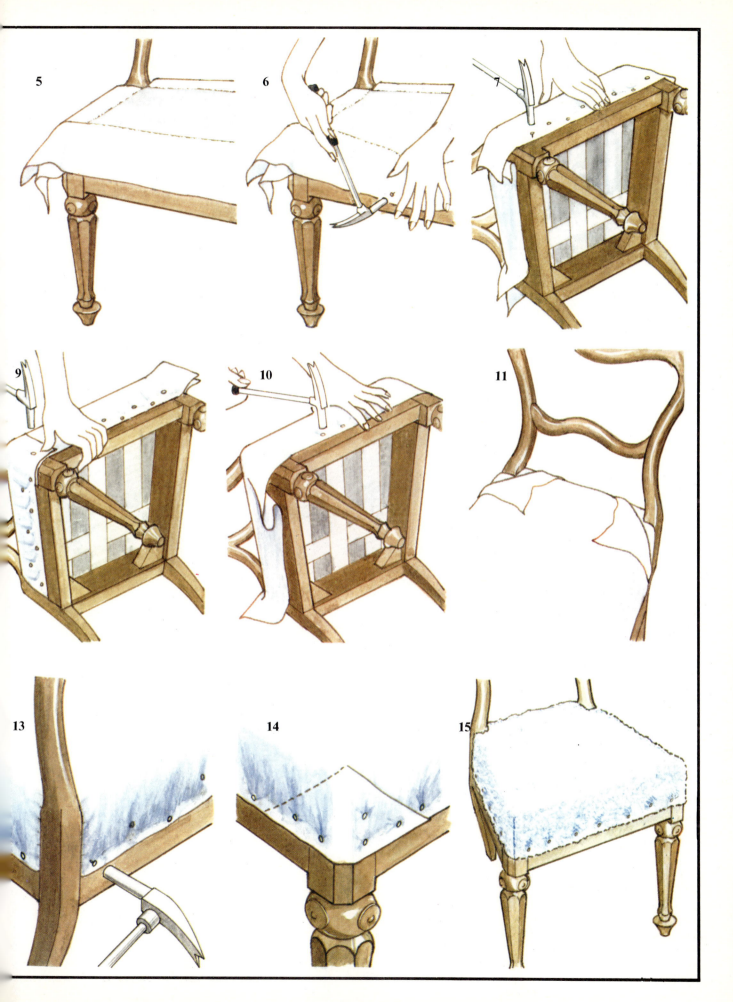

5

6

7

9

10

11

13

14

15

Re-upholstering antique chairs

Victorian dining chairs can often be bought quite cheaply from a junk shop and you can turn them into something both useful and decorative simply by re-upholstering them and giving a little attention to the woodwork.

Tools needed

Coil springs: four 10cm (4in) in 12mm (gauge 10) wire.

Regulator. This is a type of needle 20cm-25cm (8in-10in) long which helps to form the stuffing into a good shape. It has one pointed and one flat end. A kitchen skewer could be used for this purpose, although if you are planning to do a lot of upholstery it is worth investing in the proper tool, which is not expensive.

Needles. For making the bridles you will need a spring needle which is a heavy-duty needle 13cm (5in) long, curved along its length, so that it can be pulled in and out easily. For stitching the edge you will need a 25cm (10in) straight upholsterer's needle.

Materials

Stuffing. Horsehair is the traditional stuffing but, because it is difficult and expensive to obtain today, it is often mixed with hog hair. Old hair mattresses can sometimes be bought cheaply at jumble sales or from junk shops. If you tease out the hair before washing it will return to its original life.

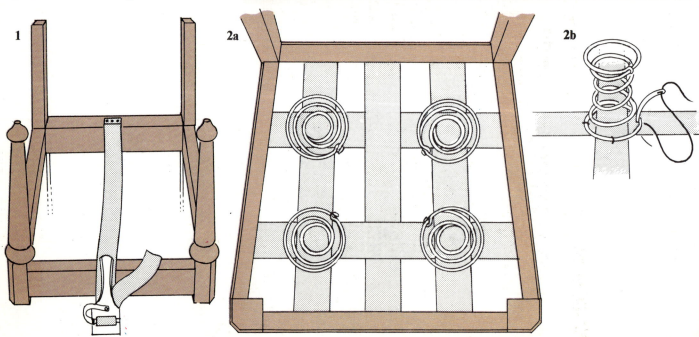

Alternatively, use Algerian fibre. This comes from the Algerian palm grass and, provided that it is teased out thoroughly, it makes a good, inexpensive stuffing.

For a small chair with about 7.5cm (3in) depth of padding you will need about 1kg (2lb) of either type of material.

Webbing. Buy sufficient to replace the original webbing: plain brown twill weave or upholsterer's webbing.

Most ordinary chairs will need three or four strands of 5cm (2in) webbing placed back to front plus two strands across the seat.

Twine, a very strong, smooth string made from flax and hemp, is used for making bridle ties around the edge of the seat which help to hold the stuffing in place. Twine is also used for stitching on the springs and for stitching up the edge, another process which holds the stuffing in place and ensures a straight and firm edge.

Laid cord, a thicker twine, used for lashing the springs.

Scrim, a loosely woven material which is used for covering the first layer of stuffing. Allow enough to cut one piece the same size as the seat plus 15cm (6in) larger all around to allow for the depth of the padding.

Calico is used for covering the second layer of stuffing; you will need a piece approximately same size as scrim.

Wadding is used over the calico to prevent the stuffing from working through; allow the same amount as for the scrim.

Canvas, a heavy furnishing variety, is used over the springs. You will need a piece the size of the seat plus about 2.5cm (1in) all around for turnings.

Main cover. It's wise to choose a dark colour in a proper upholstery grade fabric which will wear well and not show the dirt quickly. Patterned fabrics or those with a raised surface stay crisper-looking for longer than plain fabrics. Allow the same amount as for the scrim.

Stripping the upholstery

Follow the method described previously. As you work make a note of the way the original top cover was attached, the number of springs and webbing strands and the height of the original padding. If you wish, the padding can be made a little higher or lower.

Check that all the old tacks have been removed from the frame. You should fill the old holes with plastic wood to give a firm basis for the tacks. Repair the frame and treat it for woodworm, if needed, and let the fluid dry completely before you start work.

Replacing the webbing

The webbing is the basis for the rest of the upholstery and must be secured tautly and really firmly. As the chair has springs the webbing is attached to the underside of the frame. You will find it easier to turn the chair upside down on the work surface.

Use the webbing straight from the roll. Without cutting it, fold over the end for 2.5cm (1in) and place it centrally on the back rail so the cut edge is uppermost and the fold is 1.5cm ($\frac{1}{2}$in) from the outer edge of the rail as shown in fig.1. Tack down, using five 15mm ($\frac{5}{8}$in) improved tacks placed in a row about 1.5cm ($\frac{1}{2}$in) from the fold, with the line of tacks staggered in the form of a shallow 'W'. If the wood tends to split use 1.5cm ($\frac{1}{2}$in) fine tacks instead (fig.1). Stand on the opposite side of the chair by the front rail and, using the web strainer, put the webbing down in position on the front rail. Press the edge of the strainer on the side of the frame to give leverage. If the frame is polished use a pad of wadding to prevent damage from the strainer.

Tack down on the rail through the single thickness of webbing, using three

1. Webbing is attached to underside of frame for a sprung seat
2. Springs are arranged in a square on top of webbing before sewing down
3. Springs are lashed together with twine and attached to the frame.
4. Springs are covered with canvas and stitched in the same way as to the webbing, using the spring needle.

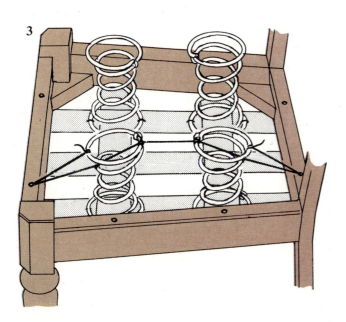

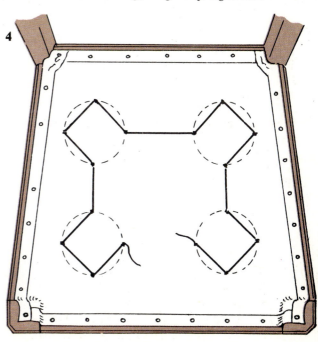

189

tacks placed in a row.

Cut off the webbing 2.5cm (1in) from the tacks.

Turn back the excess over the tacks, placing them in a staggered 'W' formation as before.

Attach the remaining strands from the back to the front in the same way, then secure the side webbing (which runs across the seat), interlacing it with the first strands.

Attaching the springs

The springs must be sewn to the webbing, and then lashed together securely at the top to prevent them from moving about in the seat. This lashing also gives the chair a rounded shape.

Turn the chair the right way up and evenly space the springs in a square on top of the webbing intersections (fig.2a). The beginning and ends of the springs should be towards the middle.

Thread the spring needle with a long length of twine.

Using the fingers of your left hand to feel the positions of the spring from the underside of the chair, insert the needle into the webbing from underneath so that it comes out level with the outside of one spring. Pull the needle through, leaving a short tail of twine, and insert it into the webbing again from the top, catching the bottom ring of the spring with a single stitch (fig.2b).

Knot the tail of the twine to the length

pulled through, but do not cut it.

Still with the needle on the underside of the chair, move to the other side of the ring and stitch it to the webbing there.

Move back to the outside again and make another stitch. This makes three stitches in all, in a 'V'-shape.

Without cutting the twine move to the next spring and repeat the operation. Continue around in this way for the remaining springs then make a knot to finish off and cut the twine.

To lash the springs, attach two 15mm ($\frac{5}{8}$in) improved tacks on all four sides of the frame, each one in line with the centre of a spring, hammering them half-way in.

Cut off enough cord to stretch twice around the frame. Leaving a tail which will stretch easily to the top of the nearest spring, plus another 5cm (2in) for knotting, tie the cord around a tack on the back rail, and hammer the tack in the rest of the way.

Working towards the front of the chair, take the main length of cord to the nearest spring and knot it around the coil which is second from the top of the nearest side. Take it through the spring to the other side and knot it around the top coil. Use a clove hitch knot (fig.7).

Move to the other spring in the row and knot the cord around the top coil on the nearest side, keeping the distance between the springs the same as at the

bottom. Take the cord through the spring and knot it around the coil which is second from the top on the front edge. Tie it off tightly around the tack on the front rail and hammer it in (fig.3).

Take the tail of cord at each tack back to the nearest spring and tie it around the top coil on the outside, pulling tightly so that the spring slightly leans down towards the frame.

Repeat this process on the other pair of springs with the cord running parallel to the first length, and then again with two lengths running across the chair. The springs will now have a rounded shape.

The main stuffing

Centre the canvas over the springs. Fold over 2.5cm (1in) on one side of the canvas and place this centrally on the back rail with the raw edge uppermost. Tack down 15mm ($\frac{5}{8}$in) tacks, placing them 2.5cm (1in) apart and 1.5cm ($\frac{1}{2}$in) from the fold. Fit it neatly around the back uprights, cutting if necessary.

Smooth the canvas over the springs by pulling it quite taut and temporarily tack it to the front rail through a single thickness, keeping the grain of canvas absolutely straight. Smooth out the canvas to the side rails, and temporarily tack through the single thickness.

When satisfied that the canvas is completely smooth and the grain straight, hammer the tacks in completely. Trim off the excess canvas to

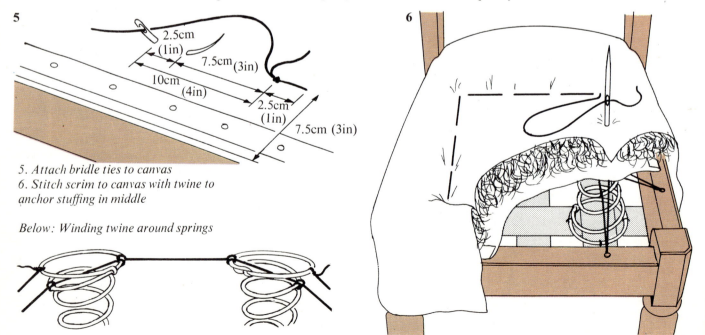

5

2.5cm (1in)

7.5cm (3in)

10cm (4in)

2.5cm (1in)

7.5cm (3in)

5. Attach bridle ties to canvas
6. Stitch scrim to canvas with twine to anchor stuffing in middle

Below: Winding twine around springs

6

within 2.5cm (1in) of the tacks, then fold this over and tack it down at about 5cm (2in) intervals.

Stitch the springs to the canvas in a similar way as they were attached to the webbing, but make a single knot at each stitch to lock it in position (fig.4).

To make bridle ties for the stuffing, thread the spring needle with enough twine to go 1½ times around the chair. The stitch used is rather similar to back stitch. Start by making a stitch in the canvas about 2.5cm (1in) long and 2.5cm (1in) from the edge. Pull it through, leaving a 7.5cm (3in) tail. Tie the tail in a slip knot (fig.7) to the main length at the point where it emerges from the canvas.

Go forward and insert the needle about 10cm (4in) away, but pointing it backwards. Pull it out about 7.5cm (3in) from the starting point (fig.5). Leave the stitch on top of the canvas loose enough for a hand to be inserted.

Continue around the whole edge in this way, making sure that a 2.5cm (1in) stitch falls at each corner. You may have to adjust the length of the bridles to do this.

Finish off by tying a knot.

Take a good handful of stuffing and tease it out thoroughly, removing any lumpy pieces. Put it under one of the bridle threads, working it together well to prevent lumps. Do this for all the bridles, then fill the middle with more stuffing, teasing it well to make an even shape and to overhang the edge slightly by the same amount all around.

Place the scrim centrally over the stuffing and fix one temporary tack in the middle of each side to hold it. Put two other temporary tacks either side of the central tack. At this stage the scrim should be rather loose on the surface of the stuffing.

Thread an upholsterer's needle with a long piece of twine and stitch through from the scrim to the canvas in a rectangle about 7.5cm (3in) from the edges of the seat. To do this, pass the needle through the scrim and stuffing and pull it out between the webbing on the underside of the chair, leaving a tail of twine on top for tying off. As soon as the needle is completely through the canvas, keep the unthreaded end pointing down, and push needle back through the canvas with the threaded end 1.5cm (½in) further on. Withdraw it on top and tie to the main length in a slip knot.

Push the needle back into the scrim making a stitch about 7.5cm (3in) long on top. Continue around in this way, leaving a 1.5cm (½in) gap between stitches (fig.6).

Pull the twine tightly so that the scrim is pulled down and be careful not to catch the springs as the needle passes through. Even out any lumps in the stuffing with the regulator. This process anchors the hair in the middle.

Remove the temporary tacks securing the scrim to the frame – on the front of the seat first, then the sides, and lastly the back. Even out the hair which is along the edges of the seat. Add more if necessary to make a fat roll which just protrudes beyond the edge of the frame. Tuck the raw edge of the scrim under the hair, smoothing it over the roll. Use 9mm (⅜in) tacks to fix the folded edge of the scrim to the grooved edge of the frame. Do not pull it too tightly over the roll.

Stitching the edge

This is done in two stages. The first,

7

Slip knot

Clovehitch knot

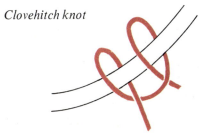

Top to bottom: Remove tacks, cut the stitching, and remove twine holding springs. Lift hair stuffing, remove springs and webbing. Final step is to lift out the remaining tacks.

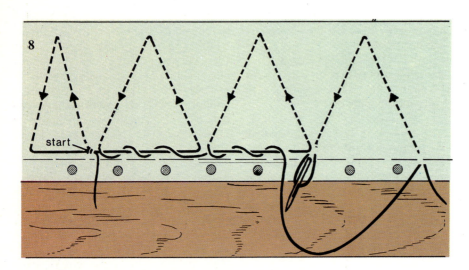

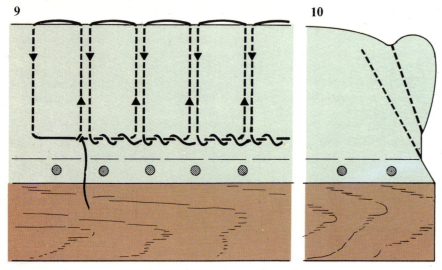

8. *The loop made by blind stitches pulls the stuffing to the edge of the seat*
9. *Top stitching forms stuffing into roll*
10. *A profile of the stitches.*

which is called blind stitching, pulls enough stuffing to the edges to enable a firm edge to be built up. The second stage, top stitching, forms a roll from this section of stuffing. The roll has to be really firm because the covering fabric is pulled over it, and any unevenness would spoil the shape.

Start the stitching at the back on the left side of chair and work around seat anti-clockwise to include back.

To do the blind stitching thread the upholsterer's needle with a good length of twine. Insert the unthreaded end of the needle into the scrim just above the tacks and about 4cm (1½in) from the corner. Insert the needle into the stuffing at an angle of about 45°. It will emerge on the top of the chair about 5cm (2in) in from the edge and 1.5cm (½in) nearer the corner.

Pull the needle through, stopping as soon as you see the eye, so that it is not completely withdrawn. Push it back into the stuffing again, altering the angle so that it emerges through the side on the same level as where it first entered, but 2.5cm (1in) nearer the corner. You have, in effect, made a V-shaped stitch or loop in the stuffing (fig 8).

Pull the twine through so that there is a tail of about 7.5cm (3in). Tie to main length with a slip knot and pull tight. Insert the needle about 5cm (2in) further along the edge, slanting in the same way as before and bringing it out on the same level on top as the first stitch. Bring it down again at an angle to emerge on the side about 2.5cm (1in)

back. Before withdrawing the needle completely, wind the twine hanging in a loop below it, around the needle twice. Pull needle right through.

Put the unthreaded end of the needle into the centre of the chair top to anchor it temporarily. Hold the edge of the stuffing with your left hand so that the fingers are on the top and the thumb is on the side. Wrap the twine around your other hand and pull the stitch really tight, pressing down with your left hand at the same time; you should be able to feel the filling being pulled towards the edge.

Continue working around the edge in this way, being careful not to place the twisted section of a stitch so that it has to go around a corner. To finish, knot the twine carefully and tightly.

Correct any unevenness in the stuffing with the regulator, then re-thread the upholsterer's needle with a long length of twine.

Top stitching is similar to blind stitching, the main difference being that the needle is completely pulled through on top of the stuffing so that a stitch can be made on top. This means that the needle should be inserted vertically into the scrim and not inclined to the left as with blind stitching. Starting at a corner, insert the needle about 4cm (1½in) away and about 1.5cm (½in) above the blind stitching. Push it through so that it emerges on top about 2.5cm (1in) in from the edge.

Re-insert the threaded end of the needle about 2.5cm (1in) to the left of this point, keeping it parallel to the first entry so that it emerges 2.5cm (1in) away (fig.9).

Tie the end of the twine in a slip knot as before. Insert the needle again and complete the stitch, reinserting it about 2.5cm (1in) to the left as before so that it is just short of the first stitch. Before withdrawing the needle completely from the second half of the stitch, wind the twine around it and then pull tight in the same way as for blind stitching. Continue all around the edge in this way. The stitches on top of the chair should form a continuous line, following line of chair.

The second stuffing

Make bridle ties in the scrim as with the first stuffing. Fill the cavity which has been formed by the roll edge with more stuffing tucked under the bridle ties, and cover the chair with a piece of calico, temporarily tacking this with 9mm (⅜in) fine tacks to the front of the frame, then the back and lastly the sides. If the original upholstery finished on this face, rather than on the underside of the chair, be careful to place the tacks clear of the line where the wood begins to show. Cut into the calico at the back corners to fit around the uprights of the chair back, following the method given in the previous chapter.

After the calico has been positioned, tack it in place.

If the corners of the chair are rounded, make a double pleat or an inverted pleat (as in the photographs), or a single pleat if the corner is square. To keep a smooth line the calico has to be pulled hard over the roll edges, but be careful to keep the grain of the calico absolutely straight, putting most of the pressure from back to front as illustrated.

The top cover

Cover the calico with wadding to prevent the stuffing from working through. Cut a piece of cover fabric on the straight grain large enough to cover the seat in the same style as the original upholstery. Temporarily tack it down with 9mm (⅜in) fine tacks through a single thickness. Finish the corners as for the calico cover, using the flat end of the regulator to make a smooth finish at the back.

Tack down.

Trim off the excess fabric.

Top left: Work stitching anti-clockwise
Top right: Check grain of fabric
Bottom left: Pleat to finish corners
Bottom right: Upholstery is complete

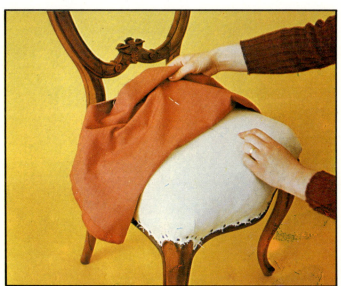

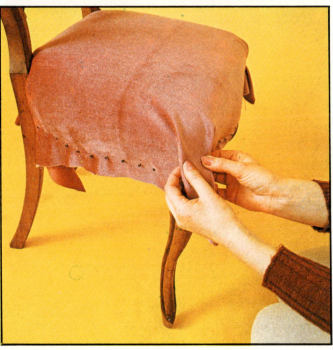

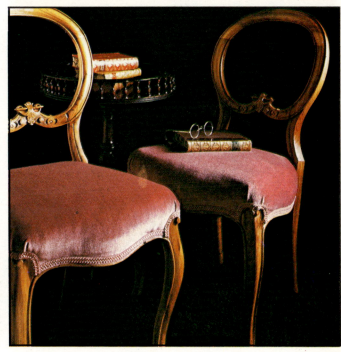

Upholstered bedhead

Right: One of the most useful tools for padding is a staple gun.

Below: Cover your padded headboard with a colour-coordinated fabric.

If you have an ugly wooden bedhead, one way of smartening it up is to pad it with foam and cover it with fabric to match your bedspread or other fabrics used in the room. The cover may be a loose one so that it can be removed for cleaning or you could make it more permanent if you choose fabric which can be dry-cleaned in position. This method of upholstery can also be used for bedheads with struts or for new bedheads cut from 1.5cm ($\frac{1}{2}$in) plywood or blockboard. It is not suitable for intricate shapes because you will not be able to achieve a smooth outline round the edges. For these it is simpler to inset the padding, leaving an un-padded border of wood around the edge. The gun is a heavy duty stapler which is designed to fire staples into a hard surface like wood. It is useful in modern upholstery where several rounds of tacks might splinter the chipboard or ply-woods now being used (in traditional upholstery hardwoods, such as beech or birch, were always used).

If you want to attach the cover per-manently, choose hard-wearing fabric which will not show the dirt quickly and which can be cleaned when it is in position by using an aerosol dry clean-ing liquid. For a loose cover most kinds of soft furnishing fabrics can be used although if you choose a loosely woven one you may need to back the pieces with lining fabric.

To calculate the amount of fabric to buy, measure the length and width of the bedhead and add 15cm (6in) each way for turnings and ease of working. If the bedhead is wider than the fabric, double the amount and add on one pattern repeat to allow for matching design. If you are covering the back of the board, allow the same amount. The fabric for this can match the front of the board or you could use a cheaper plain fabric such as calico or curtain lining. Allow the same amount if you are making a removable cover to allow

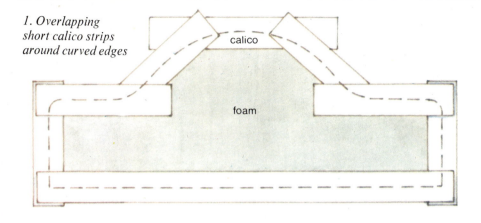

1. Overlapping short calico strips around curved edges

2. Tacking the calico to the wood

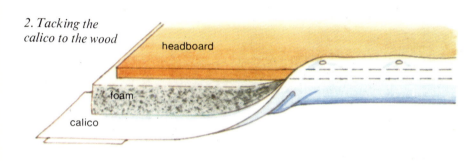

3. Attaching the bottom strip to the front of the board

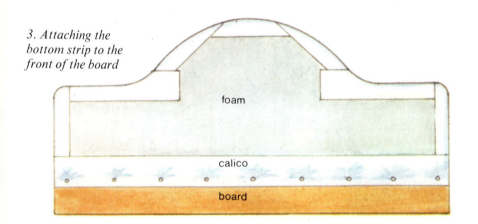

4. Finishing the calico strip

Folding the strip around

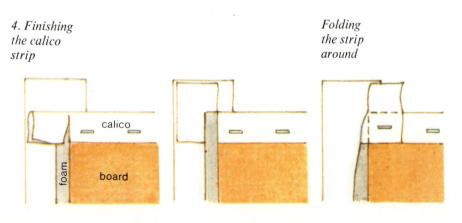

for the back.

Foam padding is used is used, 5cm (2in) thick and cut 2.5cm (1in) larger all around than the area to be padded. If the foam would make the bedhead difficult to fix on to the bed again, leave an unpadded section at the bottom of the same depth as the mattress so that the bedhead can slot into the base.

To mark the foam for curved edges, place the headboard on to the foam and trace round with a felt-tipped pen. Make another line 2.5cm (1in) outside this for the cutting line.

Buy enough calico to tear into 10cm (4in) strips to fit around the perimeter of the foam with a piece to cover the foam completely, plus an extra 15cm (6in) each way for turnings. Adhesive (such as Bostik 1) for attaching the calico strips to the foam.

Preparing the foam

Tear strips of calico 10cm (4in) wide to fit each side of the foam plus 2.5cm (1in) to overlap at each corner. To fit shaped sides, cut several short lengths of calico. Fold the strips in half lengthwise and apply the adhesive from the edge up to the crease line to within 2.5cm (1in) of each end. Mark a border with a felt-tipped pen 5cm (2in) wide inside the edges of the foam on one side and apply adhesive up to the line.

When the adhesive is tacky stick the strips to the foam keeping the crease line level with the edges. On the curved edges overlap the strips (fig.1).

Attach the foam, remove the struts from the back of the headboard (they are normally screwed in place). Place the foam on your work surface with the calico strips downwards. Place the headboard front-side down onto the foam so that there is a 2.5cm (1in) border of foam showing around the edges (or along the top and sides only if an unpadded section is being left at the base of the board to allow for the mattress).

Squash up the edges of the foam so that they are level with the edges of the headboard; bring the strip at the top of the board over onto the back and secure with temporary tacks placed at 15cm (6in) intervals. Do the same at the sides and bottom (fig.2). If you are leaving an unpadded section tack the calico onto the front of the board (fig.3).

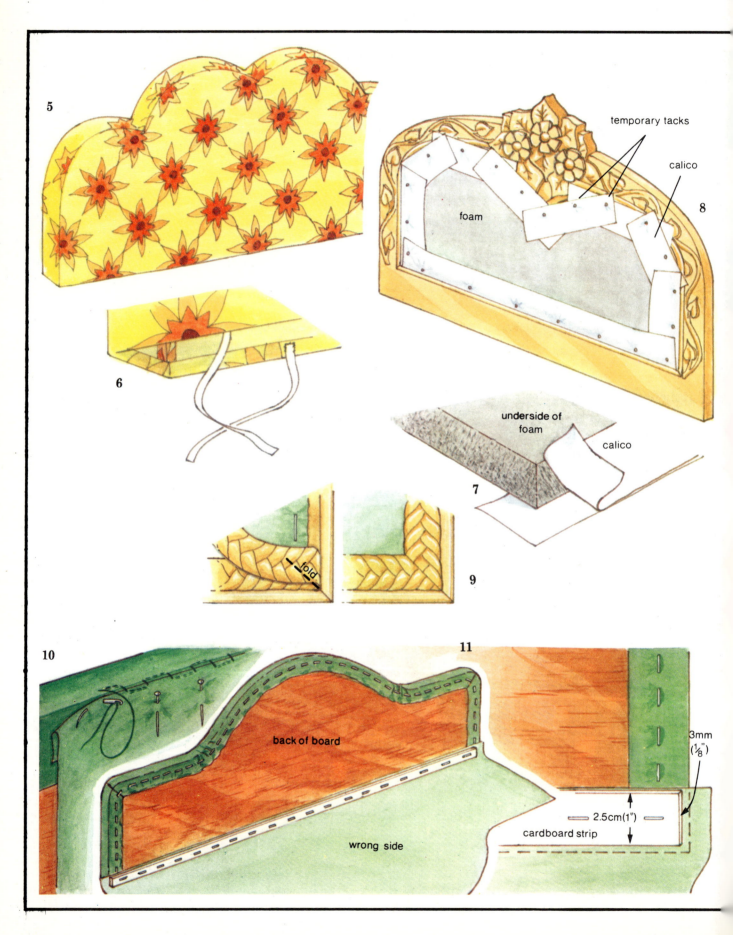

5

6

7 underside of foam

calico

8 temporary tacks

calico

foam

9 fold

10 back of board

wrong side

11 3mm (⅛")

2.5cm(1")

cardboard strip

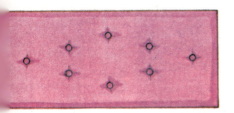

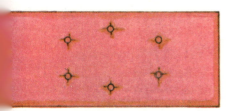

Above: The variety of patterns that can be produced by shallow buttoning is enormous. The selection above is a small cross section. When the buttons are positioned, they compress the padding slightly.

5. *Top view of loose cover in position*
6. *The loose cover is attached with tapes which are tied under the board*
7. *Foam piece for inset padding*
8. *Tack the calico close to the foam*
9. *Mitring the corners of braid*
10. *Slip stitching*
11. *Back-tacking one straight edge of the back panel firmly into place*

Beginning at the centre and working out to the sides, completely secure the top and bottom edges with staples, placing them about 2cm ($\frac{3}{4}$in) apart and about 6mm ($\frac{1}{4}$in) from the edge. Release the temporary tacks as you complete each side.

Check that all the staples lie flat on the surface and tap them down lightly if necessary. To remove a staple, lever it up with the point of a regulator or skewer and pull it out with pincers.

At the corners, slash the overlapping calico level with the sides of the board to the corner of the wood and then to the front edge of the foam. Open the slashed portion out and refold it the other way so that it wraps around the sides and some extends at the corners (fig.4). Tack it down and trim off the surplus calico flush with the edges of the board. Tack and staple the side strips in the same way.

Fitting the lining

Cut a piece of calico 15cm (6in) longer and wider than the board and place it centrally over the foam. Temporarily tack it to the back of the board in the centre and 7.5cm (3in) from the corners at the top and bottom. Place more temporary tacks in between and then tack the sides. When the lining is completely taut and smooth, secure it with staples, placing them about 1cm ($\frac{3}{8}$in) from the edge, and remove all the temporary tacks.

Fitted top cover

Attach this as for the lining, but placing the staples 1.5cm ($\frac{1}{2}$in) from the edge and 6mm ($\frac{1}{4}$in) apart, and finishing corners on an inverted pleat. Trim off the excess fabric close to the staples.

If you have left an unpadded section at the foot of the board, cut a strip of fabric to cover that section plus about 5cm (2in) all around. Back-tack (see diagrams) the top edge so that the fold comes level with the bottom of the padding. Take the remaining three edges around onto the back of the board and tack and staple.
Replace the struts on the back.

Covering the back

If you want to cover the back of the headboard to make a neat finish, cut out the fabric to the same size as the foam.

The fabric is attached by back-tacking on one edge and slip-stitching the remaining three edges. Both techniques are commonly used in all kinds of upholster and are useful to learn.

Decide which edge is to be back-tacked. Usually this is the top edge if this is straight, but if this edge is curved it should be done along the bottom edge. When the fabric is in position, replace the struts on the back of the board, piercing the fabric with fine pointed scissors to make a small hole for the screws.

Loose top cover

The method for making this is not unlike that for making a welted cushion. It can be pulled over the padding and fastened under the bottom of the board with tape.

For the front and back panels cut two pieces of fabric the same size as the board, plus 1.5cm ($\frac{1}{2}$in) at the top and sides and 2.5cm (1in) at the bottom for turnings. Where the fabric has a one-way design or pile which must run vertically on the board and it is not possible to cut the panel from a single width of fabric, cut a main centre section from the full width and join two narrower sections to each side, so that the pattern matches.

For the welt strip cut a long strip of fabric equal to the depth of the board including padding plus 2.5cm (1in) for turnings by the length of the sides and top plus 2.5cm (1in).

With right sides together, pin the strip to the sides and top of the front panel, taking 1.5cm ($\frac{1}{2}$in) turnings. Clip into the turnings at the corners to make a smooth outline and machine stitch the seam.

Join the back panel to the opposite edge of the strip in a similar way and press all the seams. Turn to right side (fig. 5). Turn up 2.5cm (1in) all around the bottom of the cover and make a 2cm ($\frac{3}{4}$in) hem. Stitch on lengths of tape in corresponding positions on the hem so that the cover can be tied in place (fig.6).

Inset padding

On elaborately shaped headboards or those which have a polished wood surround, it is often better to inset the padding, leaving an unpadded border round the edge.

Mark the area on the front of the board to be padded and make a paper template of the shape. Cut the foam to this shape. Prepare the foam by grooving the side edge from the underneath (i.e. cut away the edge at an angle of 30°) and stick on a strip of calico along the grooved edge for strength (fig.7). Then stick on calico strips around the perimeter as for boards with all-over padding. Place the foam onto the board so that it is in exactly the right position, pull the calico flat onto the surface of the board and hold in place with a few temporary tacks along each side, placing them as close to the edge of the foam as possible (fig.8).

When you are satisfied with the shape of the foam, replace the temporary tacks with staples. Trim off the calico close to the staples.

Cover the foam with a calico lining and then the main cover, attaching them in a similar way with tacks and staples. Keep the staples as close to the edge of the foam as possible and place them 3mm ($\frac{1}{8}$in) apart on the top cover. Trim off all the excess fabric. Cut a piece of furnishing braid to fit the perimeter of the padding and stick it over the raw edges of the fabric and staples with a clear adhesive. Mitre all corners for a neat effect (fig.9).

Slip stitching

This is a technique commonly used in upholstery for attaching outside panels. Thread a curved needle with strong thread, and knot the free end.

Insert the needle into the fold from the open end and pull out about 1.5cm ($\frac{1}{2}$in) further down. Make a straight stitch across to the fabric on the other side and make a small stitch towards the opening. Bring the needle out and make a straight stitch across to the fold. Run the needle along the fold in the direction of the area to be covered, making a stitch of about 1.5cm ($\frac{1}{2}$in). Make a small stitch across to the other side and make another 1.5cm ($\frac{1}{2}$in) stitch. Continue all around (fig.10) till all the folds are stitched.

To back-tack

For this you need a piece of cardboard, 2.5cm (1in) by the width of the head-

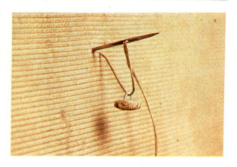

Left: Passing needle through the hole
Above: Making small stitch at front

board less 6mm ($\frac{1}{4}$in). Place the edge of the fabric, right side down, onto the edge of the wood, on the side to be covered, so that it overlaps by 2.5cm (1in) and the remaining fabric is beyond the edge. Place the strip of cardboard over the fabric so that one long edge and the two short edges are 3mm ($\frac{1}{8}$in) in from the edges of the wood (fig.11). Secure the cardboard and fabric to the wood with staples placed about 2.5cm (1in) apart.

Fold the fabric down onto the board, pulling it firmly over the cardboard so that a neat edge is formed. Turn under the remaining three edges of fabric, snipping around curves for a smooth line, so that the fold is 3mm ($\frac{1}{8}$in) from the edge of the wood. Pin in place, putting the pins at right angles with the heads towards the outer edge so that the fabric is kept taut. Slip stitch the fold to the cover fabric, using the curved needle and strong thread.

Shallow buttoning

Shallow buttoning adds extra interest to a plain padded surface and is not difficult to do. It can be used for a wall panel, for padded bedheads and on chairs and stool tops.

Basically the buttons are placed on to the surface of the board in a regular pattern and pulled down into the padding with twine which is taken through the padding to the back of the board, through a drilled hole, and fastened off securely.

Unlike deep buttoning where the buttons are sunk into the padding by some 5cm-7.5cm (2in-3in), the buttons in shallow buttoning merely compress the padding by about 1.5cm ($\frac{1}{2}$in). The fabric is not distorted much beyond forming a few wrinkles (in deep button-

ing the fabric is distorted so much that it is generally formed into pleats between the buttons), so the buttons can be added when the front cover has been completely attached.

Use metal buttons, of about 2cm ($\frac{3}{4}$in) diameter, which can be covered in fabric

---

To make a buttoned surface:
You will need:
Buttons.
Upholstery twine and long upholstery needle.
Two 1.5cm ($\frac{1}{2}$in) improved tacks for each button.
Drill and wood drill bit (No. 8 size).

---

to match the main cover. The buttons should have a metal shank on the back so that the twine used to secure them can be slotted through. The shank sinks into the padding and is completely hidden when the buttoning is complete. The buttons can be made professionally by a soft furnishing supplier or you could make them yourself using a button kit.

The buttoning design

With shallow buttoning the buttons can be placed exactly as you want them and you can have as many or as few as you like. You could place them in a rectangle, in a large diamond, a triangle or even a circle.

Attaching the buttons

When the padding and cover are complete, place the board, padded side down, onto your work surface. Place two improved tacks on opposite sides of each hole and hammer them halfway down.

Thread the needle with a length of

Left: Shallow buttoning adds a touch of luxury to this bedhead.

twine and tie one end round one of the tacks. Hammer the tack completely home then pass the needle through the hole and padding to the front of the board, checking that you are keeping the needle straight. Pull the needle completely out on the padded side and thread it through the button shank. Push it back into the padding and hole, making a small stitch on the surface of the cover.

On the back of the board pull the twine as tightly as possible so that the button compresses the padding, and wrap it around the second tack (it often helps to have an assistant at this stage).

Hammer the tack home, keeping the twine wound around the tack as tight as possible. Cut off the excess twine, leaving a tail of about 2.5cm (1in).

Buttoning onto webbed foundations

Shallow buttoning is normally worked onto padding with a firm foundation but, with care, it can also be worked onto padding with a webbing foundation, such as a dining chair. Mark the design for the buttoning lightly in pencil or tailor's chalk onto the cover of the padding.

Attaching the buttons

Thread the needle with a long length of twine. Pass the needle through the padding from the top on the marked position and bring it out on the underside, passing it through a strand of webbing. Leave a long tail of twine on the top side of the padding.

Return to this length and thread the needle with it. Pass the needle through the button and pass the needle through the padding again, making a small stitch on the surface of the padding. Pull the twine right through and remove the needle.

Roll up a small piece of spare webbing or canvas and place it between the two lengths of twine on the underside of the webbing. Tie the ends in a slip knot (page 191) and tighten knot around little roll. The roll helps to prevent the knot from pulling through the webbing. Secure the knot firmly to prevent it from slipping and then cut off the excess length.

Padded footstool

Use the following technique to make a really useful and economical footstool from a wooden box.

You will need:

Wooden box, such as an old bottle crate, with a firm base.
The box is inverted so that the base forms the top of the stool.
Fine glasspaper.
Tack hammer and lifter.
Staple gun (optional).
Drill and 3mm ($\frac{1}{8}$in) drill bit.
Scissors, tape measure.
Several 1cm ($\frac{3}{8}$in) fine upholstery tacks.
Adhesive (such as Bostik 1).
Foam (two pieces are required): measure the base of the box and buy a piece of 5cm (2in) thick foam to the same dimensions plus 1.5cm ($\frac{1}{2}$in) each way. Measure the perimeter of the box and the height, add 5cm (22in) to the height and buy a piece of sheet foam to these dimensions.
Calico. For the lining allow enough calico to cut separate pieces for each side and the base of the box plus 10cm (4in) all around each piece. For attaching the 5cm (2in) thick foam allow enough to cut a 7cm (3in) strip to fit each side plus 2.5cm (1in)
Cover fabric. Buy the same total amount as for the calico.
Piping cord (No. 3 size) and adhesive tape (any width) to fit the perimeter of the box plus about 5cm (2in).
Handles (optional).
Sewing thread to match calico and cover fabric.

The padding
Smooth the sides and base of the box by rubbing all over the outside with the glasspaper. Drill 6-8 holes through the base at 15cm (6in) intervals to allow ventilation for the foam.
Fold each calico strip in half lengthwise and crease fold with your fingers.
Open out the strips and spread adhesive on one of them from the raw edge up to the crease line. Spread adhesive on the corresponding edge of the foam.
Press the sticky part of the calico onto the sticky edge of the foam so the non-sticky part of the strip extends beyond the edge of the foam (fig.1).
Repeat for the remaining strips.

Attaching the foam
Turn the box so that the base is uppermost and place the foam onto it so that the calico strips are hanging down.
Temporary-tack the strips to the sides of the box about 1.5cm ($\frac{1}{2}$in) from the top of the box, placing one tack in the centre of each side, then one at each end and then at 5cm (2in) intervals in between (fig.2). The foam should be completely flat on the top and the calico strips should be smooth.
If you are using a staple gun, replace each tack with a staple and then fill in with more staples so they are as close as possible. If you are not using staples, hammer the tacks down and add more tacks so they are 1.5cm ($\frac{1}{2}$in) apart. Trim off the excess calico.

Padding the box sides
Wrap the sheet foam round the sides of the box so that the foam covers the calico strips and the bottom edge is level with the open end of the box. Secure with a few staples or tacks on each side (fig.3).

Covering the box
Re-measure the sides of the box to include the foam padding. Cut pieces of calico to fit the top and each side allowing 1.5cm ($\frac{1}{2}$in) for turnings all around except at the bottom edges of the side sections where you should allow 2.5cm (1in).
Machine stitch the side sections together down their corresponding edges to within 1.5cm ($\frac{1}{2}$in) of the top and 2.5cm (1in) of the bottom. Press.
With right sides together, pin the calico top section to the top edge of the stitched side section so that the corners of the top section match the seams on the sides (fig.4). Machine stitch and press the turnings onto the side section and turn right side out.
Fit the lining over the box and pull down firmly (it will be a snug fit). Staple or tack it to the box just above the open end and trim excess.

Main cover
Cut out the main cover fabric as for the calico lining and stitch the side sections

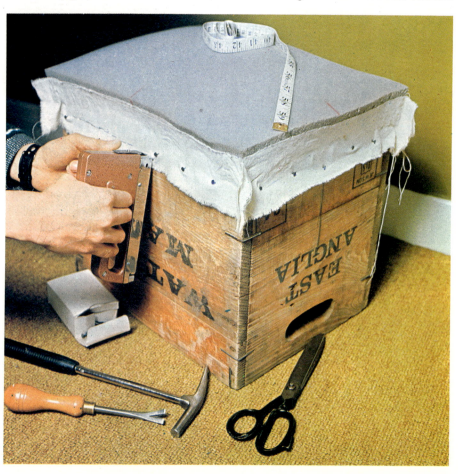

200

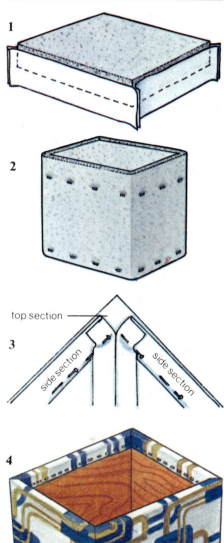

1. Calico strips stuck to the foam
2. (Opposite) Replace tacks with staples
3. Sheet foam wrapped around sides
4. Pinning side section to top
5. Cover stapled inside the box

together as before. From the remaining fabric cut 4cm (1½in) wide bias strips for piping.

Make up the piping to fit along the top edge of the side section and machine stitch in place. Clip into the turnings of the piping casing at each corner. Stitch the top section to the sides as for the lining, but with the piping sandwiched between the two layers.

Fit the cover onto the box, pull the raw edge over the open end and staple or tack inside the box (fig.5).

Cover the raw edges of the fabric with the adhesive tape.

Attach handles to the sides of the box

Needlepoint furnishing designs

Florentine embroidery is the name applied to a whole range of needlepoint designs which are worked in straight stitch. Also known as Hungarian Point or Bargello, most forms of Florentine stitch are worked over four or six threads in a variety of patterns, creating strong, geometrical shapes and striking visual effects. As straight stitch does not distort the canvas unduly, you will not require a frame when making small objects.

Although Florentine stitches can be used to create very elaborate and complicated designs, the simplest and two of the most characteristic patterns, zig-zag and flame, look impressive but are very straightforward and quick to work. Each row of a separate colour is worked horizontally across the canvas, with either a step up or down from stitch to stitch. Once one line of colour has been worked, all the others will follow suit. If you have to join the yarn midway

across a row, finish off the old thread by threading it through the back of the stitches and begin a new thread in the same way.

Zig-zag is the simplest pattern of all. The zig-zag base· line forms regular peaks, which can be either very deep or fairly shallow. For small objects, a pattern that repeats about every ten stitches is suitable (fig.1). The stitches are usually worked over four threads and back two, which gives a pleasing regular pattern.

Zig-zag stitch looks good either in subtly shaded colours, or in vivid, contrasting colours.

Flame patterns

Flame patterns are slightly more complicated, forming steep peaks of varying heights to give a variety of designs. This stitch is usually worked over four threads and back one (fig.2). Flame stitch looks best when worked in a range of toning colours for a subtly shaded effect.

Stitching notes

The easiest way to stitch Florentine is in two movements – put the needle in at the front and take it out from the back, putting it into the next position from the back. Repeat from the front. Working in this way it is easier to see the threads for counting. If you do make a mistake, cut it out rather than unpick it – the yarn gets so worn with unpicking it is impossible to use it again.

Base line

Most Florentine designs are begun with

Yarn	Length per skein or ball	Canvas size	Needle size
Anchor Tapisserie Wool	13.7m (15yd)	14 threads per 2.5cm (1in) single canvas	18
DMC Laine Tapisserie	8m (8yd)		
Appleton's Tapestry Wool	13.7m (15yd)		
Appleton's Crewel Wool (4 strands)	27.5m (30yd)		
Anchor Tapisserie Wool	13.7m (15yd)	16 threads per 2.5cm (1in) single canvas	18
DMC Laine Tapisserie	8m (8yd)		
Appleton's Tapestry Wool	13.7m (15yd)		
Appleton's Crewel Wool (3 strands)	27.5m (30yd)		
DMC Retors à Broder	10m (11yd)	16 threads per 2.5cm (1in) single canvas	18
Coton du Pinguin	160m (175yd)		
Appleton's Crewel Wool (2 strands)	27.5m (30yd)	24 threads per 2.5cm (1in) single canvas	22
Clarks Linen Embroidery	15.5m (17yd)		
Anchor Stranded Cotton	8m (8yd)		

one row worked right across the width of the design – called the base line, although it is often worked in the centre of the canvas to keep the pattern symmetrical. Zig-zag and flame can be started with a base line anywhere on the canvas and all other rows will follow automatically above and below.

Pattern repeats

An important aspect of all Florentine designs is to make sure that the base line consists of a complete number of pattern repeats and that each side of the design is symmetrical. Both zig-zag and flame stitch build up their patterns from one base line in such a way that

they can be started at any point on the canvas. Once the first row has been worked, the others follow almost automatically. The pattern is repeated above and below the base line. Where necessary, work half-stitches at the edges to fill in the finished square or rectangle.

Estimating yarn length

As zig-zag and flame stitch are always worked in horizontal rows, by calculating the amount of yarn needed to work one complete row it then becomes easy to estimate the total amount of yarn required to work a design of a given size. Working with a 46cm (18in) length of yarn, stitch as much of the pattern

1. Front and back of zig-zag stitch
2. Sample of flame stitch

3. Above: Base line for bricking and Below: for a simple zig-zag pattern

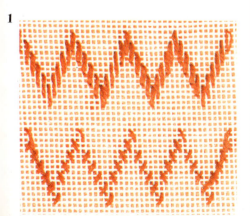

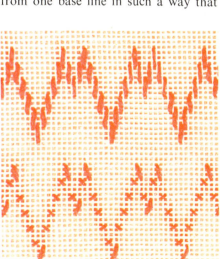

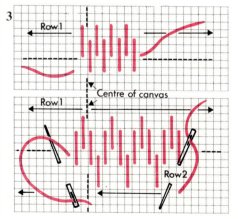

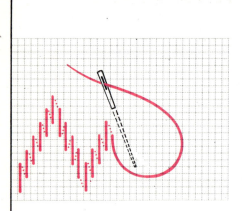

4. Zig-zag stitch detail

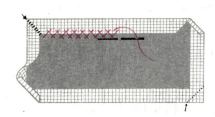

5. Finishing piece of work by mitring the corners, and using herringbone stitch to secure the edges.

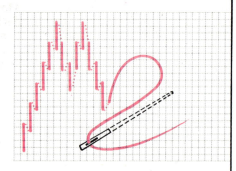

6. Detail of flame stitch

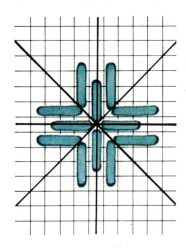

7. Centre stitches in the same hole

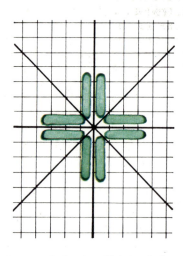

8. Centre stitches in adjoining holes

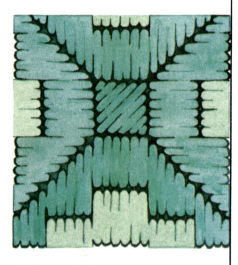

9. Blocks of stitches at the centre

repeat as this will work. Count the number of lengths needed to fill the row. Multiply again by the number of rows to be worked in each separate colour – each stitch covers four horizontal threads, so divide the total number of horizontal threads by four to get the number of complete rows. This gives the total amount of yarn required. The chart shown here gives the lengths of different manufacturers' skeins, so you can work out how many skeins you need.

Varying canvas sizes

A basic stitch like zig-zag or flame can easily be translated onto larger or smaller canvas, using the appropriate yarn (see chart).

The base line is worked as before, but the number of pattern repeats will be different if covering the same area on larger or smaller canvas. However, if working a pair of objects, one larger and one small, then the smaller object can be worked on a smaller size canvas with exactly the same design reduced in scale.

To calculate the pattern size on different sizes of canvas, count the number of threads covered by one pattern repeat. For example, in the patterns shown here

the zig-zag covers 10 threads and flame covers 14.

All canvas is measured by the number of threads per 2.5cm (1in), so divide the number of threads across the width you want to work by the number of threads covered by one pattern repeat. This will give the number of pattern repeats you can work in the base line. Remember to work an exact number of pattern repeats and to keep the base line symmetrical.

Pattern symmetry

If you are making a small object like a spectacles case, you can achieve stitch symmetry by counting how many pattern repeats can be worked in the base line, as described above. You can start at one side of the canvas and work in horizontal rows straight across. However, for larger objects lke cushions this system is unsuitable because of the number of threads to be counted. So, for larger embroideries which need to be symmetrical, begin stitching at the marked centre lines of the canvas. Stitch the first row only from the centre outwards. Subsequent rows can be stitched straight across the whole width of the design, beginning at the point where the first row ends (fig.3).

Check carefully the number of stitches in the base line. A mistake is hard to spot in the early stages, but will ruin the completed embroidery.

If your base line is accurate there is no need to count stitches again.

Four-way Florentine

Four-way Florentine is a fascinating development of the traditional Florentine needlepoint technique. It is also known as radial Bargello because the stitches appear to radiate from the centre of the canvas.

This effect is achieved by working in a circular fashion, beginning at the centre of the canvas and moving outwards. The canvas is turned in order to work each side so that the tops of all the stitches point towards the centre.

Designs

Most traditional Florentine patterns may be used for the radial technique but it is worth plotting the design on graph paper to make sure of its success.

The designs work best if the overall shape is a square, a circle or a hexagon, but the technique can be adapted for rectangles or other shapes by working the radial pattern as a motif and completing the shape with a border or a background colour.

Materials

Use the materials described on the chart and calculate the amount of yarn required for the project.

Plotting designs

When you have chosen your pattern and have decided on the gauge of canvas, draw on graph paper an outline of the item you are making so that each line

on the paper corresponds to one thread of canvas. If your shape is not a square or circle, draw a square within of the required size. For circles, draw a square with sides equal to the diameter of the circle round the outside of the circle.

Find the centre point of each side of the square and draw lines across the square between the centre points on opposite sides. Draw diagonal lines across the square.

Using coloured pencils to represent the shades of the pattern you have chosen, draw the first stitches at the centre of the square. These first stitches should correspond to the centre stitches of

Above: Ideas for radial designs.

your chosen pattern. If the diagonal lines cross in a space on the graph paper, the centre stitches will be worked into the same hole (fig.7). If the diagonals cross on a junction of the graph lines, the centre stitches will be worked as shown in fig.8. (This will leave a tiny space at the centre.)

Where the design has a block of stitches in the centre, as shown in the scoop pattern overleaf, the blocks can be arranged in a square around the centre (fig. 9). In this case the space left is filled by diagonal stitches.

Florentine chair seats

The quantities and instructions are given for a dining chair with a larger than average drop-in seat but they can easily be adapted to fit your own chairs.

Below: Once you have learned the basic techniques of Florentine, you will feel confident about tackling projects such as the one below. It is in fact a very simple stitch, but has an amazingly dramatic impact. If you have a chair with a worn drop-in seat, this is the ideal way to make it brand new again. You can devise your own colour scheme if you wish, the possibilities are infinite.

Materials required

Clark's Anchor Tapisserie wool: 5 skeins each Tangerine 0311, 0313, 0315, Chestnut 0350, Black 0403, 2 skeins Flame 0334.
0.70m ($\frac{3}{4}$yd) single thread tapestry canvas, 7 threads to 1cm (18 threads to 1in) 68.5cm (27in) wide.
Tapestry frame (optional).
Tapestry needle No. 18.
Paper for making template of chair seat.
Upholstery tacks, 1cm ($\frac{3}{8}$in) long.
Tack hammer.
Wood plane (if necessary).

Making the template

1 Remove the seat from the chair, place it on to the paper and draw around.
2 Draw a second line 2.5cm (1in) outside the first line to allow for the depth of the padding. Draw 2.5cm (1in) squares in each corner for mitred corners. The stitching should not be worked in these squares. Cut along the outside line.
3 Pin the template onto the canvas and draw around the edge using a felt-tipped pen. Allow at least 2.5cm (1in) unworked canvas all around so that it can be attached to the under-side of the seat.

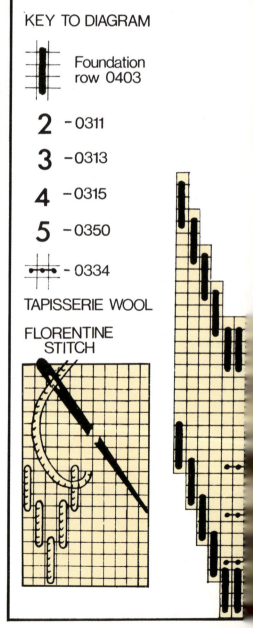

KEY TO DIAGRAM

Foundation row 0403

2 - 0311

3 - 0313

4 - 0315

5 - 0350

- 0334

TAPISSERIE WOOL

FLORENTINE STITCH

Marking the design

1 Mark the centre of the canvas in both directions with tacking.
2 Following the chart, mark the pattern onto the canvas starting at the centre (indicated by the arrows) and working outwards. Repeat the design until you reach the outside edges.
3 Mount the canvas onto a tapestry frame if you are using one.

Working the design

1 The design is worked in Florentine stitch and satin stitch over four threads of the canvas. Work the foundation row first in the colour shown on the chart, starting at the centre and going out to the sides in both directions.
2 Work the next row below the foundation row in the colour shown on the chart. The tops of the stitches in this row should be worked into the same holes as the bottom of the stitches in the foundation row.
3 Work following rows in same way.
4 When the colour sequence is complete, start again with the foundation row and continue as before, working to the outline shape.
5 To complete the design work the horizontal straight stitches.

Attaching the canvas

1 Place the canvas onto the seat and fold the excess onto the underside Try the seat in position on the chair.
2 If the canvas is too thick for the seat to fit back into the chair, remove the tacks holding the original fabric. Plane the sides of the frame by the required amount and re-tack the fabric.
3 Mitre the corners of the canvas and attach the canvas centrally to the seat as for the cover fabric.
4 Replace the seat on the chair.

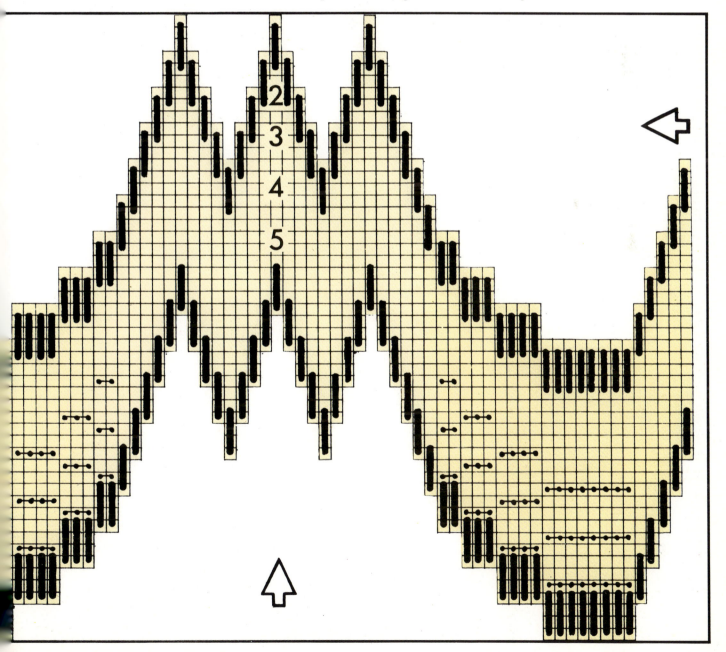

Making loose covers

It is quite simple to make your own loose covers and it is considerably less expensive than having them made. Complicated patterns are not required. The fabric is cut directly on the chair or sofa and 'moulded' to fit the contours of the upholstery by pinning. It is a satisfying experience to see the shape emerging as you work.

Although the shapes and sizes of upholstered furniture vary, the same basic techniques are used for all styles both to estimate the fabric required and to cut and fit covers.

One particular chair has been used here for the purpose of illustration. Different shapes or additional insets are treated in the same way but it is important to follow the seam lines of the original upholstery as closely as possible.

This chapter is devoted to calculating

fabric and cutting out covers. Stitching and finishing is dealt with in the next chapter.

With the exception of velvet and leather almost any upholstered chair or sofa can be fitted with loose covers.

Before you start always clean the chair or sofa with dry upholster shampoo so that no dirt rubs onto your fabric.

Choosing the fabric

Choose furnishing fabrics which are tough and hard wearing, firm in weave, colour fast and pre-shrunk. Avoid very thick fabrics as these will be difficult to

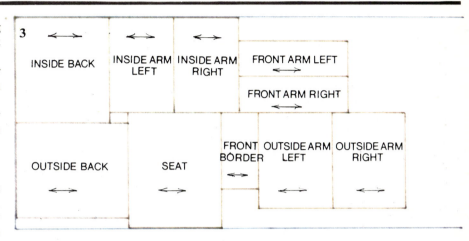

3

INSIDE BACK	INSIDE ARM LEFT	INSIDE ARM RIGHT	FRONT ARM LEFT
			FRONT ARM RIGHT
OUTSIDE BACK	SEAT	FRONT BORDER	OUTSIDE ARM LEFT / OUTSIDE ARM RIGHT

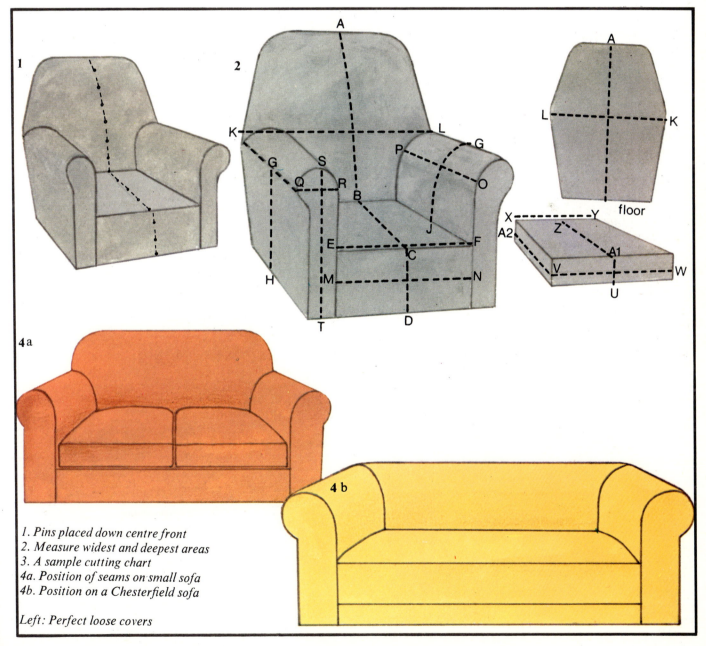

1. Pins placed down centre front
2. Measure widest and deepest areas
3. A sample cutting chart
4a. Position of seams on small sofa
4b. Position on a Chesterfield sofa

Left: Perfect loose covers

work with, especially if you are piping the seams. Medium weight cottons and linens treated for crease resistance are ideal but do not attempt to use dress fabrics as they are not strong enough.

Taking the measurements

Before buying the fabric and cutting out, the separate sections must be measured. Write all measurements down as they will be needed for calculating the amount of fabric to buy and again when cutting out the individual sections of fabric.

Remove the cushion or cushions if there are any and mark a line with glass headed pins up the centre of the outside back of the chair, down the inside back and long the seat from the back to the front border (fig.1).

Using a fabric tape measure, measure each section, including cushions, at its widest point (fig.2). If your particular chair or sofa sections are not pictured here, these should be measured following the same principle.

Outside back: from A to floor; from K to L.

Inside back: from A to B plus 15cm (6in) for tuck-in; from K to L.

Inside arm: from G to J plus 15cm (6in) for tuck-in; from P to O plus 15cm (6in) for tuck-in.

Outside arm: from G to H; from K to Q.

Seat: from B to C plus 15cm (6in) for tuck-in; from E to F plus 30.5cm (12in) for tuck-in.

Border: from C to D; from M to N.

Front arm; from Q to R; from S to T.

Cushion top: from X to Y; from Z to A1.

Cushion front inset: V to W; from A1 to U.

Cushion side inset: from A2 to V.

Fabric requirements

Most furnishing fabrics are 122cm (48in) wide and to cover a chair you will require about five times as much fabric as the height of the back. However, a more precise estimate is needed for each individual piece and this can be accomplished using the measurements just described.

Draw a small chart to scale on a sheet of paper or graph paper. (Large quantities of fabrics will be involved.)

Draw two parallel lines to scale to represent the width of the fabric. Use a simple ratio such as 1mm for every centimetre or $\frac{1}{10}$ in for every inch.

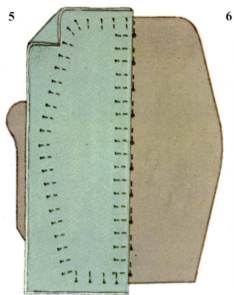
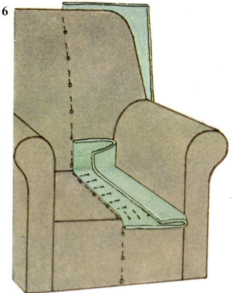

Using the measurements you have taken draw out rectangles to scale to represent each section needed for the cover, adding 2.5cm (1in) to each measurement for seam allowances (fig.3). Label each piece and mark the dimensions as you progress. Remember that some sections such as sides, arms and cushion parts have to be cut twice.

Extra allowances. Should the fabric you choose have a repeated design this will have to be taken into consideration and extra fabric bought. The quantity depends on the size of the design.

Allow an extra 1.40m (1½yd) for cutting bias strips if you intend to pipe a chair. Increase this estimate proportionately for a sofa.

Special allowances for sofas must be made for joins in the fabric if necessary to obtain the correct width (figs.4a and 4b). A repeated pattern must always match at the seams.

Extra fabric will also be needed should you want a frill or pleated finish to the bottom.

For a frill, you will need twice the circumference of the bottom of the chair by the depth of frill plus seam and hem allowance.

For a plain tailored skirt with a pleat at each corner you will need the circumference of chair or sofa plus 81.5cm (32in) by the depth of trim plus seam and hem allowance.

Having drawn all the pieces out to scale on paper, measure the total length and convert to full scale to find out the amount of fabric required.

Cutting the fabric

Following the chart you have made, mark out with chalk and cut a rectangle of fabric for each area to be covered. Make sure that the lengthwise grain of each piece runs with the grain of the fabric, and that the pattern, if any, matches. Be sure to add 1.5cm (½in) seams around each piece.

Fitting the cover

The method of fitting the fabric to the chair is to fold the rectangles of fabric in half with strong sides together and, working from the centre marked with pins, fit, pin and trim closely. The fabric is then opened out and the pieces stitched together inserting piping in the appropriate seams.

Starting with the outside back pieces fold in half and place the folded edge level with the pins down the back of the chair, the allowances made for turnings should project at the top, side and bottom. Pin down the fold then smooth the fabric out to the side of the chair and pin it to the padding, placing the pins at right angles to the edge of the fabric. Keep the fabric smooth and taut with the grain of the fabric straight in both directions (fig.5).

Pin the seat piece to centre of seat in the same way, so that the allowance for the tuck-in lies at the back and side and a

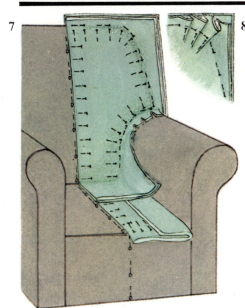

7

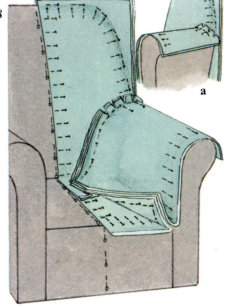

8
a

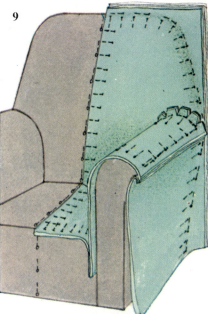

9

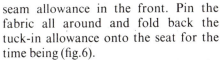

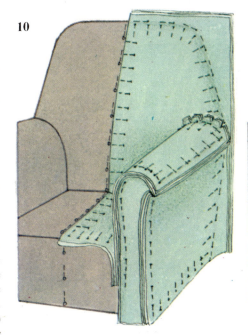

10

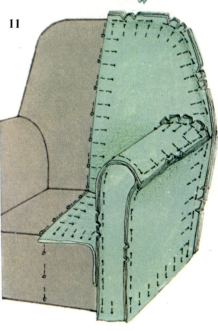

11

seam allowance in the front. Pin the fabric all around and fold back the tuck-in allowance onto the seat for the time being (fig.6).

Fold the inside back piece, pin it to the centre line, smooth it out and pin it to the padding as before. Then pin to the outside back piece at the top of the chair following the shape of the chair exactly.

With some fabrics you may be able to ease in the fullness. With others, such as linen on a curved back, you may have to make small darts at the corners.

Pin the pieces together down the sides working from the top down. As you reach the arm cut into the fabric from the sides so that the inside back can be wrapped around smoothly to join the back. Carefully cut the fabric over the arm to fit the curve and then extend gradually outwards to the full 15cm (6in) tuck-in allowance at the bottom of the section (fig.7). Clip into the seam allowance on the curve.

Fitting the arms

Place the two inside arm pieces together with wrong sides facing, then place them onto the inside arm. Pin the front edge to the padding first and the top to the 'sight line'. This is an imaginary line (fig.8a) where a seam must be made in loose covers and does not already exist in the upholstery. The seam allowance should overlap the front and the 'sight line'. Smooth to back of arm, with grain parallel to side of chair. Pin the bottom

edge to the tuck-in edge of the seat and cut the back edge of the arm to correspond with the inside back tuck-in. Clip the seam allowance over the top curve of the arm where necessary (fig.8).

Place the outside arm pieces together with wrong sides facing, keep the straight crosswise grain of the fabric parallel to the floor. Pin the top edge to the inside arm on the 'sight line'. At the very back of the arm where the padding is less rounded, more fabric may have to be pinned into the seam. Pin the back edge of the outside arm piece to the outside back, leave front edge free (fig.9).

5. *Outside back fabric is pinned into place, keeping it smooth and taut*
6. *Seat piece in position. Fold back the tuck-in allowance*
7. *Inside back pinned to outside back. Fit fabric carefully over the arm*
8. *Inside arm pinned and trimmed.*
8a. *Dotted line represents sight line*
9. *Outside arm pinned at top and back. The front edge is left free*
10. *Arm front in the correct place. Follow the shape of the chair.*
11. *Seam allowance trimmed and clipped with notches in groups of two and three on corresponding seams*

Fitting the arm fronts

Position both front arm pieces together, wrong sides facing, to the widest part of the arm front and pin carefully to the outside arm piece following the shape of the chair as closely as possible. Continue pinning to the inside arm as far as the end of the tuck-in (fig.10).

The front panel or border. This cannot be cut until after the other pieces have been cut and all the main seams have been stitched and tuck-in positioned correctly.

Trimming the seam allowance

If you are satisfied with the fit of the cover so far, trim all the turnings exactly to within 1.5cm ($\frac{1}{2}$in) of the pinned fitting lines. Cut notches in the corresponding seams in groups of two and three, so that you will be able to fit the pieces together again (fig.11).

Remove all the pins, take the sections off the chair and open them out.

Piping

Piping has several advantages. It gives a stronger seam and a more professional finish. If you are not confident of stitching very straight seams piping will hide minor inaccuracies.

Bias strips

A quick way to cut the bias strips and make up piping is as follows:

Above: A wing chair

Right: Arm chair with cushions

1 FOLD

2

3

Take a rectangle of fabric about 23cm (9in) by 45.5cm (18in). The length of the strip should be at least twice the width.

Fold up the bottom right-hand corner to obtain the crossways grain (fig.1). Cut off this corner and join to other edge with right sides facing and 6mm ($\frac{1}{4}$in) seam (fig.2).

Press the seam open and trim off any

4 5mm ($\frac{1}{4}$in) seam allowance A

B

5

6

selvedges (fig.3).

Make a ruler in card to the width of the piping strips. In soft furnishing the width is usually 4cm (1$\frac{1}{2}$in) wide.

Using the ruler and tailor's chalk mark lines on the right side of the fabric, parallel to the ends. Then mark a 6mm ($\frac{1}{4}$in) seam allowance along each side. Mark points A and B as shown (fig.4). Stick a pin through the wrong side of fabric at point A and bring it across through point B. Pin the two sides together very accurately, right sides facing.

Continue pinning along the marked seam to make a sort of cylinder. Tack, and check that the horizontal lines meet exactly. Stitch then press seam open using a sleeve board (fig.5).

Turn to the right side and start cutting along the horizontal lines (fig.6).

Piping cord

Use piping cord No.3 or 4. As piping cord shrinks when washed boil and dry the cord twice before making up.

212

Completing loose covers

In the previous chapter instructions for cutting out a loose cover are given, and here the loose cover is stitched and completed.

Piping

Piping will give a neat, well defined edge and at the same time strengthen the seams of covers to provide greater durability. First measure all edges of the chair which will be piped. Include the edges of cushions, and the base of the chair if it is to be piped as well.

Buy piping cord in one long length as joins in the cord are to be avoided.

Make up lengths of piping by enclosing the piping cord in the bias strips. Use Number 3 or 4 piping cord or check with your fabric retailer.

Attaching piping. Pin and tack the piping on the right side of the fabric sections shown (fig.1). Make sure raw edges are together. These include the top and sides of the outside back, the front arms and the top edges or 'sight line' of the outside arms. The front border will be cut and piped later.

Stitching and pressing

You are now ready to assemble the cover. You will find that a neat and crisp finish will be easier to achieve if you press seams as you work.

Remember to take 1.5cm ($\frac{1}{2}$in) turnings throughout and before stitching the sections together always pin and tack them first.

1. Piping tacked to the outside back, top of outside arm and front arm

outside back

front arm

outside arm

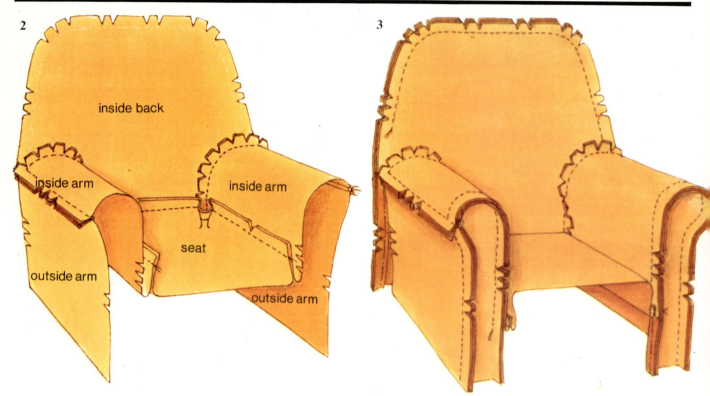

2

inside back

inside arm

inside arm

outside arm

seat

outside arm

3

Stitch all seams with right sides facing and neaten the raw edges by stitching them together with a zig-zag stitch, or oversew by hand. Press all seams away from the front of the chair.

First tack and stitch the tuck-in seam at the back of the seat and the bottom of the inside back. This is an unpiped seam. Next stitch the outside arms to the inside arms stitching the piping into the seam.

Stitch the bottom of the inside arms to the sides of the seat tuck-in, then stitch the arm to the inside back. (This seam is not piped.) Fig.2 shows seams stitched together thus far.

Stitch the outside and inside back together along the top and down one side, then stitch the other side to about 10cm (4in) above the top of the arm, leaving an opening so that the cover can be fitted onto the chair. The length of the opening depends on the shape of the chair as you must be able to slip the cover on easily. This is a piped seam.

Stitch the front arm pieces in place. Stitch from the outside arm inwards and finish at the tuck-in on the inside arm (fig.3).

Fitting the front border. Put the cover onto the chair right side out. Tuck in the sides and back tuck-in pieces, and leave the seam allowance protruding at the front edge. It is at this stage that you will

be able to decide how long the back opening should be.

Place the front border in position (fig.4). Pin it to the front of the seat cover and to the seam allowance of the tuck-in at both sides and to the lower front arms wrong side facing. Trim the seam allowance to 1.5cm ($\frac{1}{2}$in), mark position with notches and remove the cover from the chair.

Unpin the front border and insert piping along the seam line of the top edge from tuck-in to tuck-in (A to B in fig.4). Pin together, right sides facing. Tack and stitch the front border into position. The piping will run from A to B along the front of the seat and below A and B on the front arms.

Back opening

The opening down the back of the cover can be finished with a zip fastener, hooks and eyes or press studs – they are all equally suitable.

Strong upholstery zips are available and furnishing tape with large press studs or hooks and eyes already inserted can be bought by the metre (yard). If the chair or sofa has a very curved back, separate hooks sewn on by hand with hand worked bars will give a neater finish. It depends upon the finish at the bottom of the chair how long the zip or tape

2. Sections stitched together
3. Openings left for zip or tape
4. Pin front border to seat and arms
5a. The back opening here is fastened with a special furnishing zip
5b. Tape which has been already fitted with studs stitched into opening
5c. Special tape fitted with hooks and bars stitched into the opening
5d. The opening on a very curved chair back with hand-sewn hooks and bars.

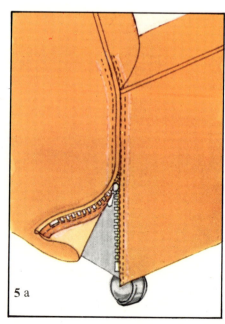

5 a

4

opening.

With the two pieces of tape fastened together, pin the tape into the opening making sure there is a stud or hook just above the bottom of the chair. One edge of each tape should be on the seam line. Now open the tape and tack and stitch each tape into position. The back tape is stitched on both sides flat against the back but the tape attached to the side bends around to the back of the chair. Stitch side tape close to the seam line. Work another row of stitching on the tape 5mm ($\frac{1}{4}$in) from the first (fig.5b and c).

With the tape fastened neaten the top raw ends of the tape and stitch together. Hooks and hand worked bars on plain tape. If the back of the cover is very curved it will be neater to use this method. The tape is attached to the cover in the same way as tape with hooks and eyes or studs. Hooks are then stitched on at about 5cm (2in) intervals and bars worked by hand in strong thread to correspond with the hooks. On some curves it will be necessary to place the hooks and bars closer together so that the opening does not gape (fig.5d).

Box cushion. To cover a box cushion see page 160. Make both sides alike so that it is reversible.

Finishing the bottom

There are a number of ways to finish the bottom of a loose cover depending upon

should be. Take the zip or tape to the planned bottom seam line.

Fitting a zip fastener. Measure the length required. The zip should not come to the bottom corner as the zip pull may protrude.

Clip the front seam allowance at the top of the opening. Press the seam allowance on both edges to the wrong side and tack on the folds.

Place the closed zip to the cover with the

right side of the zip to the inside of the cover, and the open end down. From the right side tack the zip into place close to the teeth of the zip. The piping cord will be over the teeth.

Using a piping foot, machine stitch close to the teeth and again near the outside of the tape to add strength and prevent the zip tape catching in the zip (fig.5a).

Tape with press studs or hooks. Clip the front seam allowance at the top of the

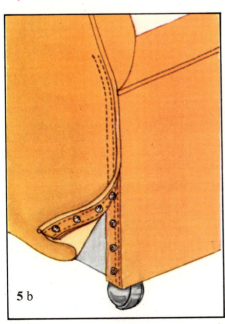

5 b

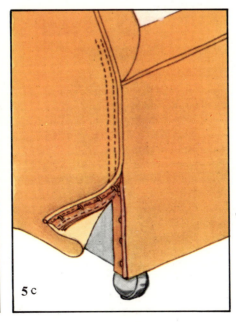

5 c

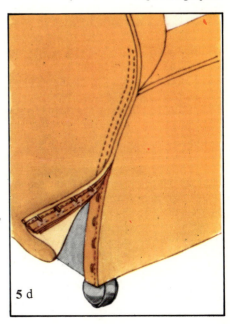

5 d

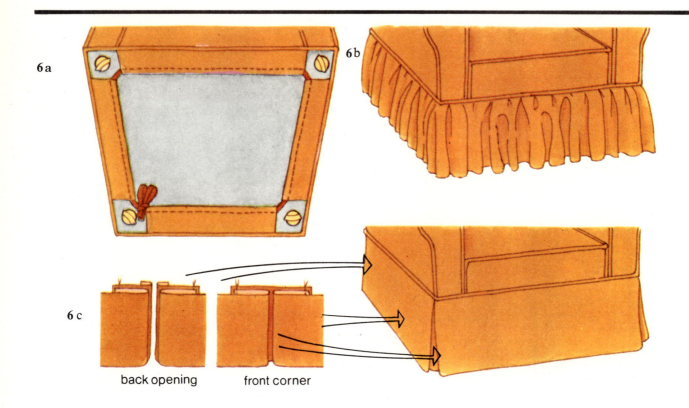

6a *Piped finish to bottom of chair*
6b *Frilled finish attached with tapes*
6c *Plain finish with box pleats*

the style of the chair or sofa and your own personal taste.

A plain finish can either be piped or left plain. It consists of strips of fabric fitted under the chair between the legs, with a narrow hem forming a channel (fig.6a). It is not difficult to do.

If the bottom is to be piped attach the piping to the loose cover with raw edges together and tack into place before proceeding.

Cut four strips of fabric about 10cm (4in) wide and the correct length to fit between the legs.

Make a narrow hem at the ends of each piece and a channel 1.5cm ($\frac{1}{2}$in) wide along one long side to hold the tape.

Stitch the raw edges of the strips to the bottom of the cover, sandwiching any piping in between. Neaten the raw edges and press up onto the cover.

Insert a long piece of tape through the channel. Place the cover on the chair and tie the tape in one corner.

For a frilled finish (fig.6b), decide upon depth of frill required and add 1.5cm 1.5cm ($\frac{1}{2}$in) for seam allowances at the top and 2.5cm (1in) for a small hem.

Measure around the bottom of the chair and double this measurement. This will be the length of frill required.

Cut fabric into strips the required depth

and join the strips to obtain the right length taking 1.5cm ($\frac{1}{2}$in) turnings. Clip the selvedges and press the seam open.

Make a small hem along the bottom of the frill by turning up 2.5cm (1in). Make a small hem on the short ends for the opening in the same way, mitring the corners.

Divide the frill into four equal sections and mark with pins. Run a gathering thread between the pins. The open end will go to the back opening.

With the cover on the chair mark the position of the stitching line for the frill with pins, measuring from the floor. Trim the cover to 1.5cm ($\frac{1}{2}$in) below the pins and pipe the bottom of the cover.

Divide the measurement around the piped edge of the cover by four and mark with pins.

Take the cover off the chair. Draw up the gathers on the frill and with right sides and raw edges together matching the pins, pin and tack the frill to the cover, distributing the gathers evenly. Stitch and press up, neaten the raw edges together.

A plain tailored finish can be attractive. To make the skirting, a border of fabric is placed around the chair or sofa with a pleat at each corner (fig.6c). Measure the bottom front, back and sides of the

chair or sofa, and add 10cm (4in) to each measurement.

Cut strips of fabric to these lengths and to the depth of border required plus seam and hem allowance; mark each piece. Cut these strips 10cm (4in) by the depth of the border and two strips 6.5cm (2$\frac{1}{2}$in) by the depth of the border, These are for the corners.

With the cover on the chair mark the depth of border required with pins and trim the cover to 1.5cm ($\frac{1}{2}$in) below the pin line. Pipe the edge all around the bottom of the cover.

Join the border pieces together placing a short piece to each corner and the two very short pieces to the back opening. Take 1.5cm ($\frac{1}{2}$in) turnings. Clip the seam allowance and press open.

Make a small hem along the bottom and turn in 1.5cm ($\frac{1}{2}$in) at the ends. Neaten and press.

From the right side make a 4cm (1$\frac{1}{2}$in) inverted pleat at each corner and tack. The seams will sit inside each pleat.

Tack and stitch the border to the cover with right sides together, sandwiching the piping, neaten and press up.

LAMPSHADES

Nothing reveals more about your personality and life-
style than your home. Yet those individualistic touches
such as lampshades can be surprisingly expensive. Also,
it can be very difficult and time-consuming, if not quite
impossible, to find exactly the lampshade that fits in
with your decor. Sometimes it's a matter of making sure
that you use a certain fabric, or else combining a special
style with a particular colourway. The following
projects give you a gratifying range of choices, from
Tiffany to classically shaped shades. The instructions
are very easy to follow, so that even if you've never
made a lampshade before, you'll achieve super results.

Basic techniques

Fabric lampshades can be made in many shapes and sizes but in most cases the basic techniques involved are the same and once you have learned how to make one shape you can easily go on to make the others.

The frame

The frame forms the structure of every type of lampshade. Frames are available in several different styles and sizes with various fittings for attaching them to the lamp. They are made from tinned or copper wire and joined by spot welding or – on better made frames – by soldering.

Each frame consists of two rings, one of which contains the fitting for attaching the lampshade to the base. The rings are joined by struts or staves, which may be curved or straight. The relative diameters of the rings and the length of the struts determine the size of the lampshade and the shape of the rings and the struts governs its shape. The most common shapes available are shown below. When you buy your frame, check that the struts are evenly spaced and firmly fixed to the rings and their shape has not become distorted by storage. If you cannot find the shape and size of frame you want ready made, some lampshade-frame suppliers will make a frame.

The fitting

Frames are made with a variety of fittings and you should choose the correct one for your purpose.

Pendant fitting (fig.1) is used for hanging shades. It consists of a small ring held by two or three arms which are joined to opposite sides of the top ring. The small ring fits onto the lampholder (this is the fitting which holds the bulb and has a small ring which is unscrewed so that the lampshade can be put on). Some frames are fitted with a dropped pendant (fig.2) which ensures that the lampholder is hidden. Some straight drum frames have this type of fitting so that the frame can be used with the pendant at the bottom for a table lamp.

Duplex fitting (fig.3) is designed for standard lamps or big table lamps. It consists of an inner ring of about 10cm (4in) diameter which is attached to the top ring by four arms and positioned 7.5cm (3in) below the top ring. The inner ring sits on a separate shade carrier (fig.3a) which is screwed to the lampholder. Shade carriers are available in different heights and you should choose one which will position the shade so that the bulb is in the middle of it.

Butterfly clip fitting (fig.4) is used on small shades for wall fittings or multiple ceiling fittings as well as small table lamps. The clip fits over the bulb.

The fabric

Most medium to lightweight natural-fibre fabrics can be used to make lampshades, although for those styles which are fitted on the bias or cross of the fabric some printed fabrics with a definite design – such as flowers with stems – may not be suitable.

Choose the fabric initially to suit the decorative scheme of your room but bear in mind the fact that some colours change when seen under artificial light or they may vary the type of light which the shade will give. Dark colours, for example, tend to absorb the light whereas pale colours reflect it and allow the light to pass through. Lining a dark colour with a white, pink or beige fabric will help to give more light. If possible hold your chosen fabric with the lining over a switched-on bulb to get an idea of the effect before you buy it.

Silk is the traditional fabric for lampshade-making and although it is the most expensive of the fabrics you might choose, it is worth the extra cost because it is pliable and easy to fit, it does not sag or split easily, it washes well and does not shrink. Most kinds of pure silk can be used and there are some imitation silks, such as taiho and dupion, which are also suitable.

Most lampshade frame suppliers have a selection of suitable silks but you may find a wider selection among dress fabrics. Beware of using furnishing fabrics which are stiff and do not have much give.

Cottons of all kinds can be used for most styles of lampshade, although you may be restricted to frames with straight struts if you choose a design which cannot be used on the bias.

Linens are normally too firmly woven to be good for lampshades and they are difficult to fit smoothly and may not allow much light to pass through. Some of the finer embroidery linens, however, may be used for drum or panelled shades, particularly where a lace effect has been worked, perhaps by drawn or pulled thread work.

Man-made fabrics such as nylon or polyester are not usually suitable be-

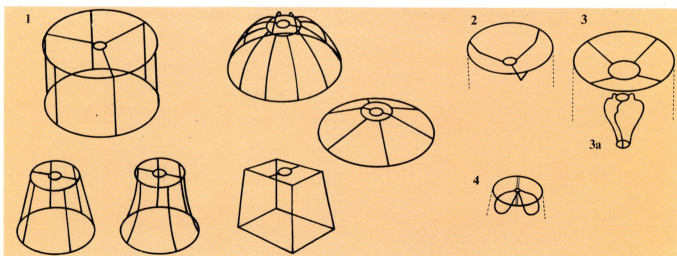

cause they tend to shrink or sag and some weights split.

Fabric requirements
For a tailored cover on frames with straight struts, such as the drum or the straight empire, the fabric is fitted on the straight of the grain. Measure half the circumference of the bottom ring of the frame (or its widest measurement) between two struts on opposite sides and then measure the height of the frame (fig.5). Allow enough fabric to cut two rectangles to these measurements plus about 7.5cm (3in) all around for fitting. For frames with curved or bowed struts, such as the bowed empire, the fabric is fitted on the bias. Measure the frame diagonally between struts on opposite sides of the frame from the top ring to the bottom ring (fig.6). Allow enough fabric to cut two squares of the fabric along the grain to this measurement plus about 7.5cm (3in) for fitting.

For a panelled cover measure the width of each panel across the widest part and then measure the height. Allow enough fabric to cut a rectangle on the straight of grain to these measurements plus about 7.5cm (3in) all around for fitting (fig.7).

Covering methods
There are three main methods of making the cover for a fabric shade.

A semi-fitted cover is the simplest fitted and also the quickest. The cover is made to fit the widest part of the frame and is gathered or pleated to reduce the fullness on either or both rings if they are narrower than the widest part.

Use balloon shades for Tiffanys (like a Tiffany, but spherical) and any type of frame with straight struts.

A panelled cover requires some skill in achieving a smooth finish. The fabric for each section is fitted and stitched to the frame individually and the stitching on the struts is neatened by a trimming. It is the only method where the cover is stitched to the struts as well as the rings. Use for square shades, bowed drums and straight empire shades. It is also a good method if you want to incorporate panels of embroidery or appliqué.

Fully fitted or tailored covers require more skill and time. The cover is made to fit the frame tightly all over so that the finished lampshade is smooth and taut. With the exception of the drum shape, this is normally achieved by using the fabric on the bias although some pliable fabrics can be used on the straight grain. The cover is normally made in two halves, one for each side of the frame. The seams joining the halves should be placed exactly over the struts of the frame.

Use for all styles of shade with circular rings.

The trimming
The trimming is the finishing touch of all lampshades and is fitted around the rings to hide the stitching and raw edges of the fabrics.

You can fit braid to both rings or you could fit the braid to the top ring only and use a co-ordinating fringe for the bottom ring.

Suppliers of lampshade materials have large selections of trimmings and it is preferable to use these rather than furnishing trimmings.

For a more tailored finish you could use velvet ribbon in a colour to match your fabric or you could make your own trimming from spare pieces of bias fabric to match your cover.

To calculate how much trimming to buy, measure the circumference of the rings and add on 2.5cm (1in).

Tools
You do not need any specialized tools for lampshade-making and those you do need you probably have already. Scissors with sharp blades, for cutting the fabric and trimming the edges.

Pins – use rustless steel dressmaker's pins or the glass-headed type for fitting the cover. Lills pins are useful when stitching the fabric to the frame as they are less likely to scratch you.

Sewing thread to match your cover fabric.

Needles. 'Betweens' needles are ideal because they are short and stiff and unlikely to bend or break when they touch the frame.

Clear, non-staining contact adhesive for finishing seams and for attaching the trimming.

Washing lampshades
Using a soft brush, carefully remove any dust, and then dip the shade into warm, soapy water. Rinse the shade in clean water, and leave it to dry

1-7. Frames are sold in a variety of shapes, with appropriate fittings to match.

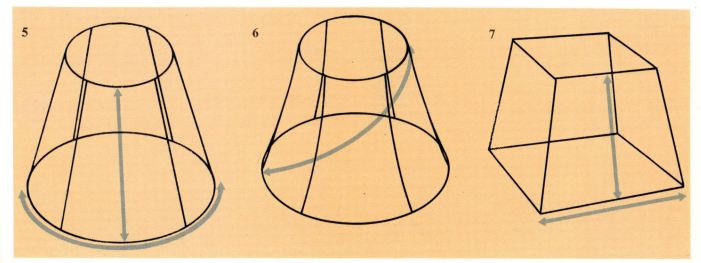

5   6   7

Tiffany lampshade

Careful preparation of the frame is essential for lampshade making because it determines the final appearance and long-lasting wear of the shade. The preparation is done in two stages: cleaning and painting the frame to ensure that it does not tear the fabric and stain it through rusting when the lampshade is washed, and binding it with tape to give a foundation to which the fabric can be pinned and stitched.

1. Starting to bind the rings so that the end of the tape is completely covered and secured firmly.

2. Wrapping the tape around the ring an extra time before each strut

3. Starting to bind the struts by looping the end of the tape around the T-joint at the top

4. Finish off at the foot of struts by wrapping around the ring on both sides and putting the ends through

To prepare the frame

You will need

Metal file, steel wool, old newspapers. Paint in white or to match your cover fabric. Use a quick-drying cellulose paint (such as is sold for touching up car bodywork) or an enamel (such as used for painting models).

Small soft brush.

White cotton tape, 1.5cm ($\frac{1}{2}$in) wide. Use a loosely-woven tape sold for the purpose (this can be dyed to match your cover fabric). You can use bias binding (with one crease opened out) but it is not recommended because its edges tend to fray and it is more bulky han the special tape.

Needle and sewing thread to match the binding.

Examine the frame carefully and use the file to remove any sharp points where the struts are joined to the rings. Clean the frame by rubbing with the steel wool. Stand the frame on newspaper and paint it. You may have to do this in two or more stages so that you can reach all sides of the rings without smudging. The paint is usually touch dry quite quickly but leave the frame for 24 hours so that it can harden before you bind it.

Binding the frame. This is the most important stage of the preparation. The binding must be very tight or it will slip and the fabric will not be tautly stretched over the frame however much time you spend on the fitting. For most styles of lampshade the rings and two struts, on opposite sides of the frame, are bound so that the fabric can be pinned and fitted onto them.

The binding on the struts is then removed because it is no longer needed but it is kept on the rings so that the cover can be stitched in place. This is a modern development of lampshade making: traditionally all the struts were bound and the binding remained on the finished lampshade, which sometimes had the disadvantage of showing through as ridges.

The main exceptions to this are square and other panelled styles where the fabric is fitted and stitched to each side of the frame individually, in which case all the struts are bound before the rings. To bind the top ring cut a piece of tape equal to twice the length of the circumference. Place one end of the tape under the ring at the top of a strut, bring the tape over the joint and bind over the end of the tape. Continue binding the ring as tightly as possible, keeping the tape at an acute angle and overlapping the previous wrap slightly (fig.1).

At each strut, wrap the binding around the ring an extra time before you reach the strut and then go on to the next section on the other side of the strut (fig.2). To finish, stitch down the end of the tape on the outside of the ring.

Turn the frame upside down and bind the bottom ring in the same way.

To bind the struts, cut a piece of tape twice the length. Start at the top and loop the end around the T-joint (fig.3). Bind over the end and continue winding tightly down the strut. Finish by winding around the ring on both sides of the

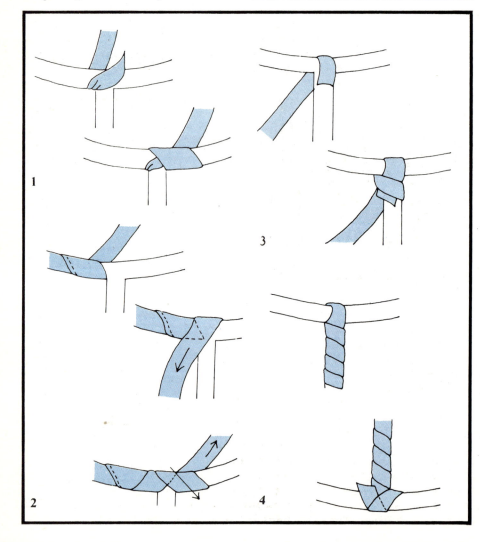

strut and pull the end through a previous loop (fig.4). There is no need to trim off the excess tape unless the binding is to remain on the finished lampshade.

Easy Tiffany cover
One of the easiest and quickest ways of covering a Tiffany frame is to make a detachable cover. This method has the extra advantage in that the cover can easily be removed for washing, and you do not need to bind the frame because the cover is not fitted or stitched directly to it. It is, however, advisable to paint the frame. If you don't want the paint to show, use plain white.

To assess fabric, measure the frame at its widest part (this is not necessarily the bottom ring). If the measurement is less than the width of the fabric, the cover can be made in one piece. If it is

Above: Broderie anglaise makes a pretty cover for Tiffany lampshade. When you are cutting the trimming, place the edge along the scalloped selvedge of the fabric to give a neat finish. The effect is very feminine.

more, the cover should be made in two halves.
Measure the length of the struts and add 9cm ($3\frac{1}{2}$in). If you are making the cover from one piece of fabric, allow enough to cut one piece along the grain to the length of the struts plus 9cm ($3\frac{1}{2}$in) × the measurement of the circumference of the widest part plus 2.5cm (1in). If

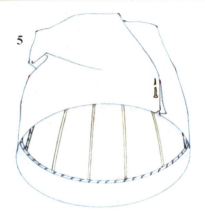

5

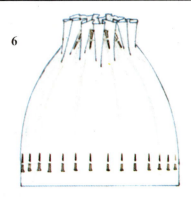

6

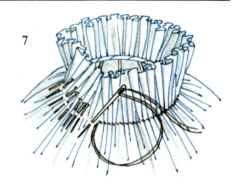

7

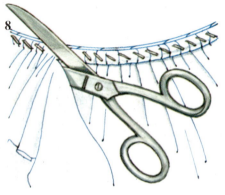

8

you are making it in two halves, allow enough to cut two pieces along the grain to the length of the struts plus 9cm (3½in) × the measurement of half the circumference plus 2.5cm (1in). If you are making a scalloped fabric trimming. allow enough to cut a strip of the measurement of the circumference of the bottom ring plus 2.5cm (1in) × 13cm (5in).

Start as if you were making a semi-fitted cover and join the fabric so that it fits the widest part of the frame.

Fold over 6mm (¼in) onto the wrong side along both the edges of the fabric and press. Fold over 1.5cm (½in) again to make casings and tack and machine stitch, leaving openings in the stitching of about 1.5cm (½in)

Pin and machine stitch the trimming 2.5cm (1in) above the lower edge of the cover (if you have a scalloped trimming, fold under the raw edges and topstitch them to the cover as in fig.11 – it is not necessary to use ribbon to cover the stitching).

Thread the elastic through the casing along the lower edge of the cover, draw up the elastic and pin the ends together. Thread the tape through the casing along the upper edge of the cover.

Place the cover on the frame so that the trimming is positioned on the lower ring. Draw up the elastic tightly to draw the margin of fabric under the frame. Pin and stitch the elastic at the required place and trim off the excess. Arrange the gathers of fabric neatly.

Arrange the fabric neatly on the frame at the top and draw up the tape so that the cover is firmly held over the frame making sure the trimming is still correctly positioned. Tie the tape neatly and trim off the excess length. Stitch up the openings in the casings.

Tiffany lampshades

These are the simplest kinds of lampshade to cover because they do not require the elaborate fitting of a fully tailored style.

The frame is traditionally bow-shaped and has twelve struts. The cover is semi-fitted so that it fits the bottom tightly but is gathered to fit the much narrower top, and it looks prettiest in a light cotton or broderie anglaise fabric. It is often trimmed with a heavy fringe which gives it its distinctive character, or a scalloped or lace trimming could be added for a lighter effect.

You will need
Prepared frame
Fabric (for the amount see above).
Sewing thread
Trimming (see below)

Fitting the cover. Cut out the fabric to the measurements given. If you are using one piece, fold it in half with the shorter edges together and mark the fold with tacking. If you are using two pieces join them using one of the methods given below.

Place the fabric with the right side facing out onto the frame so that the seam or line of tacking is level with one of the bound struts. Centre the fabric on the length of the strut so that 4.5cm (1¾in) extends at the top and bottom. Pin the seam or tacking line to the bound strut in one or two places in the middle.

Wrap the fabric around the frame and pin the edges together in line with the opposite bound strut so that the cover fits tightly at the widest part of the frame but does not distort the fabric (fig.4). Remove the fabric from the frame and tack along the straight grain

level with the pin.

Joining the fabric. The fabric may be joined in one of three ways, depending on your own preference and the fabric you are using.

The two main methods are either to use a plain seam and trim the turnings to 3mm (⅛in) and finish the edge by oversewing or a machine zig-zag stitch; or you could use a French seam. Alternatively, if you are using broderie anglaise with a scalloped edge, you could overlap the scalloped edge over the plain edge by 6mm (¼in), join and machine stitch.

Stitching fabric to frame

Place the cover on the frame as before, with the right side facing out, and pin it to the binding along the bottom ring. Place the pins so that the points face into the body of the lampshade so that you are less likely to scratch yourself. Smooth cover up the line of the struts, keeping the grain straight, and pin at the top of each strut.

Fold away the fullness between the struts into tiny pleats and pin them. Repeat along the bottom ring if this is narrower than the widest part of the frame (fig.6).

Start stitching the fabric to the binding on the outside of the rings using a small

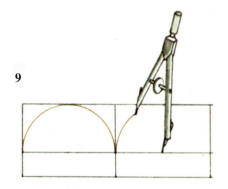

9

10

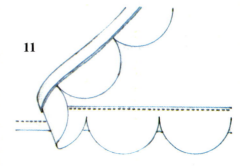

11

5. In order to fit the fabric neatly, first pin it around the frame
6. Gather the fullness into pleats and pin into place
7. Stitch fabric around the top ring, removing pins as you proceed
8. Turn surplus fabric back over and trim after stitching
9. Drawing the scallop pattern
10. Tacking pattern to the fabric
11. Top stitching the edging.

oversewing or hemming stitch. Work in a clockwise direction around the ring, making sure that you catch the gathers firmly in position. Use double thread and begin and fasten off securely, using several small back stitches (fig.7).
Turn the surplus fabric back over the stitching so that the fold is level with the edge of the rings, and stitch through all thicknesses. Trim surplus fabric close to

Scalloped edging

You will need
Fabric, 13cm (5in) wide, the measurement of the circumference of the bottom ring plus 2.5cm (1in)
Strip of paper, 10cm (4in) wide, the measurement of the circumference of the bottom ring
Compasses, ruler, pencil
Velvet ribbon, the measurement of the circumference of both rings plus 1.5cm ($\frac{1}{2}$in) for turnings
Clear adhesive

stitching (fig.8). To finish, see scalloped or fringe edging for alternative ideas. Both look very attractive.

Cutting out scallops
Measure the distance between the struts

on the bottom ring and divide the paper into sections of this measurement. Draw another line half this measurement away from one long-edge of the paper.
Using a radius of the same half measurement, place the point of the compasses on the long line in the centre of each division and draw a semi-circle (fig.9). Repeat along the length of the paper.
Place the fabric strip around the bottom ring with the wrong side facing out and pin the short edges together so that the strip fits the ring exactly. Remove the strip and machine stitch along this line. Press the turnings open.
Fold the circle of fabric along the length to make it 6.5cm (2$\frac{1}{2}$in) deep with the wrong side facing out. Place on the paper pattern so that the edge with the curves is 6mm ($\frac{1}{4}$in) from the fold and the short edges of the paper meet on the seam line. Tack to the fabric along each edge (fig.10).
Machine stitch along the curves through all thicknesses, following the drawn line. Tear away the paper carefully and trim the fabric to within 3mm ($\frac{1}{8}$in) of the stitching. Clip into the angle between each scallop.
Turn right side out and tack along the curved edge so that the seam is exactly on the edge. Press.
Place the trimming onto the lampshade so that the raw edges are in line with the turned-up edges of the cover. Stitch in the same way as the cover.
Fold under one edge of the ribbon for 6mm ($\frac{1}{4}$in) and place in line with the seam of the cover so that it covers the raw edge and stitching of the trimming. Smear some adhesive along the underside of the ribbon and smooth the ribbon down onto the ring, keeping it as straight as possible. At the end, fold under to meet the first fold and press

firmly to make sure that it is securely fixed.
Place the ribbon around the top ring to cover the raw edges and stitch in the same way, keeping it as straight as possible and smoothing it around the top ring firmly.

Fringe edging

You will need
Fringe, the measurement of the circumference of the bottom ring plus 1.5cm ($\frac{1}{2}$in) for turnings.
Co-ordinating braid, the measurement of the circumference of the top ring, plus 1.5cm ($\frac{1}{2}$in) for turnings.
Clear adhesive.

Fold under one end of the fringe for 6mm ($\frac{1}{4}$in) and stick down with a spot of adhesive. Place the fold onto the bottom ring so that it is level with a seam and the top edge of the fringed section is level with the edge of the ring. The braided or solid section along the top edge of the fringe must cover the binding on the ring, the raw edges and stitching of the fabric.
Apply adhesive for about 10cm (4in) along the underside of the braided section and place it in position on the ring, stretching it slightly. Secure with a pin. Apply adhesive to the next 10cm (4in) and stick down as before. Keep checking that the braid is level with the rings as you progress. When you reach the other end, fold it under to meet the first fold exactly and stick down. Secure with a pin.
The braid is attached to the top ring in a similar way but the outer edge should be pinched up slightly with your fingers so that the inner edge will lie flat.

Lined lampshades

The cover for tailored, lined lampshades is made in two sections, one for each half of the frame. One of the sections is fitted and shaped on the frame itself and then used as a template for the other section. The pieces are then seamed together and the whole cover replaced on the frame and stitched to the rings.

Usually you have a choice of whether to fit the cover on the straight or bias grain. Of the two methods, fitting on the bias is easier because the fabric is more pliable, but it is more wasteful and some patterns do not look right when used this way.

Straight drum shapes should always be fitted on the straight grain because it helps to maintain the correct shape. Very waisted shapes – where the circumference is less in the middle of the frame than at the top – must be fitted on the bias grain so that the fabric will be stretched at the top ring when it is replaced on the frame.

The fabric for the lining can be cut on the bias grain but if you use a pliable fabric, such as crêpe-backed satin, it can easily be fitted on the straight grain which is less wasteful. For estimating the amount of fabric see page 219.

The lining

This type of lampshade should always be fitted with an internal lining which hides the struts and gives it a professional finish. Internal linings are known as balloon linings because although they are fitted on to the outside of the frame, in the same way as the cover, when they are stitched in place inside the frame they 'balloon' away from the struts.

Fitting the cover

In order to achieve a really smooth, taut cover, take good care with the fitting. It is essential to keep the grain of the fabric straight without distortion and to place the seams exactly over the struts of the frame.

Fold one of the fabric squares in half diagonally with the wrong side facing out and press the fold lightly with your fingers at each end.

Place the frame on your work surface with the bottom ring facing you and the two bound struts to the left and right. Place the fabric on to the frame so that the fold is level with the centre of the top

half: if the frame has eight struts, place the fabric onto it so that the fold is in line with the centre strut (fig.1); if the frame has six struts, place the fabric onto it so that the fold is in the centre of the two top struts.

Open out the fabric, keeping the fold in line with the centre strut or in the centre of the two top struts. Pin it to the rings at the top and bottom of the crease, keeping it taut but without stretching it. Smooth the fabric out to the bound struts with your fingers to mould it to the shape of the frame. Pin it to the tops and bottoms of the bound struts, so that the pin points are facing in.

Place more pins at about 1.5cm ($\frac{1}{2}$in) intervals down the left-hand strut, easing out any fullness in the fabric. Place the pins at right-angles to the strut with the points facing in. Starting at the top of the left-hand strut, follow the grain line of the fabric diagonally across the frame. Keeping the line completely straight and tight, pin it where it meets the right-hand strut or the bottom ring (fig.2).

Go back to the next pin down on the left-hand strut and follow the grain down in the same way. Tighten the fabric and pin. Continue in this way, pinning and tightening the fabric away from the left-hand strut diagonally across to where it naturally falls on either the right-hand strut, or the bottom ring (fig.2a).

Working upwards along the grain in the opposite direction, tighten the fabric from the left-hand strut to the top ring and pin at the top of the intermediate (unbound) struts (fig.3). Remove the pin at the top of the right-hand strut, tighten the fabric in the same way and replace the pin.

Complete the pinning down the right-hand strut and along the remaining part of the bottom ring, smoothing out any remaining fullness or wrinkles with your finger by running it in the direction of the grain. Never run your finger along the bias grain or you will distort the fabric and possibly stretch it.

Using a pencil, lightly draw down the fabric in between the pins over the outer bound struts. Draw lines about 1.5cm ($\frac{1}{2}$in) long inwards from the bound struts along the top and bottom rings. Mark a dot on the rings at the top and bottom of each intermediate strut.

Remove all the pins and remove the fabric from the frame.

Marking the second section. Place the marked section onto the second section with right sides together so that the edges are level and the grain, pattern or slub is running in the same direction on both pieces. Pin the sections together along the pencilled strut lines. Work tailor's tacks at the outer ends of the short pencil lines and at each dot.

Cut around the shape adding about 4cm (1$\frac{1}{2}$in) all around.

Machine stitch the pieces together down the pencilled strut lines and fasten off securely.

Cut through the tailor's tacks and open out the fabric. Press the turnings open lightly with your fingers. Spread adhesive along the turnings, press the turnings together so that they adhere and trim to within 3mm ($\frac{1}{8}$in) of the stitching.

Put the cover to one side while you fit the lining.

Fitting the lining

Fold one of the lining pieces in half lengthwise along the straight grain and crease the ends of the fold lightly with your fingers. Open out the fabric and place with wrong side facing upwards (with crêpe-backed satin this is usually the crêpe side) onto the frame so that the crease is level with the centre of the frame. Pin the fabric at each end of the crease to the rings and then smooth out to the side struts and pin at the tops and bottoms. Do not overtighten at these points or the fabric will not keep to the shape of the frame.

Pin the fabric halfway down the left-hand strut. Tighten along the grain and pin halfway down the right-hand strut. Working up from these points, pin up to the top ring, tightening the fabric horizontally by pulling from the left and right, and working first on one strut and then on the other (fig.4). Work downwards to the bottom ring in the same way.

When the sides are pinned, pin the fabric to the rings, tightening only enough to remove any wrinkles. Check that the grain line is completely square and avoid overtightening vertically or you will lose the shape.

Mark the fabric as for the main fabric and remove from the frame.

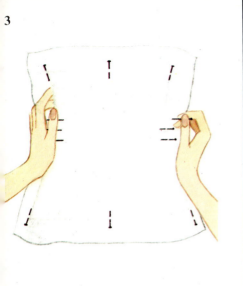

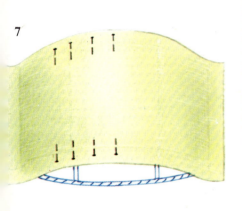

3

7

1. *Placing the fabric on the frame*
2. *Following the grain line across*
2a. *Tightening the fabric along the grain onto the bottom edge*
3. *Tightening the fabric along the grain up to the top ring*
4. *Tightening the lining horizontally between the struts*
5. *Tacking the curved stitching line to form the balloon lining*
6. *Stitching the cover to the rings*
7. *Slitting the lining to fit around*
8. *Stitching the lining to the outside*
9. *Pinning the fabric strip to hide the slits in the lining*
10. *Tightening the cover vertically*

Mark the second section of the lining in the same way and stitch the two pieces together down the sides so that the stitching starts 3mm ($\frac{1}{8}$in) in from the marked line at the top and bottom and curves in to about 1cm ($\frac{3}{8}$in) from the line in the middle (fig.5). This forms the balloon shape of the lining.
Finish as for the cover.
Remove the binding from the struts.

Attaching the cover

Turn the cover right side out and place onto the frame so that the seams lie over the struts which were originally bound and the tailor's tacks line up with the ends of the struts and are on the rings. Pin the fabric to the rings at the tops and bottoms of the intermediate struts. Do not put any pins into the fabric down the length of the struts – they must be placed in the rings only.
Check that the turnings are lying flat over the struts and are not twisted and make any adjustments needed. Working alternately on each side of one of the seams, start tightening the cover on the frame by adjusting the pins. When you make one alteration to one side of the seam, go to a similar place on the opposite side and make the same alteration. Keep checking the seam and grain lines. Insert more pins into the rings between the struts so that the cover is lying taut against the frame.
Stitching the cover to rings. When you are satisfied with the fit of the cover, it can be stitched to the rings. The most comfortable way of doing this is to sit with the frame on your lap with a pad of fabric beneath it to prevent your legs from being scratched.
Start stitching at a strut and work towards your free hand so that you can hold the fabric taut onto the frame with your fingers as you stitch (fig.6).
Use each length of thread doubled and start and finish with two or three back stitches. Work in a close, firm hemming stitch, placing the stitches on the outer edge of the ring.
When you have stitched around both rings, cut off the excess fabric close to the stitching.

Attaching the lining

Place the lining into the frame and align the seams with those of the cover. Position the tailor's tacks correctly on the bottom ring and pin. Draw the fabric up the shade and pin on the inside of the ring at the top of each strut. Roll back the excess fabric at the top inside ring and clip into it in line with the arms of the light fitting and at intervals in between if the fabric seems tight (fig 7). Roll the fabric over the top ring, fold under the fabric at each side of the slits for the fitting, and pin all around to the outside edge so that the pins are over the previous stitching.
Stand your frame upside down (with the top ring at the bottom), check that the seams are over the struts and pull the fabric on both sides of the seams to tighten it over the bottom ring. Working alternately on each side of the seams, pin the fabric to the ring.
Stitching the lining to rings. Stitch the lining in a similar way to the cover, placing the stitches on the outside of the ring. Cut off the excess fabric close to the stitching (fig. 8).
Finishing the slits. To finish the slits for the light fitting, cut a bias strip for each one, 5cm (2in) long × 2.5cm (1in). Fold in the raw edges so they meet in the middle and then fold the strip in half again.
Slip stitch all the folds together lightly Place each strip loosely around a fitting so that it covers the slit and pin the ends on the ring. Secure with a few stitches and trim off any surplus fabric level with the raw edges of the lining (fig.9).

Trimming the shade

Finish the shade by trimming with braid, a bias strip or velvet ribbon.

Straight drum shapes

A straight drum frame is one which has top and bottom rings of the same size – the rings can be circular or oval. Both the cover and lining fabric should be fitted on the straight grain. The method is similar to that previously described, but it is essential that the tightening is done vertically and not horizontally, in order to maintain the correct shape. To do this, place the fabric onto the frame, and pin it to the top and bottom rings so that it is really tight (fig. 10). Then pin it to the side struts, pulling only enough to remove any wrinkles. Finish the shade as for other shapes, but without shaping the seams on the lining.

Instant lampshades

Among the simplest and quickest lampshades to make are those using stiff-backed fabrics.

A fabric with a stiffened backing is only suitable for lampshades with straight or sloping sides because it cannot be stretched or moulded to one with curved sides.

Although the standard frames with struts can be used for firm lampshades, all you actually need are two rings for the top and bottom of the shade – the structure in between is formed by the rigidity of the fabric. These rings are sold in a wide range of diameters.

The fabric

Many stores which sell lampshade frames also sell a selection of fabrics already bonded to the stiffening. Alternatively, you can buy the bonding separately and iron it onto the back of your own fabric. To calculate the amount of fabric to buy; if you are making a lampshade with rings of the same size at top and bottom, decide on the height of shade you want, measure the circumference of the rings and buy enough to cut a rectangle of the same size plus about 2.5cm (1in) each way.

If the rings are of different sizes, make a paper pattern, following the method below. Place the pattern on another rectangle of paper so that one short side of the pattern is level with the edge of the paper and measure across the pattern at its widest and highest points. Allow a piece of cover fabric of the same size plus about 2.5cm (1in) each way.

You will also need enough 2cm ($\frac{3}{4}$in) self-adhesive cotton tape to fit around both rings, a tube of clear adhesive and some braid or trimming to fit around the rings to finish off the lampshade neatly.

Right: If you decide to use a frame to make a lampshade from stiffened fabric do be sure that the shape you choose is very simple. Complex shapes are not suitable since stiffened fabric does not bend readily, and you would find it very difficult to mould.

Left: This delightful lampshade has been made from a fresh modern print, and the shape has been kept utterly simple. The effect is stunning.

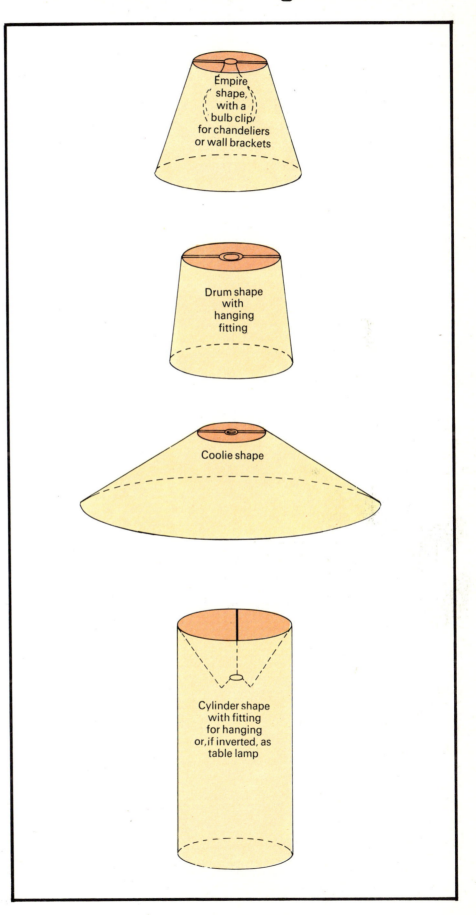

Making a paper pattern

Near the bottom left-hand corner of a large sheet of graph paper draw a horizontal line (A-B) equal in length to the diameter of the bottom ring. Find the centre of the line (point C) and draw a perpendicular line upwards from it to the required height of the shade (point D).

At point D draw another horizontal line (E-F) equal to the diameter of the upper ring and with D as the centre.

Join A-E and B-F and extend these lines upwards until they intersect at G.

Using G-E as the radius, draw a large arc from E equal to the circumference of the top ring (the arc can be measured with a piece of string).

Using G-A as the radius, now draw another arc from A equal to the circumference of the lower ring. Add 2cm ($\frac{3}{4}$in) to the length of each arc for turnings and then join them (H-I). Cut around A-E-H-I and this gives the paper pattern.

Preparing the frame

Unwind enough of the self-adhesive tape to fit the circumference of the bottom ring and press the centre of the sticky side around the inside of the ring. Overlap the ends by 1.5cm ($\frac{1}{2}$in) and cut off. Turn over one edge of the tape on to the outside of the ring and press down. Turn over the other edge in the same way and press down firmly so that it overlaps the first edge smoothly. This ensures that the overlap will be secure and hidden when the cover fabric is in position.

Preparing the fabric

If you are using backed fabric, cut out the fabric from the paper pattern.

If you are an using unstiffened fabric, cut out the fabric from the paper pattern and then cut out the stiffening, making it the same size.

Lay out your fabric on an ironing board with the right side facing down.

Position the stiffening on the main fabric with the adhesive side down so that the sides are level.

Iron the pieces together using a fairly hot temperature and allow to cool.

Check that the pieces are bonded firmly and re-iron if necessary.

Attaching the cover

Using clothes pegs, not dressmaker's pins which would leave holes, peg the cover around the rings as tightly as possible and overlap the ends by placing one short edge over the other edge. Check that the seam is straight, then apply a little adhesive to the wrong side of the top section and press firmly onto the other edge. Allow to dry (fig.4).

Remove about half of the pegs along the top ring and spread a little adhesive along the ring in that portion. Press the cover firmly and carefully back into position so that the ring is 3mm ($\frac{1}{8}$in) below the edge. Secure with clothes pegs. Repeat for the other half of the ring and allow to dry before sticking the bottom ring in the same way.

Adding the trimming

Cut pieces of trimming to fit around the top and bottom of the shade, allowing 1.5cm ($\frac{1}{2}$in) extra. Turn under 6mm ($\frac{1}{4}$in) at each end of the trimming and stick down.

2. Making the paper pattern and cutting out the fabric
3. Butt the joins exactly so that the ends meet without overlapping
4. Fitting and glueing the cover, using clothes pegs to secure it.

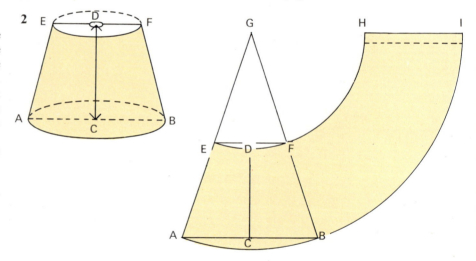

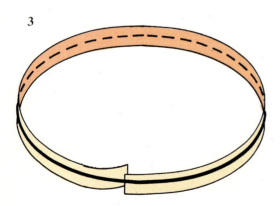

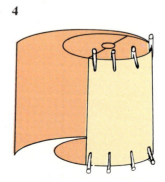

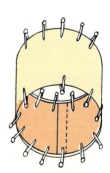

If you can thread beads then you can make bead fringes. This simple form of decorative beadwork transforms ordinary lampshades into really original home furnishings.

Because beads are available in so many different shapes and sizes, before embarking on a project think carefully about where your beading is to be used. Think about weight, size and use. For example, large wooden beads could look cumbersome.

Working a fringe

It is much easier to work a fringe separately from the object you want to fringe, rather than working on the object itself. You will need a base of some kind, however, so choose a suitable cord or ribbon. Some examples include brown soutache braid, white piping cord, red fancy braid, black velvet ribbon and navy, flat silk binding. Use these as bases.

Pin the cord to a polystyrene block or some similar type of material and sew your beads onto the cord. Once the fringe is made it can be applied by either sewing or gluing.

Note: When working these beaded lengths do not pull the thread too tight or the string will not hang correctly.

Some fringe patterns

Figs. 1-5 show the methods of producing the fringes in the photograph.

Lattice fringe is worked on braid using bugle (cylindrical) beads, rocaille beads and drops at ends.

Start on the right, fasten thread back up through beads as shown and thread on more bugles and small beads to complete left side of lattice.

Pass thread along braid to next starting point. Proceed as before but pick up small bead from first strand to make the lattice design.

Striped fringe is worked onto piping cord and is simple to do.

Fasten the thread to the cord and thread up 18 medium-sized brown beads, one large bead, one stop bead.

Work back through beads to piping cord to pass thread to next starting point. Begin next strand by threading 20 small white beads, one large brown bead and the stop bead.

Pass the needle back through all the beads in the strand and into the piping cord. Now repeat the first strand. Continue working in this way.

For a jet fringe, fasten thread onto fancy braid and thread up 24 rocaille beads. one drop and 6 rocaille. Re-insert needle into 18th bead from the top, and pass back up the beads to the beginning. Move along braid.

The second length consists of 20 rocaille, one drop and 6 rocaille. Reinsert your needle at the 14th bead. The third length has 14 rocaille, one drop and 6 rocaille and the needle is re-inserted at the eighth bead.

The pattern continues by repeating (b), then (a), then (b) and (c) again.

For chevron fringe, from a velvet ribbon base, thread 6 white, 6 red, 6 black beads. Pass needle back through beads; work 6 more lengths.

To make chevron add a black bead at the top of the next length and increase this in each of the following 5 rows by adding one more than the row before. The final length should have 6 black beads at the top.

In the next 5 rows decrease by one the number of black beads at the top of each length so that the sixth row has none. Continue from the beginning.

For a daisy fringe, thread a random number of blue, then 8 white beads.

Pass needle back through first white bead, thread one yellow and pass through fifth white bead. To form daisy, pull thread tight.

Thread some more blue beads – then white and yellow as directed above. Pass needle through fifth, sixth, seventh and eighth white beads and tighten.

Re-insert needle into blue beads and work back up through first daisy to beginning of length. Continue to work random length strands in this way.

Left, top to bottom: Bead fringes like these can be very effective, and the designs are intended to make the most of each different sort of bead. The lattice fringe uses amber drops, and next down, the striped fringe has rows of starkly contrasting colours. The centre picture shows a jet fringe. These beads, much beloved by the Victorians look super attached to braid. Below the jet fringe is the chevron fringe. It is great fun to make, and simple too, just follow the sequence on the chart. The bottom fringe is a daisy design.

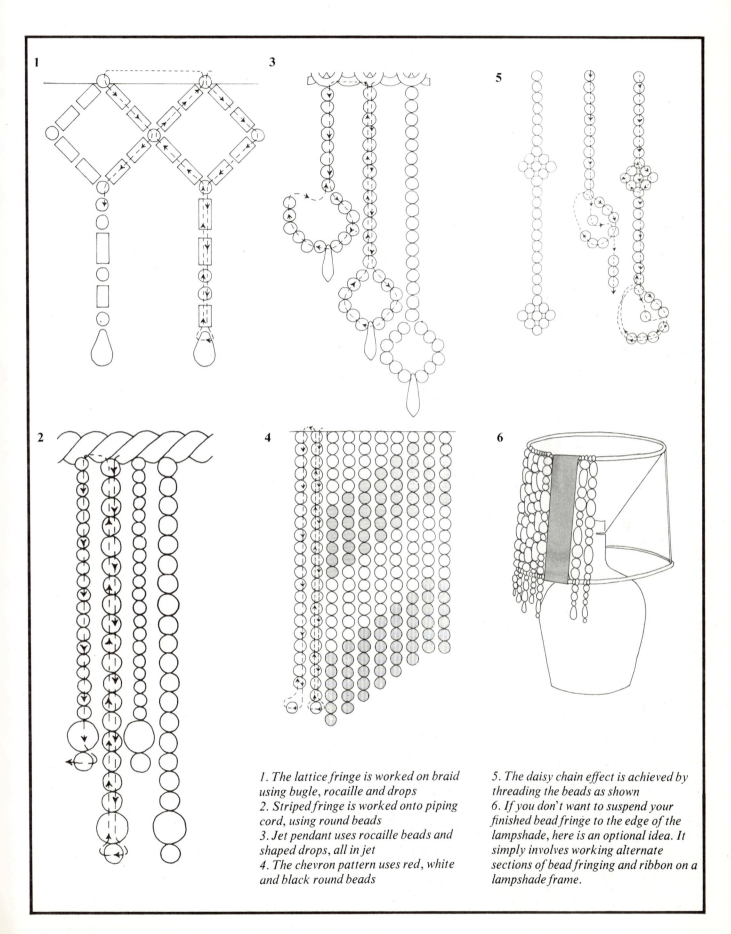

1. The lattice fringe is worked on braid using bugle, rocaille and drops
2. Striped fringe is worked onto piping cord, using round beads
3. Jet pendant uses rocaille beads and shaped drops, all in jet
4. The chevron pattern uses red, white and black round beads

5. The daisy chain effect is achieved by threading the beads as shown
6. If you don't want to suspend your finished bead fringe to the edge of the lampshade, here is an optional idea. It simply involves working alternate sections of bead fringing and ribbon on a lampshade frame.

BUDGET IDEAS

Running a home nowadays requires a considerable
amount of ingenuity to make the most of your budget.
Before you succumb to the temptation to buy expensive
home accessories, take a look at the following projects.
Not only are they super items in themselves, but they'll
suggest other ideas – for example the rugs can be
used as throw covers for beds, or as wall hangings.
Wall tidies can be used all over the house – make one
for the bathroom out of your worn or faded towels.
You should try to get into the habit of saving every
scrap of spare fabric – most of your old clothes can
be recycled and cut into strips and squares.

Tortoise cushion

Opposite: Worn out denim jeans can be transformed into some really fun soft furnishings. Here you can see a tea cosy, a hanging pocket, cushions, a tablecloth appliquéd with floral cotton – even a wall hanging. These are just a few ideas to start you off.

Below: The economy-minded will already save every scrap of leftover material. Here's one way of using it really creatively with basic appliqué skills.

Make your cushions as pretty as a picture in next to no time using appliqué. This mischievous turtle has been appliquéd with a machined zig-zag stitch.

The success of this picture stems from the delicate mixture of patterned fabrics. The blue and white spots of the strawberries are echoed by the stronger blue and white spots on the turtle's back, in the flower centre, and again in the unifying border which acts as a frame.

The combination of spots and checks makes an unusual design.

The flower stem and the turtle's features have been embroidered. The use of a quilted background fabric gives a subtle variation in texture.

Use illustrations of favourite characters from children's books as inspiration, and make a whole family of animal cushions. If you don't know how to appliqué, instructions are given on pages 126-148.

Matching kitchen accessories

Fabric required

0.45m (½yd) PVC fabric, not less than 114.5cm (45in) wide.
0.25m (¼yd) contrasting PVC fabric at least 114.5cm (45in) wide.

You will also need

Thread to match main fabric.
One piece 1.6cm (⅝in) diameter dowel rod, 56cm (22in) long (dowel rod is obtainable from any wood merchant).
One piece 1.6cm (⅝in) diameter dowel rod, 45.5cm (18in) long.
Two cup hooks to fit dowel rod.

Size

56cm (22in) long × 45.5cm (18in) wide. This size can be adjusted to fit your own cupboard door.

Cutting out

1 From the main fabric, cut out the piece for the main panel and the large pockets to the sizes shown in fig. 1.
2 From the contrasting fabric cut out the pockets to the sizes shown in fig. 2.
3 From the remaining main fabric cut strips 2.5cm (1in) wide to fit the tops of the contrasting pockets.
4 From the contrasting fabric cut two strips 63.5cm (25in) long by 2.5cm (1in) wide. From the remaining fabric cut strips 2.5cm (1in) wide to fit the tops of the pockets cut from the main fabric.

Making up

1 Fold the two longest strips in half lengthways with the wrong side inside and crease firmly with your fingers. Place the strips over the long edges of the main panel so they are completely enclosed.

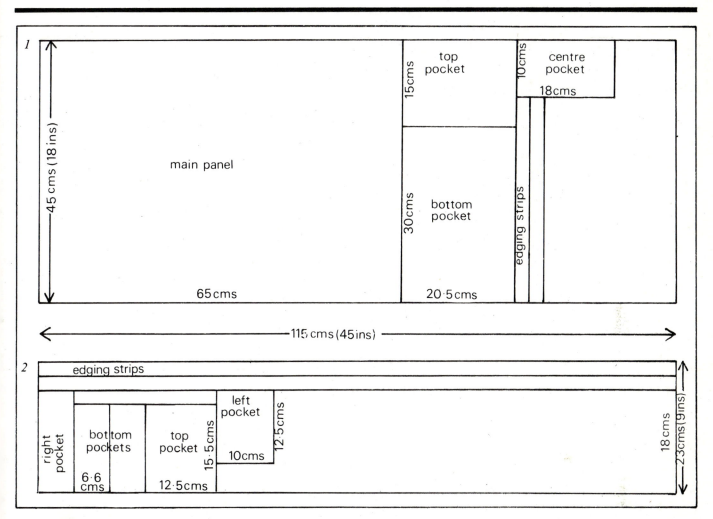

1. *Diagram for cutting main panel*
2. *Diagram for strips and small pockets*

Above left: Covering sides of the long panel with contrast fabric

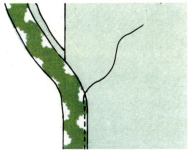

Below left: Making a tuck in the bottom pocket. Tack and tape in position.

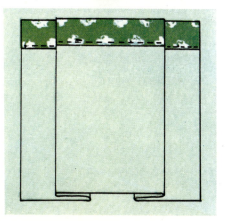

Opposite: The complete set looks super.

Tack and machine stitch through the three thicknesses.

2 Bind the tops of the pockets in the same way.

3 Turn the shorter edges of the main panel onto the wrong side for 4cm (1½in). Tack (do not pin as this will leave holes and machine stitch.

4 Place the pockets for the middle row in place, checking you have left enough space for the top and bottom rows. Tack and machine stitch down the sides and bottom edge. Start and finish the machine stitching by reverse stitching for about 2.5cm (1in) to add strength.

5 Along the bottom edge of the large bottom pocket, measure in 2.5cm (1in) from the sides and make tucks to reduce the width of the pocket by 10cm (4in). Crease the tucks firmly with your fingers to the top edge and hold down temporarily with adhesive tape.

6 Place the pocket in position on the main panel and tack and machine stitch down the sides and along the bottom edge. Remove the tape.

7 Make tucks in the larger top pocket in a similar way and stitch in position. Stitch the remaining pockets in position.

Finishing off

1 Insert the longer dowel rod into the casing at the top of the panel so that an equal amount extends at each side. Insert the shorter rod into the casing at the bottom of the panel.

2 Try the panel in position on your kitchen door and mark the positions for the hooks 2.5cm (1in) from the ends of

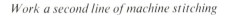
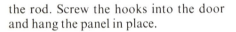

Work a second line of machine stitching

Fold strip to form a loop

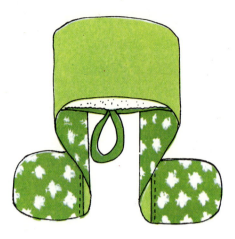

Tack pockets in position

the rod. Screw the hooks into the door and hang the panel in place.

Ironing board cover

This cover is made with fabric on both sides of the padding so that when one side fades it can be turned.

The fabric

Buy a linen or strong cotton fabric which will withstand hot ironing temperatures. Allow enough fabric to cut two pieces 7.5cm (3in) larger all around than the ironing surface. You will also need a piece of 6mm ($\frac{1}{4}$in) thick foam rubber or thick synthetic wadding the same size as the ironing surface, a long length of 6mm ($\frac{1}{4}$in) wide elastic, 0.90m (1yd) tape, 1.5cm ($\frac{1}{2}$in) wide and a piece of paper for cutting the pattern.

Making the pattern

Lay out the paper flat, place the ironing board face down onto it. Draw around the edge of the ironing surface and draw another line 7.5cm (3in) outside this. Cut along the second line.

Cutting out

1 Using the paper pattern cut two pieces of fabric on the straight grain.
2 Trim the pattern to the first line and cut out the padding to this size.

Making up

1 Place the padding onto the wrong side of one of the fabric pieces so that there is an equal margin all around. Tack and stitch 6mm ($\frac{1}{4}$in) from the edge.
2 Place the second piece of fabric to the padded piece so that the right sides

are together and machine stitch around, taking 6mm ($\frac{1}{4}$in) turnings. Leave an opening of about 15cm (6in) and turn the cover right side out through this.
3 Fold under the turnings along the opening and tack the folds together, leaving a small opening of about 1.5cm ($\frac{1}{2}$in) for the elastic to be inserted.
4 Machine stitch all around the edge of the cover, leaving the small opening. Work a second line of machining 1.5cm ($\frac{1}{2}$in) in from the first line.
5 Cut a piece of elastic about 15cm (6in) shorter than the perimeter of the board and thread it through the casing formed by the rows of machine stitching around the edge of the cover.
6 Place the cover onto the board and draw up the elastic to fit so that the unpadded border is underneath the ironing surface. Pin the elastic at the correct length, take the cover off the board and stitch the ends of the elastic together, trimming off any extra. Stitch opening.
7 Divide the tape into four and sew two pieces on opposite sides of the cover in the middle and two pieces at the top. Replace the cover on the board and tie the tape underneath to hold the cover in position.

Double oven gloves
Fabric required
0.45m (or $\frac{1}{2}$yd) cotton fabric, 91cm (36in) wide.
23cm ($\frac{1}{4}$yd) contrasting cotton fabric, 91cm (36in) wide.

You will also need
23cm ($\frac{1}{4}$yd) thick synthetic wadding.

Cutting out

1 Cut the main fabric in half lengthways and round of all corners on one strip, using a small plate as a guide. Round the corners of contrasting fabric to match.
2 From the remaining fabric, cut two 18cm (7in) lengths for the pockets and round off the corners of one long side on both pieces to match the main strips.
3 Round of all the corners on the wadding to match those on the main strips.

Making up

1 Place the wadding onto the wrong side of one of the main pieces and tack in position all around the edge.
2 Make narrow hems on the pocket pieces along the opposite edges to the shaped sides.
3 Place the pockets, wrong side down, at each end on the right side of the contrasting strips so that the shaping matches. Tack in position.
4 Place the two strips together with right sides facing and tack and machine stitch round the edge taking 6mm ($\frac{1}{4}$in) turnings. Leave an opening of about 18cm (6in) in the middle of one long side and turn the gloves right side out. Fold under the turnings.
5 From the spare fabric, cut a length 4cm ($1\frac{1}{2}$in) wide by 15cm (6in) long. Fold under the raw edges and stitch the folds together to make a strip.
6 Fold the strip in half to form a loop and insert the ends into the opening. Stitch to the turnings.
7 Stitch the folds of the turnings together.

Patchwork oven gloves

Few things are as annoying as trying to grip a hot pan firmly using a small padded square without burning yourself – these gloves are a pretty solution. They are quick to make, and are ideal as a gift for a newly-wed.

You will need:
Scraps of cotton fabric for patchwork.
45.5cm (18in) plain cotton fabric for lining.
45cm (18in) of 110gm (4oz) polyester wadding.
91cm (36in) cotton binding.
Matching sewing thread.
Old newspaper for pattern.

To make up
Make the pattern by drawing around your hand on the newspaper. Add 3.5cm (1¼in) all around for seams and cut out the pattern.
Fold lining fabric in half and cut out glove pattern twice.
Cut four glove pieces from the wadding.
Make a piece of cut and stagger patchwork to measure 86cm × 30cm (34in × 12in). Cut out glove pattern in doubled fabric as for lining.
Open out lining pieces so that you have two left-hand and two right-hand pieces. Tack wadding to each piece and then stitch together in pairs of left and right with the unpadded sides together and taking 15mm (⅝in) seams.

Trim wadding from seam allowance. Clip around the curves and inside thumb.
Make loops for hanging the gloves by folding a small length of binding in half, then tack it to the right side of one patchwork piece, raw edges together. Repeat for other glove.
With right sides together, stitch each pair of patchwork pieces together taking 9mm (⅜in) seams.
Clip around the curves and turn to right side.
Slip wadded lining into the patchwork gloves, wrong sides together, and tack the wrist edges together.
Finally, fold binding over raw edges and stitch in place.

Plaited rug

For maximum impact at minimum cost, plait yourself a hard-wearing rag rug. This old cottagers' technique may be called "poor man's loom", but the effect is a rich explosion of colour which can be haphazard or as planned as you please.

Making the plaits

It is possible to use most fabrics except the very finest or thickest to make a plaited rug, so search through your rag bag.

Cut the fabric into thin strips. Each strand of the plait should be of a similar thickness, so make wider strips of a thin fabric and narrower strips of a heavy fabric.

Make a sample plait to begin with, keeping the tension fairly firm. The plait should be the same width all the way down and all the plaits should be of a similar thickness.

To start a plait, fasten the three strips of fabric to a piece of string with a safety pin and tie the string to a chair back. The plait can then be kept taut while it is being worked.

Do not have the strips too long; it is easier to keep adding on new strips as they get shorter. The new strips are sewn on and the edges turned in so that the right side of the plait is even.

Forming the circles

The rug illustrated has a centre made up of five rows of seven circles in each row. Each of these circles is approximately 16.5cm (6½in) in diameter. The gaps in between the large circles are filled in with 24 smaller circles.

When the plaits are long enough, wind them into circles, using strong thread to sew them together as you go around. Join the large and small circles together in rows to complete the centre of the rug.

Making the border

The centre of the mat is surrounded by four lengths of plaits, two plain and two multi-coloured. Sew them together in rows, moulding them around the outer circles to achieve a scalloped effect.

Outside this border is another border of circles alternating with twin circles. The twin circles are plaits approximately 70cm (27in) long wound together from each end.

Finally, sew three more lengths of plaiting around the outer edge of the rug to complete the border.

Opposite: Economy ideas need not be drab. This super rag rug is made from brightly coloured fabric scraps, and looks good enough for any home. The technique used here is called 'poor man's loom', and has been used for generations. It can be adapted for making covers for beds, even wall-hangings — the coils can be arranged in very interesting patterns and colour combinations.

1. To make a plait, first secure the three strips to a piece of string with a safety pin, then tie to chair.
2. Once you have made a fairly long plait, you can start making coils. These are stitched with strong thread.
3. The border of the rug is composed of braids arranged in a contrasting pattern. Coils are wound from each end.

Memo board

Size
66cm (26in) long × 30.5cm (12in) wide.

Fabric required
0.45m ($\frac{1}{2}$yd) cotton fabric

You will also need
Mounting board or thick card, 66cm (26in) × 30.5cm (12in).
Matching thread.
Fabric adhesive.
Scraps of felt in dark and light green.
One eyelet and cup hook.
Note pad, 12.5cm (5in) wide.
0.25m ($\frac{1}{4}$yd) elastic, 1.5cm ($\frac{1}{2}$in) wide.

Cutting out
Draw the carrot shape on board or card and cut out.
Place the card shape on to the fabric and cut two pieces, allowing 1.5cm ($\frac{1}{2}$in) extra for turnings all around.
From the remaining fabric cut a strip 30.5cm (12in) long × 6.5cm (2$\frac{1}{2}$in) wide for the elastic casing and two strips 15cm (6in) long × 5cm (2in) wide for the pencil tube and for binding the note pad opening.
Trace the shapes for the leaves and cut from the felt.

Making the carrot
1 Mark the centre line in tacking down the length of one of the main fabric pieces.
2 Mark the opening for the note pad 21.5cm (8$\frac{1}{2}$in) from the top edge and 13.5cm (5$\frac{1}{4}$in) wide, placing is so that it is centred on the width of the fabric.
3 Place the binding strip right side down so that it is centred over the marked opening and machine stitch in a rectangle 0.6cm ($\frac{1}{4}$in) from the line. Cut along the line and diagonally into the corners of the rectangle. Turn the binding onto the wrong side, press and top-stitch on the right side.
4 To make the tube for the pencil, fold over the short ends on to the wrong side for 0.3cm ($\frac{1}{8}$in) and machine stitch along

the fold. Fold under the long ends in the same way but without machining and press. Fold the tube in half lengthways with right side facing out and pin and top-stitch along the folds to the fabric 2.5cm (1in) above the bound opening.

5 Prepare the casing for the elastic in a similar way. Trim the elastic to 23cm (9in) and insert it into the casing, gathering up the casing to fit. Place the casing onto the board 9cm (3½in) below the top edge so that it is centred on the width. Stitch at each end through all thicknesses. Arrange the gathers evenly and stitch at 4cm (1½in) intervals across the casing to form individual pockets.

6 Place the two fabric shapes together with right sides facing. Taking 1.5cm (½in) turnings machine stitch from the widest point at the top on one side, down and around to the widest point on the opposite side, leaving an opening at the top. Clip turnings and turn right side out.

7 Insert the card, fold under the turnings of the opening on each side of the leaves and slip-stitch.

8 Glue the felt shapes to the card at the top for the leaves so that they cover the remaining raw edge on the front of the carrot. Fold under the remaining raw edge on the back and glue down.

9 Finish by inserting the eyelet in the top of the leaves and hanging on the cup hook in the required place. Insert the note pad into the bound opening.

Herb bags

Below: Make these delightful herb bags. Neaten the edges of the hessian first by overcasting or zig-zag stitches to prevent fraying. Then wash to remove any dressing, and iron while damp.

Size
Approximately 25.5cm (10in)
× 20.5cm (8in).

Fabric required
Remnants of medium or light-coloured hessian, large enough to cut out pieces approximately 30.5cm (12in) × 45.5cm (18in) (these measurements allow for shrinkage which may vary according to the hessian used).

You will also need
1 × 25ml ($\frac{7}{8}$fl oz) bottle Dylon Colourfun in Raven Black.
1 bottle Colour-fun in Polar White.
Artist's soft paintbrush.
Cardboard stencil of alphabet with letters 2.5cm (1in) high (obtainable from an art shop).
Soft pencil.
Dish for mixing colors.
Clean cotton cloth.
Thread to match hessian.
Thick cord 30.5cm (12in) long for each bag.

Marking the design
1 Draw the name of the herb you require onto paper using the stencil. Cut around the outside of the word.
2 Lay the hessian with the longer edges at the top and bottom and place the word on the left-hand half, about 5cm (2in) from the bottom. Check that it fits and that there is enough room for the border design, plus 6mm ($\frac{1}{4}$in) seam allowance along the left-hand edge and bottom. If necessary the fabric can be turned around so that the shorter sides are at the top and bottom.
3 Mark the area of the border and then draw the word in pencil onto the hessian. Add leaves or other decoration if desired.

Applying the paint
1 First mix the colours. Shake both bottles well. Pour a little of the white paint into the dish, then add the black paint, a few drops at a time until you obtain a strong charcoal grey. Mix well, and apply a little to a spare piece of hessian. Correct the colour if necessary. Make sure you have enough of the mixed paint to complete the design.
2 Practice painting a few letters on a spare piece of hessian.
3 Paint the letters onto the bags and then fill in the border design. (To keep the fabric stationary, first tape the edges to the work surface.)
4 Leave the painted pieces of hessian to dry. If possible, hang them in a place where air can circulate around them.
5 Wash the brush well in water and recap the bottles.
6 To fix the colour, cover the design with the cotton cloth and iron it for one or two minutes, using a very hot temperature. Keep the iron moving over the fabric.
7 Wash the pieces of hessian, and iron them smooth while still damp.

Finishing the bags
1 Place the two short sides of the bag together with the right side inside and machine stitch down the sides and bottom taking 6mm ($\frac{1}{4}$in) seam allowance.
2 Fold 2.5cm (1in) to the wrong side at the top and finish with a 2cm ($\frac{3}{4}$in hem) either by machine or by hand.
3 Tie cord around top of bags.

Pot holders

Make something useful that is also decorative. These potholders are a good example – no more scorched hands and they make an attractive addition to kitchen decor if hung on the wall in a group.

You will need:
Scraps of cotton fabric for patchwork.
Terry towelling for lining.
227g (8oz) synthetic sheet wadding for padding.
Contrasting bias binding.
Small brass ring.

The photograph shows various ideas for patchwork shapes. Cut out and make up the ones of your choice, using the techniques described in Patchwork chapters.
Using the finished patchwork as a pattern, cut out the towelling lining.
Cut wadding the same shape and size.
Pin and tack wadding to the wrong side of the patchwork then zig-zag stitch along seam lines to hold in place.
Tack lining to the back.
Pin and tack bias binding around edges and zig-zag stitch in place.
Sew a ring to the edge for hanging finished potholder.

Index

Patchwork in rows P. 103.

Appliqué cushion. P. 119

Sunflower motif P. 137.

Ribbon Cushion interlacing 136

Felt Motif P. 129.

Staggered Patchwork.